The Model Rules on EU Administrative Procedures. Ad...

[redacted]

[redacted]

Europa Law Publishing, Groningen 2016

[redacted]

[redacted]

The Model Rules on EU Administrative Procedures: Adjudication

Edited by Matthias Ruffert

European Administrative Law Series (II)

Europa Law Publishing is a publishing company specializing in European Union law, international trade law, public international law, environmental law and comparative national law.
For further information please contact Europa Law Publishing via email: info@europalawpublishing.com or visit our website at: www.europalawpublishing.com.

Typeset in Scala and Scala Sans, Graphic design by G2K Designers, Groningen/Amsterdam

NUR 828;
ISBN 9789089521859 (paperback)
ISBN 9789089521866 (ebook)

The European Administrative Law Series hosts academic publications related to the development of European administrative law. The series aims to cover all aspects of European administrative law, reflecting the role of the European Union, the role of domestic legal orders and their mutual relation and influence.

Acknowledgements

In a way, the 2015 meeting of the Dornburg Research Group on New Administrative Law in Rome was a jubilee meeting. The Group met 10 years after its foundation in 2005 in Dornburg, and it did so for the fifth time. I can hardly conceal that all members are proud of that achievement.

This time, the Group decided to co-operate with a larger project, the Research Network on European Administrative Law (ReNEUAL) which has just published its Model Rules on EU Administrative Law, and to critically discuss an important part of these Model Rules on a comparative basis.

The meeting was hosted in Rome by our colleague and member of both groups, Prof. Dr. Giacinto della Cananea, and on behalf of the whole group I can only express my gratitude for the splendid and generous hospitality of our Italian friend. Special thanks go to his team, above all to Dr. Martina Conticelli. Dr. Anna Riddell, as always, performed an impressive copyediting of the book, Drs. Jacqueline Lensink on behalf of Europa Law Publishing managed particularly well to edit our efforts. In Jena, I am grateful towards Elena Mönning for her organising work, and of course towards Susanne Prater who gave her – as usual – perfect assistance to the organisation and brought together all bits and pieces for publication in the end. The conference received support by the *Università degli Studi di Roma Tor Vergata*, by the *Istituto Luigi Sturzo*, our host of the first day of the meeting, and by the Hohbühl-Stiftung: *Mille grazie* and *dankeschön*!

Matthias Ruffert
Jena, spring 2016

Acknowledgements

[illegible]

[illegible] 2010

About the Authors

Giacinto della Cananea is Professor of Administrative Law and European Administrative Law at the Faculty of Economics, University of Rome "Tor Vergata".

Roberto Caranta is Professor of Administrative Law at the University of Torino.

Paul Craig is Professor of English Law, St John's College, Oxford.

Gunilla Edelstam is Associate Professor, Södertörn University, Huddinge, Sweden.

Diana-Urania Galetta is Professor of Administrative Law and EU Administrative Law, University of Milan.

Pascale Gonod is Professeur à l'Université de Paris 1, Panthéon-Sorbonne, Membre de l'Institut universitaire de France.

Thomas Groß is Professor of Public Law, European Law and Comparative Law at the University of Osnabrück.

Athanasios Gromitsaris is Associate Professor of Public Law, Friedrich-Schiller-University Jena.

Wolfgang Hoffmann-Riem is Professor for research in innovation and law, Bucerius Law School, Hamburg.

Jean-François Lafaix is Professor at the Université de la Lorraine, Nancy, France.

Oriol Mir is Vice President of the Comisión de Garantía del Derecho de Acceso a la Información Pública de Cataluña, Barcelona.

Jacues Petit is Professor of Law at the University of Rennes I.

Eberhard Schmidt-Aßmann is emeritus Professor of Public Law, Ruprecht-Karls-University Heidelberg.

Jens-Peter Schneider is Professor of Public Law, University of Freiburg, Germany.

Andrew Le Sueur is Professor of Constitutional Justice, University of Essex.

Matthias Ruffert is Professor of Public Law and European Law, Humboldt University Berlin.

Francisco Velasco is Professor of Administrative Law, Universidad Autónoma de Madrid, Spain.

Jacques Ziller, Professor of European Union Law, Pavia, Italy.

CHAPTER I

The ReNEUAL Codification Project – Book III

Jens-Peter Schneider

A. The ReNEUAL Project: Background, Objectives, Concept and Overall Structure

Single case decision-making is central to any regime of administrative procedure. This is not only true with regard to national legal orders but also for EU administrative procedural law. Thus, Book III of the ReNEUAL Model Rules on EU administrative procedure[1] has attracted particular attention throughout the drafting process as well as at various conferences and workshops organized by ReNEUAL or in cooperation with other bodies – such as the European Ombudsman, the European Law Institute, ACA-Europe[2] and the Centre for Judicial Cooperation in Florence – for discussing earlier drafts of the Model Rules.

Book III follows the same overall objectives as the other books of the Model Rules. These objectives derive from a critical analysis of the state of play.[3] Today, EU administrative law is characterized by a significant fragmentation into (uncoordinated) sector-specific and issue-specific rules and procedures complemented by punctual case-law and many variations of soft law. This fragmentation leads to an overburdening complexity of overlapping rules and principles. There is, in many respects, a growing gap between, on one hand, the proliferation of new forms of administrative action in the EU and their regulatory framework and, on the other hand, their integration into a coherent system of legal protection. The result is legal uncertainty caused by the opacity and incoherence of the fragmented legal framework. Further deficiencies are gaps concerning the protection of individual rights and the EU rule of law and gaps concerning accountability and democratic legitimation as well as reduced efficiency in administrative procedures.

Another characteristic of recent EU administrative law are the so called composite procedures.[4] Despite the 'Europeanization' of many policy areas,

---

* This chapter is inspired by the Introductions and Explanations to Books I and III of the ReNEUAL Model Rules. The author is grateful to his co-authors of these introductions and explanations for permitting him to use and modify parts of these texts.

1 The English Online Version 2014 can be downloaded at www.reneaul.eu; updated (printed) versions of 2015 exist in English, French, German, Italian, Polish and Spanish; these versions are already published or will be published in due course; additional language versions such as Romanian are planned.

2 Association of the Councils of State and Supreme Administrative Jurisdictions of the European Union.

3 See also the notes of O. Mir Puigpelat, P. Leino-Sandberg and H. Jäderblom, in European Parliament, 'Workshop on EU administrative law: state of play and future prospects' (PE453.215), 2011, p. 53 (64 et seq.), p. 249 (252 et seq.), p. 269 et seq.

4 See also G. Della Cananea, 'I Procedimenti Amministrativi Composti Dell'Unione Europea' *RTDP* (2004) special edition 1, 307 et seq.; P. Craig, *EU Administrative Law* (2nd ed., OUP 2012) 79 et seq.; H.C.H. Hofmann, 'Decision-Making in EU Administrative Law – The Problem of Composite Procedures' 61 Administrative Law Review (2009) 199 et seq.; O. Jansen and B. Schöndorf-Haubold (eds.) *The European Composite Administration* (Cambridge 2011); M. Ruffert, 'Von der Europäisierung des Verwaltungsrechts zum Europäischen Verwaltungsverbund' *Die Öffentliche Verwaltung* (2007) 761 et

there is no fully fledged EU administration. Instead, implementation of EU law is generally undertaken by national bodies which are in some cases supported by EU bodies. Moreover, in cases of (single case) decision-making by EU authorities like the Commission or EU agencies, national actors are often integrated through comitology procedures, consultation, preparatory acts or as members of boards in an EU agency. The multi-jurisdictional nature and pluralisation of actors involved in the implementation of EU policies reinforces fragmentation between sector-specific procedures. This creates barriers to administrative coordination between Member States as well as between EU and national authorities. Today, the design of composite procedures is geared predominantly towards achieving efficiency and optimal use of pre-existing resources. Their multi-jurisdictional nature may however diminish protection of individual rights and possibilities of effective judicial review. Rules of administrative procedure are, therefore, necessary to prevent – when implementing EU law through composite procedures – the rights and interests of addressees and third parties from falling into the gap between situations covered by EU-level review and accountability mechanisms and those at Member States′ level.

Against this background, a first general objective of the ReNEUAL Model Rules concerns options for translating the constitutional values of the Union into rules on administrative procedure covering the non-legislative implementation of EU law and policies. Such Model Rules have the potential of contributing not only to the clarity of the legal rights and obligations of individuals and participating administrations, but also to the transparency and effectiveness of the legal system as a whole. A codification of administrative procedures could help to simplify the legal system, enhance legal certainty and to fill gaps in the legal system, thereby increasing compliance with the rule of law.

A second objective, especially addressed in Books V and VI on mutual assistance and inter-administrative information management and exchange but also touched upon in some rules of Book III on composite single case decision-making, concerns a better coordination within the EU legal order as well as between the EU legal order and national administrative law. Such better coordination certainly affects national rules, but it does not seek to harmonise national administrative law comprehensively or significantly. Instead ReNEUAL respects that "the European legal culture is made of the diversity of legal systems progressively brought closer to each other".[5]

---

seq.; J.-P. Schneider, 'Strukturen des Europäischen Verwaltungsverbunds – Einleitende Bemerkungen', in J.-P. Schneider and F. Velasco Caballero (eds.) *Strukturen des Europäischen Verwaltungsverbunds* (Duncker & Humblot 2009) 9 et seq.; J.-P. Schneider, 'Regulation and Europeanisation as Key Patterns of Change in Administrative Law', in M. Ruffert (ed.) *The Transformation of Administrative Law in Europe* (BIICL 2007) 307 (313 et seq.); G. Sydow, *Verwaltungskooperation in der Europäischen Union* (Mohr Siebeck 2004); W. Weiß, *Der Europäische Verwaltungsverbund* (Duncker & Humblot 2010).

5 The text is a quote from a speech by Vassilios Skouris, President of the CJEU, at the European Law Institute's Inaugural Congress 2011 in Paris, cited from V. Reding, 'The European Law Institute – Tracing the Path towards a European Legal Culture' Speech/11/764, p. 2.

In order to meet these objectives the ReNEUAL Model Rules follow an approach of 'innovative codification'.[6] This involves the combination of existing principles which are presently scattered across different laws and regulations or found in the case-law of courts. Where necessary, the innovative codification also modifies such existing principles and rules and may even add new ones.

The ReNEUAL Model Rules on Administrative Procedure are presented in a form adapted to their possible adoption as an EU Regulation. Nevertheless, the term 'Model Rules' highlights the academic character of the ReNEUAL project. The Model Rules provide European legal scholarship and legal practitioners with a structured framework for debating and further developing EU administrative law. The ReNEUAL Model Rules also aim to inform legislative bodies, courts and ombudspersons about legal options and best practices which they may use within their respective competences. The Model Rules may also contribute to education at universities throughout Europe and worldwide as well as to training of public officials in administrative authorities and other public entities dealing with EU administrative law.

As a consequence of the academic character of the project, ReNEUAL decided that it should not be constricted by the existing framework of legislative competences. Nonetheless, the possibility of the (future) adoption of the whole or parts of the project as EU legislation has been considered from the beginning.[7] Within the EU's system of conferral of powers, possible future EU legislation on administrative procedures requires the identification of treaty provisions providing a legal basis for the adoption of such an Act. ReNEUAL is fully aware of the importance of addressing the issue of legal basis and the Model Rules reflect these considerations in several ways: the scope of application of Books II, III and IV is, in principle, limited to EU institutions, bodies, offices and agencies; the question whether the same legal basis can be used for different types of administrative actions has been taken into account in drafting the rules in Book I; the wording of the Model Rules has been scrutinised in view of its relationship with possible legal bases.

However, solving the problem of the appropriate legal basis has not been considered to be a precondition to the academic drafting of procedural rules. The discussion on the content of those rules therefore should not be preempted by the discussion on the legal basis. It is only after having assessed the content of those rules that a political decision can be made on how to proceed. Three possibilities are envisaged: (1) finding additional arguments to sustain the use of existing legal bases such as Article 298 TFEU, (2) putting the issue on the agenda of the next treaty revision conference in order to establish a new fully

---

6 See J. Ziller, 'Alternatives in Drafting an EU Administrative Procedure Law' Note for the European Parliament (PE 462.417), 2011, p. 16-17.

7 See P. Craig, 'A General Law on Administrative Procedure, Legislative Competence and Judicial Competence', 19 *European Public Law* (2013) 503 et seq.; O. Mir Puigpelat, 'Die Kodifikation des Verwaltungsverfahrensrechts im Europäischen Verwaltungsverbund' in Schneider and Velasco Caballero (n 4), 177 (206 et seq.).

fledged legal basis, or (3) enacting the rules of some of the six books through different legal instruments, each based on an appropriate existing or future legal basis. Irrespective of any discussion on the legal basis, provisions laid down in the ReNEUAL Model Rules on administrative procedure could also be used as a type of 'stand by codification' or as a 'boilerplate' to be supplemented with sector-specific norms in policy-specific legal acts that benefit from a single legal basis such as, for example, Article 114 TFEU for the internal market.

The Model Rules were drafted by several teams composed of scholars with special expertise in national and EU administrative law as well as in comparative scholarship. Their drafts have iteratively undergone – since the very beginning – internal and external processes of consultation and debate.[8]

The ReNEUAL Model Rules of administrative procedure are organised in six 'books'. These books are designed to reinforce general principles of EU law and identify – on the basis of comparative research – best practices in different specific policies of the EU. Book I addresses the general scope of application of the model rules, their relation to sector-specific rules and Member States' law and the definitions of terminology applied in all the books. The Preamble of Book I contains a summary of principles, which guide administrative behaviour, and the interpretation of all subsequent norms in Books II to VI. The latter books cover more in-depth administrative procedures in the EU that have the potential to directly affect the interests and rights of individuals. The Books address non-legislative implementation of EU law and policies by means of: rule-making (Book II), single case decision-making (Book III), contracts (Book IV) and, very important for the composite nature of EU administration, procedures of mutual assistance (Book V) and information management (Book VI). Each book is composed of a more general introduction to the concept and structure of the respective book, the proposed model rules and more specific explanations of the concrete proposals indicating sources of inspiration and choices between alternatives considered by the respective drafting team.

B. Book I and its Relevance for Book III

Book I comprises general rules which must to be taken into account when Book III is applied or analysed, and is shortly presented in the following paragraphs. Book I is composed of a preamble and four articles with provisions on the scope of application, the relation of the model rules to sector-specific norms of the European Union and the relation to Member States' law. The fourth article defines terms which are important in all or at least more than one of the following books.

8 Details are indicated in the Editorial Note to the ReNEUAL Model Rules.

As mentioned above and highlighted by the European Parliament´s resolution of 15 January 2013,[9] rules on EU administrative procedures must be based on constitutional principles. These principles are already laid down in various provisions of the EU treaties and the ReNEUAL Model Rules do not intend to duplicate those provisions. Instead, the preamble briefly refers to them in order to remind all addressees and other readers of the constitutional background of the detailed rules.[10] The ReNEUAL Model Rules must be interpreted "in the light" of these principles.

According to Article I-1 the model rules of Books II, III and IV are generally applicable to EU authorities only. In contrast, under conditions specified in Article V-I and Article VI-1, the model rules of Books V and VI are also applicable to Member States' authorities involved in mutual assistance and inter-administrative information management activities. The procedures and activities covered by Books V and VI address issues which cannot be solved without taking into account the relationship between EU institutions, bodies, offices and agencies on the one hand, and Member States' authorities on the other hand. However, the EU legislator may also decide through a sector-specific act to extend the scope of application of Books II, III and IV to Member States' authorities when implementing EU law. This differentiation between a general restricted opt-in approach for inter alia Book III and a comprehensive approach in Books V and VI – save some opt-in requirements for more advanced provisions of these two books – is the result of intensive discussions within the drafting teams, the ReNEUAL Steering Committee and with external experts especially from national courts.

Article I-2 stipulates the *lex specialis* principle. This means that the ReNEUAL Model Rules are not intended to substitute existing specific legal provisions on administrative procedures or to prohibit the legislator from enacting new specific rules on administrative procedures. ReNEUAL is aware of the fact that in certain circumstances such specific rules are needed to cope with the peculiarities of a special field of law. In addition, sector-specific law can introduce new legislative approaches or instruments to the EU legal order thereby serving as a laboratory for legal innovations. Thus, the *lex specialis* rule provides a useful tool against the petrification of the model rules and minimises a problem often highlighted in discussion about codifications of administrative law.

Article I-3 on the relation between the Model Rules and Member States' law does not compromise the Model Rules' restricted scope of application but

9 European Parliament Resolution of 15 January 2013 with recommendations to the Commission on a Law of Administrative Procedure of the European Union (2012/2024(INI)); see also the Council of Europe Recommendation CM/Rec(2007)7 of the Committee of Ministers to member states on good administration.

10 See also D.-U. Galetta, H.C.H. Hofmann, O. Mir Puigpelat and J. Ziller, 'The General Principles of EU Administrative Procedural Law – In-depth Analysis for the European Parliament' (PE 519.224), 2015, arguing for the formulation of these principles as recitals of a regulation.

it reminds Member State officials that they can find guidance in the ReNEUAL Model Rules if Member States' law provides for discretion concerning the concrete design of administrative procedures or leaves normative gaps. Thus officials can set up and apply their procedures under their Member State's law in accordance with European best practices. Such European best practices might help those officials to fulfil their duties under the principle of sincere cooperation and to implement EU law effectively and in a non-discriminatory manner. Furthermore, the ReNEUAL Model Rules can also support law reforms at Member State level that promote EU-friendly amendments.

C. Book III on Single Case Decision-Making

I. Scope of Book III

Like all the others Book III regulates, in line with articles I-1 (1), I-4 (1) and (2), administrative procedures by which a public authority prepares and formulates a specific administrative action, in the case of Book III, a decision (see also Article III-1 (1)). Consequently, the definition of a decision in Article III-2 (1) is highly important. According to this provision 'decision' means "administrative action addressed to one or more individualized public or private persons which is adopted unilaterally by an EU authority, or by a Member State authority when Article III-1(2) is applicable, to determine one or more concrete cases with legally binding effect." This definition has several important consequences:

First, Book III covers decisions which are addressed to a State or a group of States, as well as decisions which are addressed to an individual or a group of individuals, insofar as the addressees are determined or can be determined ex ante. Examples of the first type of decisions addressed to Member States are decisions taken by the Commission in implementing the rules in Articles 107 and 108 TFEU on the control of state aids. Commission decisions may also be addressed to private individuals or entities, for instance in the field of competition law (Articles 101, 102, 105 TFEU). This broad scope of application is in line with the need to respect constitutional principles of procedural law in both situations and takes into account that many decisions addressed to Member States have direct effects on private parties. The Model Rules of Book III are flexible enough to respect the specifics of both constellations in their implementation. In addition, the legislator may provide for a *lex specialis* if the characteristics of decisions in a particular field of law addressed to Member States require derogations from the Model Rules.

Second, under Article III-2(1) a decision is adopted in the context of administrative action, a requirement which excludes legislative and judicial acts. Third, decisions are adopted unilaterally, unlike a contract, although this does not necessarily preclude some form of formal or informal agreement on the content of the decision made between the public authority and private parties.

Finally, it is important to note that decisions for the purpose of this Book 'determine' one or more concrete cases with legally binding effects. While Book III regulates certain aspects that are preparatory to the final decision, such as a 'decision' that a responsible official should be excluded from the administrative procedure, these 'preliminary decisions' do not themselves constitute decisions for the purposes of Book III, because they do not determine the concrete case with legally binding effect. The definition also means that decisions made by the Commission pursuant to an infringement procedure against a Member State are not covered by Book III. The same applies to OLAF inspections,[11] which are not covered by Book III as long as reports following from these inspections are not considered as legally binding by the CJEU.[12]

This significant limitation of the scope of Book III may be doubted. Nevertheless, it is in line with the other books of the Model Rules and most national codifications. In substance this is justified by the need for a clear definition of the scope of application. Book III provides important and significant rights and duties. While these burdens on the public authorities are certainly justified with regard to legally binding decisions this may not be the case in other administrative actions concerning the handling of a single case. Inspections by the European Anti-Fraud Office (OLAF – Office Européen de Lutte Anti-Fraude) may be considered for good reason as potentially equally intrusive on the subjective rights of persons as a formally binding determination, i.e. a decision in the meaning of Book III. An appropriate solution would be to explicitly render Book III applicable *mutatis mutandis* to this very specific type of administrative action as well as possibly to other similar, but clearly described actions. In contrast, a less clearly defined and therefore vague extension of the scope of application may result in unpredictable and negative side-effects outweighing the positive effects gained by such an extension.

In order to avoid misconceptions, the definition – read in combination with Articles I-4(2) and III-1(1) ("prepares") – and consequently Book III cover procedures which do not end in a formal final act, but are initiated with the potential intent of adopting such an act.[13] At the other end, it must be emphasized that the adoption and notification of the final act itself are captured by the terms "formulates" (Article I-4(2)) and "adopts" (Article III-1(1)) and are consequently part of the procedure regulated by Book III.

---

11 OLAF inspections instead are subject to a number of legal instruments, such as Regulation 883/2013 of the European Parliament and of the Council of 11 September 2013 concerning investigations conducted by the European Anti-Fraud Office (OLAF) and repealing Regulation (EC) 1073/1999 of the European Parliament and of the Council and Council Regulation (Euratom) 1074/1999 [2013] OJ L248/1.

12 In line with the Court of First Instance in Case T-193/04 *Hans-Martin Tillack v Commission of the European Communities* [2006] ECR II-3995, para 69.

13 See also para 19 of the explanations to Book I.

II. Book III: Structure and Overview

A first general objective of Book III is to provide a clear set of rules applicable to all stages of an administrative procedure preparing and adopting a single case decision, from its initiation (Chapter 2), through the gathering of the relevant information (Chapter 3), particularly through hearings and consultations (Chapter 4) to the making of the final decision (Chapter 5) as well as rules on its potential rectification and withdrawal (Chapter 6). Further objectives are to achieve the right balance first, between detailed rules and general principles and second, between procedural rights and administrative efficiency.

1. Chapter 2: Initiation

Chapter 2 focuses on the initiation stage (Article III-5) and also contains some general rules related to the management of the procedure, such as the duty to appoint a responsible official (Article III-7), the rights of the parties that shall be respected when managing the procedure (Article III-8), and the time-limits within which the final decision is to be adopted (Article III-9). The Chapter also highlights the specifics of application procedures (Article III-6). In addition, the Chapter deals with two other issues: the general duty of fair decision-making (as laid down in paragraph 1 of Article 41 CFR), with a particular emphasis on the duty of impartiality of all persons who are involved in making a decision on behalf of a public authority (Article III-3), and the provision of online information on the administrative procedures envisaged by the legislation (Article III-4).

2. Chapter 3: Information gathering

The gathering of information and evidence is a centre piece of any administrative procedure leading to the adoption of a single case decision. 'Administrative procedure' can thus be understood as a structured process of choice between different alternatives through acquiring, processing and evaluating information.[14] In Chapter 3 of this book the ReNEUAL Model Rules establish an investigatory concept of procedure as the generally applicable standard.[15] The Chapter is split into two sections. The first section establishes a set of general rules, the second section deals with specific issues relating to an especially important instrument of investigation, i.e. inspections. Therefore, inspections

---

[14] See J.-P. Schneider, 'The development of German APA's Standard Procedure: Towards a Comprehensive Procedural Concept' in J. Barnes (ed.) *Transforming Administrative Procedure* (Global Law Press Sevilla 2008) 313 (320).

[15] For a more detailed discussion of this principle see J.-P. Schneider, 'Basic Structures of Information Management in the European Administrative Union' 20 *EPL* (2014) 89 (93 et seqq.); see also Craig (n 4) 333 et seq.

are not conceived as an alternative to investigations, but as an important subcategory of the instruments needed for performing effective investigations.

As mentioned above, Article III-10(1) establishes the principle of investigation as the general standard for administrative information gathering. Its wording is based on several sources of inspiration from EU as well as national law.[16] It reflects the jurisprudence of the CJEU on the duty of careful consideration,[17] which is a counterpart to the principle of investigation. The principle of investigation is supplemented but must not be compromised by the duties to cooperate for the parties established in Article III-13. Public authorities continue to bear the final responsibility with regard to information gathering. This relationship between the two principles is highlighted in the wording of sentence 1 of Article III-13(1) ("assist"). The duty to cooperate varies in different types of administrative procedures. The duty is intensified in application procedures, but it also exists in any other procedure although to a more limited extent.

Inspections, regulated in Section 2 of Chapter 3, are part of the decision-making process.[18] Where inspections provided for by Union law fall within the scope of Book III they are covered by the proposed rules, regardless of whether they are referred to as inspections, on-the-spot checks or on-site monitoring visits. As discussed above, the scope of Book III and Section 2 accordingly is limited to inspections which take place within an administrative procedure intended to end in a decision "with legally binding effect". Articles III-16 and III-17 establish both the powers of inspecting officials and their obligations, thereby taking the need to protect subjective rights into account. Articles III-18 to III-21 coordinate inspections, which must take place on Member State territory by necessity and thereby automatically occur in a multilevel system. The coordination of the ensuing interaction requires rules regulating certain aspects of Member State actions. In line with the limited scope of Book III under III-1(2) this is however conditional on the agreement of the respective Member State or must be provided for in sector-specific law.

---

16 See European Ombudsman, 'The European Code of Good Administration' (2013), Art. 9; (German) Verwaltungsverfahrensgesetz in der Fassung der Bekanntmachung vom 23. Januar 2003 (BGBl. I S. 102), das zuletzt durch Artikel 3 des Gesetzes vom 25. Juli 2013 (BGBl. I S. 2749) geändert worden ist, § 24(2). See also Wet van 4 juni 1992 houdende algemene regels van bestuursrecht (Stb. 1992, 315), in werking getreden op 1 juli 1994, laatstelijk gewijzigd bij Wet van 25 juni 2014, in werking getreden op 1 augustus 2014, Art 3:2; Legge 7 agosto 1990 n. 241, Nuove norme in materia di procedimento amministrativo e di diritto di accesso ai documenti amministrativi (pubblicata nella Gazzetta Ufficiale del 18 agosto 1990 n. 192), Sec. 6(1)(b); see also Ustawa z 14 czerwca 1960 r. Kodeks postępowania administracyjnego (Dziennik Ustaw Nr 30, poz. 168), tekst jednolity z dnia 30 stycznia 2013 r. (Dziennik Ustaw z 2013 r. poz. 267), zmiana z dnia 10 stycznia 2014 r. (Dziennik Ustaw z 2014 r. poz. 183), Arts 77-79.

17 Case C-269/90 *TU München v Hauptzollamt München-Mitte* [1991] ECR I-5469, para 14. See Case T-13/99 *Pfizer Animal Health v Council of the EU* [2002] ECR II-3305 on the integration and consideration of scientific know-how.

18 Schneider (n 15) 89 (96 et seq.).

Information gathering on EU administrative procedures often results in inter-administrative information management.[19] The sharing of information is a key element of decentralised yet effective implementation of EU law within the internal market. Information-related activities are often the essence of composite decision-making procedures. In such cases, the rules on information gathering provided by Book III must be read in combination with Books V and VI of the Model Rules. Mutual assistance, as regulated in Book V, is a core element of EU administrative law and consists to a large extent in informational mutual assistance. In addition, Book VI covers a specific set of – compared to general informational mutual assistance – more complex inter-administrative information activities. Thus, Book VI supplements the other two books by regulating distinct problems of information law. The various provisions on information management of Book VI are essential pre-conditions for the realisation of the right to good administration in situations of inter-administrative vertical or horizontal information exchange.

3. Chapter 4: Hearings and consultations

Chapter 4 specifies the rights relating to the hearing.[20] Article III-22 is concerned with access to the file and Article III-23 with the basic principles governing the right to be heard by those adversely affected. Article III-24 complements the latter article in circumstances where there is a composite administrative procedure (see also below III). Article III-25 lays down the procedural rules applicable where consultation is used in relation to a single decision that affects a large number of people (see also below IV), and Articles III-26 and III-27 are concerned respectively with consultation with the Member States and EU authorities.

Article III-23 deals with the procedural rights associated with the hearing. The core right is provided in Article III-23(1), which accords a right to be heard by a public authority to every party before a decision is made that would adversely affect that person. This formulation is in accord with that in Article 41(2)(a) of some language versions of the CFR, which do not require that the contested measure should be initiated against the claimant.

4. Chapter 5: Conclusion of the procedure

Chapter 5 establishes in Articles III-28 to III-34 the procedural principles that apply to the conclusion of the administrative decision-making. That includes the duty to specify the decision, the duty to give reasons, the duty to indicate available remedies, obligations relating to the notification of decisions, and language requirements. The obligation to state the reasons that justify a certain decision in Article III-29 can help to ensure that the decision has

---

19 *Idem* (98 et seq.).

20 On hearing rights in EU administrative law see Craig (n 4) 298 et seq., 321 et seq.

been duly considered and that administrators are diligently implementing political will. From the perspective of affected parties, an obligation to give reasons can enable them to know why a measure was adopted. From the perspective of the courts, the existence of reasons facilitates judicial review of administrative action.[21] While Article III-29 reiterates – with some innovative features[22] – an obligation that derives directly from the Treaties (see Article 296(2) TFEU),[23] Article III-30 introduces a new obligation, by analogy with several national APAs of EU Member States.[24] Article III-30 does not introduce any innovation with regard to existing judicial and non-judicial remedies at EU-level. Rather, it facilitates their use by parties by introducing an obligation to provide information about them.

5. Chapter 6: Rectification and withdrawal of decisions

Chapter 6 deals with the distinct and complex problems concerning the withdrawal and rectification of decisions. While Article III-35 addresses issues concerning withdrawal or rectification of decisions that have an adverse effect, Article III-36 is directed towards such withdrawal or rectification where the decisions have a beneficial effect. The powers provided for by these articles include the option to withdraw a decision completely, or to rectify only certain aspects of a decision which cannot be qualified as obvious inaccuracies as regulated in Article III-34.

Any withdrawal of a decision may conflict with the protection of legitimate expectations and the principle of legal certainty.[25] The protection of legitimate expectations is an accepted general principle of EU law according to the jurisprudence of the CJEU but is not yet explicitly provided in a transparent manner through a legislative act of the EU. The ReNEUAL Model Rules fill this important gap of legal protection for individuals.

The ReNEUAL Model Rules differentiate – in line with the established case law – between withdrawal of decisions that have an adverse effect (Article III-35) and decisions that are beneficial (Article III-36). If a decision has adverse effects to one party and is beneficial to another party the authority has to balance the conflicting interests of both parties (Articles III-35(4) and III-36(4)). Within these two basic categories the model rules differentiate further between lawful decisions (Articles III-35(2), III-36(3)) and unlawful decisions (Articles III-35(1), III-36(1), (2)). The model rules provide a transparent and balanced set of diffe-

---

21 Case 222/86, *UNECTEF v Heylens* [1987] ECR 4097, establishing that national authorities must state the reasons for any limitation of the rights stemming from the legal order of the EC.

22 See para 103 of the explanations to Book III.

23 On the duty to give reasons in EU administrative law see Craig (n 4) 340 et seqq.

24 This obligation is of particular importance with regard to composite procedures: Schneider (2009) (n 4) 9 (23).

25 For an account of the relevant jurisprudence of the CJEU see Craig (n 4) 549 et seqq.

rent and, in part, innovative legal requirements for a lawful withdrawal of a decision for the four categories following from this structure.

III. Book III and composite procedures

The pluralisation of actors from various jurisdictions within the European administrative space requires a high degree of procedural cooperation between these actors: this is achieved by composite procedures.[26] Article I-4(4) defines a 'composite procedure' as "an administrative procedure where EU authorities and the authorities of a Member State or of different Member States have distinct functions which are inter-dependent. A composite procedure may also mean the combination of two administrative procedures that are directly linked".[27]

Under these complex forms of integrated administrative procedures the procedural steps leading up to the decision result from a mix of applicable laws by different actors. This is irrespective of whether the final decision is taken by an EU or a Member State authority. Composite procedures require joint gathering and use of information as the starting material for decentralised decision-making. Rules of administrative procedure are therefore necessary to prevent the rights and interests of addressees and third parties in the implementation of EU law being overlooked by review and accountability mechanisms at EU-level or at Member State level. These issues of composite procedures are mainly addressed by Books V and VI of the ReNEUAL Model Rules. In contrast, the rules of Book III do not apply to Member States, unless they are rendered applicable in whole or in part by sector-specific legislation. It is nonetheless necessary within the framework of Book III to deal with at least to a limited extent with composite procedures. Otherwise the ReNEUAL Model Rules would accept – or even reinforce to some extent – one of the most important gaps of the protection of individuals in recent EU administrative law.[28]

Consequently, some rules of Book III directly regulate composite procedures (Articles III-10(3), III-11(4), (5), III-18 to 21, III-24, 26, 27, III-29(2)), while other rules are only indirectly important for composite procedures (Article III-7). Articles III-10(3) and III-24 are especially noteworthy:

Article III-10(3) refers to Articles VI-21 and VI-22 and regulates the consequences of inter-administrative information sharing through EU information systems. If a composite procedure is supported by an information system the system shall not only increase administrative efficiency and effectiveness but also inter-administrative control mechanisms in order to guarantee an effective

---

[26] For references to the academic literature on this issue see n 4 above.

[27] The wording of the first sentence is based on a definition formulated in 1999 by the Committee of Independent Experts, Second Report on Reform of the Commission, 'Analysis of Current Practice and Proposals for Tackling Mismanagement, Irregularities and Fraud' (10 September 1999), vol. I, para 3.2.2.

[28] Schneider (2009) (n 4) 9 (20 et seqq.).

protection of individual rights through a duty to independently assess information provided through such an information system.

Article III-24 deals with the right to be heard in composite procedures between the EU and Member States. The article addresses three issues: first, specific procedural obligations incumbent on the EU authorities when they engage in such procedures; second, the obligations of Member State authorities where sector-specific legislation renders Book III applicable to them and thirdly, the procedural obligations of Member States where no such sector-specific legislation exists. Article III-24(1) states the general principle that the application of the right to be heard in such procedures will depend on the division of responsibility in the decision-making process. The following paragraphs of Article III-24 provide more detailed solutions to some standard situations in composite procedures

IV. Book III and multipolar administrative procedures

In many instances single case decision-making by EU authorities concerns complex issues with wide-ranging effects on multiple interests like the authorization of genetically modified organisms or substances for plant protection, the control of anti-competitive behaviour or the control of state aids. Thus EU administrative procedural law cannot be conceived as a purely bilateral relationship between the EU authority and one addressee of an adopted decision. Even a concept focused on decisions with a (great) number of direct addressees would be too limited. Instead, EU decision-making must be understood as an interaction between the EU authority and a multitude of actors with conflicting interests which may either be addressees directly, or in case of so called third-parties (more or less) indirectly, affected by the outcome of such multipolar procedures.[29] Some decisions may be relevant even for a wider interested public.

Book III takes this multipolar structure into account and reflects that structure in several ways. The starting point is a wide definition of the central term "party" in Article III-2(3). All following procedural rights are granted to the parties to the proceedings. In contrast to many national codifications this important status as a party is not limited to the addressee of the intended decision. However the status as a party is also assigned to other persons who are "adversely affected" by the decision if such "third-parties" request to be involved in the procedure. Consequently, Book III does not need to grant special rights to third-parties. The requirement that such third-parties have to request to be involved in the procedure is a way to balance participation rights with legal certainty and administrative efficiency. In any event, the public authority is obliged under Article III-10 to identify and investigate all relevant legal interests

[29] On multipolar participation in EU procedures see: H.C.H. Hofmann, G.C. Rowe and A.H. Türk, *Administrative Law and Policy Of the European Union* (OUP 2011) 380 et seq.; on multipolar structures of national administrative procedures: Schneider (n 14) 313 (320 et seqq., 331 et seqq.).

which are reasonably identifiable, and to contact the persons who possess such legally protected interests.

It is noteworthy that the definition of "party" does not cover persons who are simply interested. A person who is merely interested does not qualify as being adversely affected solely because he or she subjectively thinks that this is so. It is an objective test, determined by the body providing the procedure in accordance with the applicable substantive law, albeit subject to judicial review. This is in accord with the criterion enshrined in Article 41(2)(a) of the Charter of Fundamental Rights (CFR). In addition Article III-8(3) provides for the choice of a representative or representatives to take part in the procedure where there are many who are adversely affected in the same manner.

A related concept, but distinct from that of "adversely affected parties", is that of "interested public". Article III-2(4) specifies that this concept is relevant for the purposes of consultations in accordance with Article III-25. It means "every natural or legal person and other associations, organizations or groups expressing an interest in an administrative procedure". This definition is justified by the fact that the effects of the intended decision can sometimes be very far-reaching and affect the collective interests of a community. If a large number of people are affected by such a decision, the procedure should allow the wider public to be consulted.

D. Final Remarks

As mentioned above, single case decision-making is a centre piece of most codifications of administrative procedural law. Therefore, Book III should certainly be a starting point of any legislative attempt at EU-level to create an administrative procedural law based on the rule of law. The EU may follow the example of the Netherlands which established its *Algemene Wet Bestuursrecht*, i.e. its General Administrative Law Act, in "tranches".

In many national codifications the rules on single case decision-making are supplemented by some basic rules on mutual assistance. This follows from the fact that effective single case decision-making by one public authority depends in a significant number of cases on support by other authorities. That need for inter-administrative collaboration is a consequence of modern administrative organisation based on an efficient division of labour. The multilevel and multi-jurisdictional structure of the EU administrative space requires such a framework for mutual assistance even more than in national contexts. Thus, also Book V should be understood as a necessary component for any appropriate legal framework of single case decision-making by EU authorities, although this requires an extension of the scope of application of certain parts of this framework to Member States' authorities. The fundamental principle of sincere cooperation embodied in Article 4(3) TEU justifies such an extension because this principle remains ineffective in a significant number of cases without such a legislative framework.

CHAPTER 2

The Heritage of Otto Mayer: *Actes Administratifs Unilatéraux* and *Verwaltungsakte* in a Franco-German Comparison

Pascale Gonod

For Ernst Forsthoff, the term *Verwaltungsakte*, which designates a diversity of government acts, is a term which emerged during the second half of the 19th Century and predominantly of doctrinal origin.[1] He underlines that the notion scarcely appears in legislation before the adoption of legislative texts on the administrative court system.[2] In France, the development is rather the other way round: statutes use the expression *acte administratif* and ascribe it the same meaning – particularly to determine the scope of application of the Statute of 16-24 August 1790 – and doctrine has subsequently endeavoured to define what is covered by the notion of *acte administratif.*

It is remarkable that the second half of the 19th Century was a founding period for the approach and determination of the *acte administratif unilatéral* and the *Verwaltungsakt*, in France and in Germany, but it is not surprising given that the liberal State was developing in this period on both sides of the Rhine river. In spite of clear distinctions between their writings, the 'founding fathers' of the French and German administrative legal systems, Edouard Laferrière and Otto Mayer,[3] also display strong similarities in their analysis of *acte administratif/ Verwaltungsakt* conceived of as acts of commandment.

As this section is dedicated to the 'roots' of unilateral decision making, the brief remarks which follow are intended to address this subject, from the perspective of the works of these two jurists.[4]

A. Edouard Laferrière and Otto Mayer

From the beginning of the 19th Century, the judge endeavoured to determine the content of texts with the purpose of retaining the exact meaning of the word *administration* used in the Statute of 16-24 August 1790 and in the Decree of 16 fructidor an III, according to which it was forbidden for the ordinary judge to decide on acts of the administration and on the operation

* Translated from French by Anna Riddell and Matthias Ruffert.

1 E. Forsthoff, *Traité de droit administratif allemand* (Bruylant 1969) p. 310 ("surtout d'origine doctrinale").

2 Ibid. Above all, he quoted from the statute on administrative courts in the American zone of occupation (1946/47), from the respective statute for the British zone and Articles 42 and 113 of the German *Verwaltungsgerichtsordnung* (1960), the federal statute on administrative courts, which does not give any definition. He noted that the courts themselves referred to those statutes, and defined the act as "toute ordonnance, tout arrêté, toute décision ou tout autre mesure émanant d'une autorité administrative et destinée `trancher un problème individuel dans le cadre du droit public".

3 E. Laferrière *Traité de la juridiction administrative et des recours contentieux Laferrière* (Berger-Levrault 1887-1888); O. Mayer *Droit administratif allemand* (1st ed. Giard-Briére Editeurs 1895, 1st French ed. of 1903; used here is the translation of the 3rd ed. of 1924). On these two authors see P. Gonod *Édouard Laferrière, un jurist au service de la République* (LGDJ 1997); E. Volkmar Heyen *Otto Mayer* (Duncker & Humblot 1981).

4 Notwithstanding the title of this chapter, which recalls only the heritage of Otto Mayer and neglects that of Édouard Laferrière.

of administrative bodies.[5] The definition of the *acte admininstratif* is therefore closely linked to a pragmatic question, that of the attribution of judicial powers.

The first general criterion of this attribution is the presence of the State in a dispute: as soon as the State is a 'party' to proceedings, the ordinary tribunals, i.e. the common law judges, no longer have competence. As a result legal doctrine tried to detect from the courts' jurisprudence a guiding idea of attribution between the two categories of jurisdiction based on the legal nature of the act in question. In this respect, the courts operationalised several different criteria of attribution, and consequently hesitation and uncertainty governing jurisprudence and doctrine became apparent. In spite of this, the distinction between acts of authority and of commercial acts (*acta iure gestionis*) began to take shape in the first half of the Century: it was no longer sufficient to invoke a public interest to decline the competence of the ordinary tribunals, to give administrative form to acts which would be part of the common law according to their object. It was decisive that the administrative character stemmed from the very nature of the act and not from the quality of its author or of what it was aimed at.[6] The distinction between *actes d'autorité* and *actes de gestion* began to gain awareness in legal theory.

The legal scholar P. Henrion de Pansey[7] is considered to be the first author to have described the theory of *actes d'autorité* and *actes de gestion.*[8] He considered that a dispute would always be one of common law when it was concerning relationships between citizens and that it would only be administrative if the judgment concerned the relationship between individuals and government and if the latter was not acting in a proprietary manner.[9] From that time, the range of application of *actes de gestion* only comprised acts undertaken by the State as the owner of public real estate.

5 Original text of Article 13 of the Statute of 16-24 August 1790: "Les fonctions judiciaires sont distinctes et demeureront toujours séparées des fonctions administratives. Les juges ne pourront, à peine de forfaiture, troubler, de quelque manière que ce soit, les opérations des corps administratifs, ni citer devant eux les administrateurs pour raison de leurs fonctions", and of the Decree of 16 fructidor an III : "défenses itératives sont faites aux tribunaux de connaître des actes d'administration, de quelque manière que ce soit, aux peines de droit".

6 Laferrière (n 3) vol. 1, p. 477. Original text: "... ne suffit plus, pour faire échec à la compétence des tribunaux, d'invoquer un intérêt public, de donner une forme administrative à des actes qui, d'après leur objet relèveraient du droit commun. Il faut que le caractère administratif résulte de la nature même de l'acte et non pas uniquement de la qualité de son auteur ou du but qu'il se propose".

7 P. Henrion de Pansey *L'autorité judiciaire en France* (T. Barrois Père 1827).

8 H. Berthélémy *Traité élémentaire de droit administratif* (9th ed., Paris 1920) p. 1099, n. 1. It should be mentioned that reading Otto Mayer's *Deutsches Verwaltungsrecht* it is evident that he knew Henrion de Pansey's oeuvre (see in particular p. 73).

9 Original text: "la contestation est judiciaire toutes les fois qu'il est question de statuer sur les rapports des citoyens entre eux, et elle n'est administrative que lorsqu'il s'agit de prononcer entre des particuliers et le gouvernement agissant non pas comme propriétaire mais comme gouvernement" Henrion de Pansey (n 7) p. 296.

Later in the 1860s, in the beginning of the epoch called *d'organisation* by Hauriou, with the aim of establishing a general system explaining the scope of competence of the administrative judge, Aucoc and Ducrocq[10] both took up this approach again. Aucoc stated: "The question of determination of the competence of the administrative judge could have been solved very easily, logically and possibly in line with the ideas inspiring the *Assemblée constituante* of 1789. It could have been said that every act undertaken by government authority as a public power with respect to a public service cannot but be decided upon before the administrative courts. Indeed, what the *Assemblée constituante* wanted when formulating the principle of the separation of powers was to avoid a public service being fettered by intervention of the judicial branch. Given the silence of the texts one would only have referred disputes to this authority relating to government acts where the administration acts as the holder of property under the same conditions as private individuals and is subdued to the rules of civil law."[11] Thus, Aucoc was forced to admit that the solutions expounded by the courts contradicted this analysis.

Laferrière followed the same concept but advanced further, establishing the thesis of authority and management in a system. To do this, he gave it a slightly different scope. First of all, he distinguished within government action two types of situations: administration can appear either as bearing authority or power, which is one of the attributes of the executive, or as managing and leading public services without holding sovereignty.[12] Further, he considered that deciding on the first category of acts (*actes d'autorité*) was attributed to the administrative courts, whereas deciding on the second (*actes de gestion*), similar to disputes between individuals, was part of the competence of the common law judge. Consequently, Laferrière attributed the *actes de gestion* a much larger field of application placing disputes relating to the functioning of public services a priori outside the jurisdiction of the administrative courts.

He considered that the administration was by delegation vested with a power of enforcement: it held authority, which is one of the attributes of executive power.[13] It was vested with public power to execute the statutes, pronounced

---

[10] T. Ducrocq *Cours de droit administratif* (7th ed., Paris 1897-1900).

[11] Original text: "... aurait pu être résolue (...) d'une manière très simple, très logique, et peut-être conforme à la pensée qui inspirait 1'Assemblée constituante de 1789. On aurait pu dire que tout acte fait par l'autorité administrative comme puissance publique, en, vue de la gestion d'un service public, ne peut être discuté que devant la juridiction administrative. En effet, ce que l'Assemblée constituante a voulu, en posant le principe de séparation des pouvoirs, c'est qu'un service public ne pût pas être entravé par 1'intervention de 1'autorité judiciaire. On aurait ainsi renvoyé à cette autorité, dans le silence des textes, que les difficultés relatives aux actes où l'administration figure comme propriétaire, dans les mêmes conditions que les simples particuliers, et pour lesquels elle se conforme aux règles du droit civil." L. Aucoc, *Conférences sur l'administration et le droit administratif* (1st ed., Paris 1869).

[12] Original text: "gérant et intendant des services publics et non comme dépositaire d'une part de souveraineté", Laferrière (n 3) vol. 1, p. 3 and p. 485.

[13] *Ibid.* Original text: "l'administration est dépositaire d'une part d'autorité, de puissance, qui est un des attributs du pouvoir exécutif".

secondary rules aimed at assuring the application of the latter, regulated the market of public services and provided the citizens with the advantages of good government;[14] to this end, its acts were unilateral. The accomplishment of these goals justified, in effect, the realization of particular means: this is how government could "act by general or individual orders, injunctions or measures of defence addressed to those that deviate from the rules foreseen or do harm to the general interest".[15] These instruments bear the brand of public power: the acts which were accomplished by the administration by force of that delegation, the rules it proclaimed, the rights it conferred, the injunctions or interdictions it pronounced, were coined by an inherent power.[16] However the inherent power was lacking in the means to manage the administration, i.e. when the administration was charged with supervising the management and use of public wealth, to ensure the collection of all revenue designated for public purposes and its attribution to the public services.[17] If, when issuing acts of management, administrative action was motivated by the general interest, i.e. public interest, in contrast public power did not intervene, because the capacities the administration employed to carry out these acts did not normally exceed those possessed by citizens by virtue of the common private law, or which they could assign to themselves by free contractual relationships.[18] In other words, if the administration carries out an act comparable to that which a private citizen could carry out in his relations with other individuals, then the relationship of the administration with the individual is the same. However, if the administration employs a power that has been delegated to it, then the relationship is no longer one of equals. The principle of equality is overridden by the principle of authority: law of order on the one hand, duty to obey on the other.[19]

---

[14] *Ibid.* Original text: "faire exécuter les lois, d'édicter des prescriptions secondaires destinées à assurer leur application, de régler la marche des services publics et de procurer aux citoyens les avantages d'une bonne police".

[15] *Ibid.* Original text: "agir par voie de prescriptions générales ou individuelles, d'injonctions ou de défense adressées à ceux qui s'écartent des règles prescrites ou qui nuisent à l'intérêt général".

[16] *Ibid.* Original text: "les actes que l'administration accomplit en vertu de cette délégation, les règles qu'elle édicte, les droits qu'elle confère, les injonctions ou les interdictions qu'elle prononce, portent l'empreinte d'un pouvoir propre".

[17] *Ibid.* Original text: "veiller à la gestion de la fortune publique et à son emploi, d'assurer la perception des revenus de toute nature destinés à pourvoir aux charges communes, et leur affectation aux services publics".

[18] *Ibid.* Original text: "les facultés que l'administration exerce dans l'accomplissement de ces actes n'excèdent pas, en général, celles que les citoyens possèdent en vertu du droit privé, ou qu'ils peuvent s'attribuer par des stipulations librement consenties".

[19] *Ibid.* Original text: "qui sont égales pour tous dans les rapports des individus entre eux, le sont aussi dans leurs rapports avec l'administration, lorsque celle-ci fait, en vue d'intérêts généraux, ce qu'un simple citoyen pourrait faire en vue d'intérêts particuliers. Mais ces facultés ne sont plus égales entre les individus et l'administration, lorsque celle-ci exerce la puissance qui lui a été déléguée. Ce n'est plus

The distinction between authority and management translates to the distinction between two spheres of activity – a public and a private sphere – which are rooted in a certain concept of the State inherited by the French Revolution limiting State intervention to the guarantee of individual liberty. The power of the State and manifestation of sovereignty, i.e. "the power of a will that is not determined by anything but itself subject to no other power above or parallel to it", was conceived by the Revolutionaries as being different by its very nature from the capacities of individuals. The translation of this difference ends up in the State bearing supreme authority, a superior power that outweighs the totality of individual interests: the individual right of sovereignty is imposed only on private individual rights. Acts originating from the exercise of sovereignty are different by nature from acts performed by ordinary individuals. Further, in the liberal tradition the use of sovereignty by the State in the name of the nation is limited by the respect of the common good, i.e. by the same end that constitutes the political institutions. Consequently, the pursuit of the general interest is simultaneously the foundation and the limit of State power, as well as the justification for its authority. Bearing in mind that the public sphere is limited, the State power has the task to cater for the respect of order and to give a framework to social life; it cannot intervene in the sphere of private activities or particular interests. As soon as the government places itself in a relationship of equality and enters into the area of private activities, the State of which it is a branch appears as a civil person. This creates the effect of the duplication of the State: the State as a power, and the State as a private person.

B. *Verwaltungsakt*

According to Ernst Forsthoff,[20] the question whether the notion of *Verwaltungsakt* was borrowed from French administrative law by translating the expression *acte administratif* or if it was independently developed in Germany appears to have been subject to debate. Without discussing this in detail here, it is useful to remark that Mayer considers that the expression is taken from the French terminology to designate its quality to decide individual cases authoritatively and following the rule of law.[21] Incidentally, Mayer draws strong support from the oeuvre of French jurists from the period before Laferrière. Following the example of the latter he also quotes e.g. Henrion de Pansey and Aucoc on the notion of an 'act'. The obvious similarity in this determination deduced from the ideas of power and authority by the founding fathers of French and German administrative law can be explained by their use of the same sources, the same juridical heritage, and above all, by the liberal ideas con-

alors le principe d'égalité qui domine mais au contraire le principe d'autorité : droit de commandement d'un côté, devoir de soumission de l'autre."

20 Forsthoff (n 1) p. 310.

21 Mayer (n 3) p. 79.

veyed by that heritage. In the liberal concept, to be precise, the use of the idea of power to limit the *acte administratif* is effectuated to give a foundation to the self-limitation of the State.

Scrutinizing the State under the regime of the police (*Polizeistaat*), Mayer can draw a distinction between public law and private law to separate legal personality, in other words with reference to the idea of the *fiscus* (treasury). This lies behind the apprehension of two distinct legal persons, products of a juridical division of the State: on the one hand, the old *fiscus,* the State considered as a society of pecuniary interests or a legal person of civil law, and on the other hand, the State as such, the political association, and the legal person under public law.[22] Thus, if private law is applied in every instance in which the State manages its wealth, by contrast, the State which executes public power is excluded: where there is order and force, it is the State, everywhere else, it is the *fiscus*. When the State starts giving orders and employing public power, it is impossible to apply civil law.[23] Consequently, administrative law that governs compulsory State activity obliges power to submit to its rules. Mayer expresses this well, saying that "the *Rechtsstaat* is the State which possesses a well-ordered administrative law"[24] and that gives subjects the right to question its decisions before a judge. Expressed differently, the *Rechtsstaat* is synonymous to the principle of subordinating the administration to a judge.

C. Self-Limitation of States

The idea of self-limitation of States is evidently present in the theory of Laferrière and gives a legitimate ground to the existence and powers of administrative justice. The distinction between acts of authority and of management effectively explains the disparity of the administrative judge's powers: the nature of the act deferred to the judge determines his powers. The categorisation of remedies otherwise elaborated by Laferrière on the basis of the powers of the judge constitutes the procedural answer to the distinction of acts of authority (related to the *contentieux d'annulation* and more specifically the *recours pour excès de pouvoir*) and of management (related to the *plein contentieux*). Contrary to Laferrière, the question of distinguishing disputes from each other is not at all a matter a priori in Mayer's German concept of an *Akt,* which is instead focused on the foundation of the 'science' of administrative law. What remains is that as soon as it is admitted that administrative law is an autonomous

[22] *Ibid.*, p. 57. Original text: "deux personnes morales distinctes, produits d'une division juridique de l'Etat: d'une part, l'ancien, fisc, l'Etat considéré comme société d'intérêts pécuniaires ou personne morale du droit civil; d'autre part, l'Etat proprement dit, l'association politique, la personne morale du droit public".

[23] *Ibid.*, p. 60. Original text: "Là où il y a commandement et contrainte, c'est l'Etat; partout ailleurs, c'est le fisc. (...Quand l'Etat) se met à commander et à exercer la puissance publique, alors il n'est plus question d'appliquer le droit civil".

[24] *Ibid.*, p. 60. Original text: "Der Rechtsstaat ist der Staat des wohlgeordneten Verwaltungsrechts".

system, distinct from private law, a difficulty arises as to which of the several remedies should be applied.

For Mayer, if administrative legal scholarship wishes to become a complete juridical discipline equal to its elder sisters, it must establish a system of specific juridical institutions in the administration of the State; but in fact, the only "specific" instrument that he discussed, according to Michael Stolleis, was the order of the public power (*hoheitlicher Befehl*) towards the subjects (*Untertanen*).[25] What Mayer presented as German administrative law was a system of forms of State action as acts of authority.[26] Consequently, in the centre of his construction of administrative law, there is the *Verwaltungsakt*. In his 'Deutsches Verwaltungsrecht', Mayer indeed recommends that the particular nature of the *Verwaltungsakt* must be studied if one wishes to understand modern administrative law, because it dominates that law.[27] For this jurist, an administrative act is "an act emanating from the administration which determines towards the subject (*Untertan*) what for him must be the law in an individual case".[28] More than his predecessors – who use the term 'authoritative disposition' (*obrigkeitliche Verfügung*), Mayer stresses the effect of the act with regard to the 'subject': the latter is the citizen subdued to the power of the State, who has to obey the act of authority immediately, even if it is contrary to the law.[29]

D. Defining the Concept of Administrative Act

Differences in analysis and the concept of the administrative act become apparent when one reflects closely on the writings of both jurists.

First of all, with respect to the scope of the act: whereas in France, the *acte administratif* can equally have an individual scope and a general and impersonal scope, Mayer considers it to be an individual act. Contemporary German administrative law has not deviated from this concept, and is narrower than in French law. Paragraph 35 of the *Verwaltungsverfahrensgesetz* indeed provides: "An administrative act shall be any order, decision or other sovereign measure taken by an authority to regulate an individual case in the sphere of public law and intended to have a direct, external legal effect." In other words, a statutory instrument (*réglement*) is not a *Verwaltungsakt*. Substantially defined as a normative act of a general and abstract nature, its operational dimension is not important: the fact that it is issued by an administrative authority is not sufficient to render it a *Verwaltungsakt* which would be subject to the same legal regime as individual administrative decisions. Today, as with Mayer's concept, the statutory instru-

[25] O Mayer, 'Zur Lehre vom öffentlichrechtlichen Vertrage'' 3 *Archiv des öffentlichen Rechts* (1888) 3, quoted by M. Stolleis *Histoire du droit public en Allemagne: 1800-1914* in: *Rivages du droit* (Dalloz 2014) p. 559.

[26] Stolleis *ibid.*

[27] Mayer (n 3) 1903 edition, p. 3.

[28] Mayer (n 3) p. 120.

[29] Stolleis (n 25).

ment under German law (*Rechtsverordnung* or *Satzung*) is designed to execute or implement statutes but unlike the *réglement* as we know it in France, it is not autonomous. It is designated by the expression "legal norm" (*Rechtsnorm*) and bears an infra-legislative character. This type of act includes *Rechtsverordnungen* (statutory instrument, *réglement*) issued by the federal government (some of them being subject to the approval of the *Bundesrat*, Article 80 (2) *Grundgesetz*) or of the authorities of the *Länder*, and also corporate local byelaws (*Satzungen*) issued by bodies under public law other than the State (at federal or *Länder*-level).

Further, as far as the unilateral nature of the administrative act is concerned: there is another disparity that reveals itself with respect to public law contracts. Laferrière admits them into the field of administrative law, whereas they are radically excluded by Mayer, who is resolutely hostile to this idea.

The concept preserved by Laferrière about acts of authority and of management is the same as Aucoc's of 1878, looking at the actual state of the courts' judgments (and not of the model that he exposes). He regrets that his own analysis of the act of management did not prevail: as he does not find a theoretical justification to exclude acts of management with respect to public services from the administrative competence, he fails to justify positive law. Laferrière tries to explain this, at the cost of an alteration of the concept of distinction underlying his analysis at least in two respects.

He is forced on the one hand to recognise the existence of contractual acts of the administration under public law – which led Aucoc to reject the concept of act of management developed by Laferrière – which is absolutely incompatible with the application of the distinction between acts of authority and acts of management: for him indeed, the *acte administratif* is the unilateral act (this is the very position of Otto Mayer). On the other hand, the concept of the State which translates this distinction further presumes the irresponsibility of the power-State; the extensive understanding of the idea of an act of management permits the explanation that, without calling the principle into question, the responsibility of the State can be engaged in the management of public services. Thus, logically the distinction of acts of authority and of management implies the recognition of the competence of the ordinary judge, which is contrary to the approach of positive law. Laferrière is also forced to bring in the 'subsidiary criterion' of the applicable law: the responsibility of the State in tort cannot be governed by private law rules. Ever since, the notion of act of management which he adopts is denatured, because if private law is set aside, this is precisely because the State does not apply, in the management of public services, instruments available to the ordinary citizen. Beyond the difference of their respective positions, Laferrière and Aucoc are struggling with the same difficulty: in reality, the distinction between acts of authority and of management is based on a concept of the State which is hardly in accordance with the (interventionist) role assigned to the State in the Republic.

Today, as everybody knows, German law admits the "Admissibility of an agreement under public law" (title to paragraph 54 of the *Verwaltungsverfahrensgesetz*, interesting it its formulation): "A legal relationship under public law may be constituted, amended or annulled by agreement (agreement under public law) in so far as this is not contrary to legal provision. In particular, the authority may, instead of issuing an administrative act, conclude an agreement under public law with the person to whom it would otherwise direct the administrative act." (compromise and exchange agreements, paragraphs 55 and 56). The public law contract conserves its exceptional character and was never used for public procurement and not even for concessions.[30] For Forsthoff, "when the authorities were granted public law prerogatives to fulfil their mission, one hesitated to leave them the choice between the exercise of their prerogatives and the recourse to the contractual technique." Also, in the relationship between rule and exception, the attribution to private law is first choice.

To close this discussion some final remarks are necessary. The definition of the administrative act following the criterion of authority was replaced by the application of other approaches, and this ocurred rather quickly considering the 1899 publication of Hauriou's '*gestion administrative*'. What is important is not to present the well-known elements of ancient theories, well described and discussed by Charles Eisenmann,[31] but to underline that the approach of the *acte* continues to play another central role to fix the contours of the range of application of administrative law and is therefore placed at the heart of debates on the autonomy of administrative law: the *acte administratif* remains the manifestation of the scope of administrative law, which, together with private law, restrains the administration. Further, studying the unilateral act is an essential part of administrative law. For numerous jurists, the unilateral act expresses a power inherent to the administration and allows mere individuals to oppose such acts. Therefore, de Laubadère affirms that "the unilateral act is characteristic of public law whereas private law would be based on acts of will", and he also notes that there was nothing comparable to the executive administrative decision.[32] Following Eisenmann, Dupuis has shown that the unilateral quality of the act is not exclusive for the public sphere but that it exists in private law, in relations between individuals (such as internal rules in companies, voluntary recognition of an illegitimate child, exercise of parental authority for example).[33] Nevertheless, with strong unanimity, lawyers ascribe to public law the possibility to unilaterally perform acts which create rights and obligations to the benefit or

30 M. Fromont *Droit administratif des États européens* (PUF 2006) p. 313 (original text "n'a jamais été utilise pour les contrats de fourniture, de travaus, de services et même pour les concessions").

31 See in particular C. Eisenmann *Cours de droit administratif* (LGDJ 1982).

32 A. de Laubadère *Traité de droit administratif* (LGDJ 1980), vol. 1, p. 229. Original text: "1'acte unilatéral est caractéristique du droit public, le droit privé reposant sur l'acte des volontés ... rien en droit privé qui soit comparable à ce qu'est la décision administrative exécutoire".

33 G. Dupuis *Définition de l'acte unilateral* (Mélanges Eisenmann, 1975) p. 205.

detriment of third parties without their consent and which are in certain cases able to be executed by the government itself.[34]

Without doubt, considering the *acte* as a manifestation of the scope of administrative law invites us to undertake a study of that scope in France and Germany. The persistence of a narrow concept (individual act) in Germany and a larger one in France as the *acte administratif,* may have an abstract range (executing a *loi* or not) that makes comparing the two less pertinent. However, on can insist that in both systems, the continued importance of the function of the act is remarkable, as this is correctly reflected upon by Eberhard Schmidt-Aßmann:

Studies about the modernisation of administrative law have to undertake an in-depth analysis of all elements and all categories forming the general part in order to determine to what extent they come up to the current needs and can be used to effectuate the new functions that have been bestowed upon government. It is evident that his analysis shall not end up in rejecting the traditional model. For example, if you think that the administrative act, central institution in the classical model, is vested today as formerly with extraordinary importance and lies at the heart of the new systematisation of administrative law. Another matter that has to be checked meticulously is to determine if it necessitates certain adaptations (or innovations). The result of this examination should not be prejudiced, it is open.[35]

34 G. Dupuis, *Cours polycopiés* (Université de Paris 1, 1978-1979). Original text: "de faire unilatéralement des actes qui créent des droits et des obligations au profit ou à la charge des tiers, sans le consentement de ceux-ci, et qui sont susceptibles dans certains cas d'être exécutés par la force par l'Administration elle-même".

35 E. Schmidt-Aßmann, 'Principes de base d'une réforme du droit administratif' ("Le changement de perspective du droit administratif") 2008 *RFDA* 427 and 667. Original text: "Les études qui s'occupent de la modernisation du droit administratif devront réaliser une analyse en profondeur de chacun des éléments et de chacune des catégories qui forment la partie générale, afin de déterminer dans quelle mesure ils répondent aux besoins actuels et peuvent servir pour rendre effectives les nouvelles fonctions qui ont été confiées à l'Administration. Cette analyse ne doit pas déboucher, c'est évident, sur un rejet général du modèle traditionnel. Que l'on pense par exemple que l'acte administratif, institution centrale dans le modèle classique, est doté aujourd'hui comme hier d'une pertinence extraordinaire et qu'il se trouve au cœur de la nouvelle systématisation du droit administratif. Autre chose, qui doit être soigneusement vérifiée, est de déterminer s'il exige certaines adaptations (ou innovations). Le résultat de cet examen ne saurait être préjugé, il reste ouvert."

The Heritage of Otto Mayer: *Actes Administratifs Unilatéraux* and *Verwaltungsakte* in a Franco-German Comparison

Comment by Thomas Groß

The single case decision is certainly a common core of administrative law in Europe. Nevertheless there are important differences in detail originating from the historical background and the relation to other measures of administrative action. I will develop this aspect here in comparing French, German and European Union law, both the existing Aricle 288 TFEU and Book III of the ReNEUAL Model Rules.

In France, as Pascale Gonod has shown, the *acte administratif unilatéral* has its origin in the separation of administrative action from judicial competences. The purpose of the term is to define the scope of the area where executive measures are exempt from any control by the ordinary courts. It comprises all unilateral binding determinations, i.e. single case decisions as well as administrative rules of all kinds. The more narrow concept of *décisions administratives individuelles*, corresponding to the single case decision, is also used in two statutes on special procedural rights of citizens.[36]

In Germany the *Verwaltungsakt* as defined in § 35 VwVfG (German Administrative Procedure Act) has five determining elements: it is a binding unilateral determination in administrative law concerning a single case by a public authority with external effect. The term has been used in Germany since the first half of the 19th Century, but a systematic elaboration of the concept with a lasting influence was made by Otto Mayer at the end of that century. He focused especially on adjudication. Therefore the concept was designed to define a specific measure of public administration and exclude all others, as only the qualification as *Verwaltungsakt* brought with it legal protection by the administrative courts, which were then seen as part of the administration. The purpose of this definition was to introduce the formality of civil procedure law into administrative law.[37] The *Verwaltungsakt* is seen by him as a parallel to the judgement of a civil court. This has some similarities with the development of English administrative law where the application of the principles of natural justice to administrative measures was justified by the duty to act judicially.

This parallel to civil procedure law is one of the reasons for several shortcomings in traditional German administrative law doctrine. It does not fully take into account that the single case decision is a multi-purpose instrument of public administration with a much greater variety of situations covered than by court judgments. The parallel fosters the idea that in the average case the

[36] Loi No 79-587 du 11 juillet 1979 relative à la motivation des actes administratifs et à l'amélioration des relations entre l'administration et le public; Loi No 2000-321 du 12 avril 2000 relative aux droits des citoyens dans leurs relations avec les administrations.

[37] O. Mayer, *Deutsches Verwaltungsrecht I*, (1st ed., Duncker & Humblot 1895) 65: "Justizförmigkeit der Verwaltung".

decision can be taken only on the basis of statutory law, as usual when a court is applying, e.g., the Civil Code, but this neglects the fact that the legal requirements for administrative action are often specified step by step through secondary legislation, guidelines, concepts etc. A third shortcoming of this idea that the administration should act like a judge is that the importance of the political elements of administrative action are often underestimated.

In European Union law the 'decision' according to Article 288 (4) TFEU has a much broader profile. It is a residual category for any kind of executive action with binding force outside the regulation and the directive. It combines at least three types of decisions. One of them is the single case decision in the sense that is it discussed here, but this special profile becomes clear only in combination with Article 263 (4) TFEU referring to the addressee. The second type is the decision addressed to one, several or all Member States. Third, there are also decisions without an addressee, including measures of general application. The decision in the existing primary EU law thus comprises single case decisions in the narrow sense, supervisory measures in the European federal system and administrative rule-making.

The single case decision according to Book III of the Model Rules has a different profile. The definition in Article III-2 (1) is closer to the German tradition. It is clear that the reference to the single case excludes rule-making, which is the subject of Book II. An open question is whether decisions addressed to Member States are covered by the definition. There are more and more provisions in secondary law giving EU institutions the power to issue directions binding on national authorities. A prominent case is the new Single Resolution Board created by Regulation No. 806/2014. The term 'public person' used in Article III-2 (1) to define the addressee of a single case decision could include Member States within that definition. On the other hand the rules on the annulment of legal acts in Article 263 TFEU clearly separate the protection of Member States covered by para. 2 and the protection of other addressees and persons concerned by para. 4. Would it be useful to apply the provisions on the right to a hearing, on the access to the file or the duty to give reasons to the relationship between EU institutions and national authorities? In German constitutional law there is a parallel in the right of the federal government to give binding directions to *Länder* authorities in special fields of administration covered by Article 85 *Grundgesetz* (Basic Law). This relationship is not covered by the administrative procedure act but by the vague unwritten concept of federal comity (*Bundestreue*).

In any case, the decision according to Article III-2 (1) Model Rules is more narrow than Article 288 (4) TFEU. Therefore the question arises why the drafters did not include the term 'single case' in the definition in order to avoid misunderstandings. Certainly the better solution would be to amend Article 288 TFEU in order to create a clearer system of legal measures in European Union law but this alternative requires a consensus between all Member States. It is hoped that it will be easier to obtain the necessary political support for the adoption of the model rules.

CHAPTER 3

Unilateral Single Case Decisions: A UK Perspective

Paul Craig

UK administrative law is not constructed around the concept of the administrative act in the way that is common for some continental legal regimes. The concept of the administrative act does not therefore have the centrality that it has for these other legal regimes. The practical and normative consequences of this are interesting and worthy of a paper in and of itself. Such consequences are almost certainly an admixture of the positive and the negative: thus a positive feature of attachment to the concept of the administrative act is that it provides a focal point around which to organize administrative law doctrine; a negative feature is that the very definition of an administrative act can crab and confine administrative law and thereby hamper its development and coverage of types of behaviour that ought to be within administrative law. This Chapter is not, however, about the broad conceptual issue as to the consequences, positive and negative, of constructing administrative law around the concept of the administrative act. The Chapter addresses the more specific issue, which is the focal point of this conference, viz, Book III of the ReNEUAL Model Rules in comparative perspective. The four themes of the paper can be stated at the outset.

First, public law norms dealing with the procedure for unilateral single case decision-making have a very considerable historical pedigree, almost certainly considerably older than that in Franco-German law. Thus procedural norms are not in that sense 'strangers' to administrative law in the UK. To the contrary they have, as will be seen, a pedigree going back 400 hundred years, and there is a consistent line of case law over this period.

Secondly, although the UK does not have a general code of administrative procedure akin to that which exists in many other countries, UK law does nonetheless provide legal coverage for most of the issues dealt with in the ReNEUAL Model Rules on single case decisions, although it is certainly arguable that the UK could benefit from the greater clarity and organizational form that comes with the Model Rules. There are moreover, as will be seen, mini-procedural codes dealing with particular subject matter areas, which address many of the issues covered in the Model Rules.

Thirdly, there is in reality nothing in Book III of the Model Rules that should cause any alarm to a person schooled in a common law tradition. Finally, paradoxically or not the principal opposition to the application of Book III to Member State action that falls within the scope of EU law came from countries that have more developed all-embracing procedural codes, which felt that they had more to 'lose' if Book III was applied to such action.

A. The Fundamentals of Procedural Due Process: Historic Roots

UK Administrative law dates from the late 16th Century.[1] The courts developed a body of legal rules concerned directly with the legal con-

[1] P. Craig, *UK, EU and Global Administrative Law: Foundations and Challenges* (Cambridge University Press 2015) Ch 1.

straints that should be placed on the administration broadly conceived, and many of the core concepts that we use today would be recognized by our judicial forbears such as Coke, Holt, Hale, Abbott, Blackstone, Mansfield and Kenyon because they created them.[2] The rules were part of relations between individual and State, thereby forming the foundations for classic administrative law review, and were central also to relations between the arms of government, thereby operating as a form of structural constitutional review.

In doctrinal terms, the courts developed many of the central concepts of judicial review with which we are familiar today.[3] There was well-established case law on review of fact and law. There was doctrine dating back to the sixteenth century on legal control of discretion, which was cast in terms of rationality review and also what was termed proportionability. There was jurisprudence on due process and damages liability. There was doctrine on principles of good administration, as exemplified by case law limiting the ability of a person who possessed a de facto or de jure monopoly to charge whatever prices he liked, the courts' reasoning that such property was imbued with a public interest that limited the normal capacity to charge what the market would bear.

The doctrine was given force through judicial creativity in relation to remedies. The amplification of grounds for review took place within, and was framed by, the evolution of adjectival law. Direct and collateral challenge were the vehicles for this development, the former through the prerogative writs, the latter primarily, albeit not exclusively, through tort actions. The courts transformed mandamus, certiorari and prohibition, thereby creating the remedial mechanisms to effectuate the procedural and substantive doctrines of judicial review. The prerogative writs had existed from medieval times, but were not used to control administration in the manner that became the norm from the 17th Century onwards. The judicial creativity matches anything found in more modern doctrine.[4] While the prerogative writs were the principal medium for direct challenge, a very considerable number of actions were brought collaterally, via tort claims. Plaintiffs used actions for trespass, case, replevin, trover, false imprisonment, nuisance and negligence to challenge administrative action, more especially where they sought damages, which were not available through the prerogative writs, or where a preclusive clause purporting to exclude review rendered recourse to such a writ more difficult.[5]

The inter-relationship between judicial creativity concerning remedies and the evolution of principles of administrative law is evident in relation to proce-

---

2 S. de Smith, 'The Prerogative Writs' (1951) *CLJ* 40; S. de Smith, 'Wrongs and Remedies in Administrative Law' (1952) 15 *MLR* 189; L. Jaffe and E. Henderson, 'Judicial Review and the Rule of Law: Historical Origins' (1956) 72 *LQR* 345; E. Henderson, *Foundations of English Administrative Law* (Harvard University Press 1963); A. Rubinstein, *Jurisdiction and Illegality* (Oxford University Press 1975); P. Craig, 'Ultra Vires and the Foundations of Judicial Review' (1998) *CLJ* 63; Craig (n 1) 25-93.

3 Craig (n 1) 29-44.

4 Henderson (n 2) 46-58, 112; Craig (n 1) 51-62.

5 Rubinstein (n 2) Ch 4; Craig (n 1) 59-62.

dural constraints on the administration in the form of natural justice. *Bagg's* case so central to the development of mandamus was also of seminal significance for process rights. Mandamus was the earliest of the prerogative writs to be transformed into a more general purpose tool for the remedying of administrative error. *Bagg's* case[6] was the seminal judgment in this respect. Edith Henderson captured the importance and novelty of the decision.[7] A 'writ of restitution' existed prior to *Bagg's* case. Its primary focus was, however, to protect the privilege of a claimant who had been deprived of an office, so as to ensure that he could consult with a King's Bench counsel. If such a person was arrested while attempting to exercise this right a writ would be sought to command the prison to release the person thus detained. By 1613-15 the writ had been transformed and *Bagg's* case was of central importance in this respect. The colourful case concerned the disenfranchisement of James Bagg who had been a burgess of Plymouth. He had made a succession of abusive comments about the mayor and other burgesses. Coke CJ in the King's Bench found for Bagg, concluding that the offensive words were an insufficient cause for disenfranchisement from a freehold office. This factual conclusion was buttressed by a more important finding as to the jurisdiction of King's Bench. It was held that this court had the authority,

> '[N]ot only to correct errors in judicial proceedings, but other errors and misdemeanors extra-judicial, tending to the breach of the peace, or oppression of the subjects, or to the raising of faction, controversy, debate or to any manner of misgovernment; so that no wrong or injury, either public or private, can be done but that it shall be (here) reformed or punished by due course of law'.[8]

Coke CJ in adjudicating on the removal of Bagg from office reasoned from first principle. He concluded that it appeared that the corporation had proceeded against Bagg without 'hearing him answer to what was objected', and 'that he was not reasonably warned'. The removal was therefore void being against 'justice and right' and in breach of the *audi alteram partem* principle.[9]

Dr Bonham's case[10] is most oft-cited for Coke CJ's dictum as to the court's power to declare void statutes that offended against common right or reason, or that were morally repugnant. This dictum did not fall on fertile soil, and subsequent UK courts have not exercised that power of constitutional review. They did adopt the other central limb of process rights, the *nemo iudex* principle, to the effect that no man could be judge in his own cause. It was forcefully expressed in the instant case. Thus in determining whether the College of Physicians had

6 (1615) 11 Co. Rep. 93b.

7 Henderson (n 2) 46-58.

8 (1615) 11 Co. Rep. 93b, 98a.

9 (1615) 11 Co. Rep. 93b, 99a; *Brownlow v Cox and Mitchell* (1615) 3 *Bulstrode* 32; *Hesketh v Braddock* (1779) 1 *Dougl* 119; *The King v The Company of Fishermen of Faversham* (1799) 8 *TR* 352.

10 (1609) 8 *Co Rep* 113b.

the power to fine and imprison Dr Bonham, Coke CJ held that censors could not at one and the same time be judges, ministers, and parties: 'judges to give sentence or judgment; ministers to make summons; and parties to have the moiety of the forfeiture', since this would offend the *nemo iudex* principle.[11]

Process rights became an accepted feature of the landscape of judicial review in the UK thereafter. The importance attached to the principle was exemplified in the eighteenth century by Lord Mansfield's judgment in *Hesketh v Braddock*,[12] a case that combined due process and regulatory monopoly, arising out of a fine imposed by Chester Corporation on the defendant for breaching a by-law that precluded anyone who was not a freeman from operating a shop. The by-law was void as an illegal restraint on the common right of the subject unless there was a custom to support it, but the adjudication of such a custom had occurred in the local court where only freemen could act as jurors. Lord Mansfield was singularly unimpressed by attempts to convince him that this involved no violation of due process, responding that 'the law has so watchful an eye to the pure and unbiased administration of justice, that it will never trust the passions of mankind in the decision of any matter of right',[13] and thus would not trust the freemen as jurors. While Lord Mansfield was against the substantive restraint of trade in the instant case, the judicial approach to such by-laws differed over the years.[14]

The same principle was evident in *Bonaker*,[15] where a bishop had ordered the profits due to a vicar to be sequestered by the Consistory Court because the vicar had not resided in the parish. Nothing daunted the vicar brought a restitutionary action for money had and received against the sequestrator. He succeeded on the ground that the sequestration had issued without notice given to the vicar as to why it should not issue, and the Court of Exchequer Chamber held that this was essential before the sequestration could proceed.

The *audi alteram partem* principle thus has a long lineage and developed from various types of case. Some were concerned with deprivation of offices,[16] requiring notice and a hearing prior to the deprivation. Another somewhat later group involved the clergy: penalties or disciplinary measures to which the clergy were subjected had to be preceded by notice and a hearing.[17] In the 19th Century the *audi alteram partem* principle was applied to a wide variety of bodies, private

---

[11] (1609) 8 *Co Rep* 113b, 118a.

[12] (1766) 3 *Burr* 1847.

[13] (1766) 3 *Burr* 1847 at 1856.

[14] See, e.g., *Clark v Denton* (1830) 1 B & Ad 92; *Shaw v Poynter* (1834) 2 Ad & E. 312; *The Queen v Edmonds* (1855) 4 El & Bl 993.

[15] *Bonaker v Evans* (1850) 16 QB 163.

[16] *Bagg's Case* (n 8); *R v Chancellor of the University of Cambridge* (1723) 1 Str 557; *Osgood v Nelson* (1872) LR 5 HL 636; *Fisher v Jackson* (1891) 2 Ch 824.

[17] *Capel v Child* (1832) 2 Cr & J 588; *Bonaker* (n 15); *R v North, ex p Oakey* [1927] 1 KB 491.

as well as public. Clubs,[18] associations[19] and trade unions[20] were included within its ambit. The increase in the regulatory role of public authorities provided a further opportunity for the generalised application of the maxim.

The generality of the requirement of a hearing was evident in *Cooper v Wandsworth Board of Works*,[21] where it was held that demolition powers vested in the defendant Board were to be subject to notice and hearing requirements. The court made clear that the omission of positive words in the statute requiring a hearing was not conclusive, since the justice of the common law would supply the omission of the legislature.[22] The generality and flexibility of the *audi alteram partem* maxim, were brought out once again by Lord Loreburn.[23] He stated that the maxim applied to 'everyone who decides anything', while recognising that the manner in which a person's case was heard did not necessarily have to be the same as an ordinary trial.

The breadth of the *audi alteram partem* principle was, however, limited in the first-half of the 20th Century in a number of ways.

Firstly, some courts used the distinction between administrative and judicial decisions to limit the application of natural justice. In earlier centuries the right to a hearing was routinely applied to decisions that were administrative. In so far as the term judicial was used it was automatically implied whenever a decision was made that affected a person's rights in a broad sense.[24] Despite this the courts began to draw a dichotomy between administrative and judicial decisions, to take a narrow view of what constituted a judicial or quasi-judicial decision and to require this as a condition precedent for the application of a right to a hearing.[25]

Secondly, there was confusion as to the relationship between rights and remedies. Some courts felt that for certiorari to be available there would have to be not just a determination affecting the rights of individuals, but also a superadded duty to act judicially.[26] This view was later overruled.[27] However, while it held sway it was sometimes interpreted to mean not just that there had been a

---

18 *Dawkins v Antrobus* (1881) 17 Ch D 615; *Fisher v Keane* (1878) 11 Ch D 353.

19 *Wood v Woad* (1874) LR 9 Ex 190; *Lapointe v L'Association de Bienfaisance et de Retraite de la Police de Montreal* [1906] AC 435.

20 *Abbott v Sullivan* [1952] 1 KB 189; *Lawlor v Union of Post Office Workers* [1965] Ch 712.

21 (1863) 14 CB (NS) 180.

22 *Ibid.*, 194; *Hopkins v Smethwick Local Board of Health* (1890) 24 QBD 713.

23 *Board of Education v Rice* [1911] AC 179, 182.

24 *Hopkins* (n 22).

25 *Errington v Minister of Health* [1935] 1 KB 249 CA.

26 *R v Legislative Committee of the Church Assembly, Ex p. Haynes-Smith* [1928] 1 KB 411, 415 interpreting *R v Electricity Commissioners, Ex p. London Electricity Joint Committees Co (1920) Ltd* [1924] 1 KB 171, 205.

27 *Ridge v Baldwin* [1964] AC 40, 72–76.

breach of natural justice with no remedy available. The courts went further and said that natural justice itself was not applicable.[28]

Thirdly, some courts drew an unwarranted distinction between rights and privileges. Thus, in *Nakkuda Ali* one reason the Privy Council denied the application of natural justice was because the cancellation of a licence was characterized as the withdrawal of a privilege and not the determination of a right[29] and in *Parker*[30] the cab licence that was withdrawn was conceptualized in terms of 'permission'.

These limitations on the scope of natural justice were swept away by the House of Lords in *Ridge v Baldwin*.[31] Their Lordships held that a chief constable who could be dismissed only for cause was entitled to notice of the charge and an opportunity to be heard before being dismissed. The importance of the case lies in the general discussion of the principles of natural justice, especially by Lord Reid. His Lordship reviewed the 19th Century case law that showed the broad application of natural justice and then gave three reasons why the law had become confused.

The first was that natural justice could have only a limited application in the context of the wider duties or discretion imposed upon a minister, but the courts had, unfortunately, applied these limits to other areas where the constraints were unnecessary.[32] The second reason was that the principle had received only limited application during the war. Special considerations that might be pertinent during wartime should not affect the ambit of natural justice now. The third was the confusion between rights and remedies evident in the requirement of a superadded duty to act judicially for certiorari, and the way that this had stilted the development of natural justice.[33] For Lord Reid, the judicial element in natural justice should be inferred from the nature of the power and its effect on the individual.[34]

Their Lordships therefore revived the principles of natural justice. They rediscovered the older jurisprudence, which had applied the principle to a broad spectrum of interests and a wide variety of decision-makers. They disapproved 20th Century impediments, such as the requirement of a superadded duty to act judicially, which were said to be false constraints. The general tenor of the judg-

28 *Nakkuda Ali v Jayaratne* [1951] AC 66, 75–77; *Parker* [1953] 1 WLR 1150, 1153; *R v St. Lawrence's Hospital Statutory Visitors, Ex p. Pritchard* [1953] 1 WLR 1158.

29 *Nakkuda Ali* (n 28) 77-78.

30 *Parker* (n 28) 1153; *R v Leman Street Police Inspector, Ex p. Venicoff* [1920] 3 KB 72.

31 *Ridge* (n 27) 72-76.

32 *Ridge* (n 27) 71-72.

33 *Ridge* (n 27) 72-78. His Lordship expressly disapproved Lord Hewart CJ's requirement of a superadded duty to act judicially which had been developed in *Church Assembly* (n 26) and disapproved also of *Nakkuda Ali* (n 28) in so far as that case supported the requirement.

34 Lord Morris of Borth-y-Gest also based his judgment on the nineteenth century jurisprudence, *Ridge* (n 27) 120-121; for Lord Hodson the characterization of the decision as administrative, executive or judicial was not decisive, *Ridge* (n 27) 127-132.

ment was that the applicability of natural justice would depend on the nature of the power exercised and its effect upon the individual concerned, and this was fine-tuned in subsequent case law.[35]

The common law has always recognized two rationales for process rights in adjudication. Thus one rationale emphasizes the connection between procedural due process and the substantive justice of the final outcome. All rules are designed to achieve a particular goal, for example that liquor licences should only be granted to those of good character. Giving a person a hearing before deciding to refuse a licence can help to ensure that this goal is correctly applied. Procedural rights perform an instrumental role, in the sense of helping to attain an accurate decision on the substance of the case.[36] Other rationales focus upon non-instrumental justifications for procedural rights. Formal justice and the rule of law are enhanced, in the sense that the principles of natural justice help to guarantee objectivity and impartiality.[37] Procedural rights are also seen as protecting human dignity by ensuring that the individual is told why she is being treated unfavourably, and by enabling her to take part in that decision.[38]

These twin rationales for procedural rights have been recognised by the judiciary. *Doody*[39] was concerned with whether prisoners given a life sentence for murder should be told the reasons relating to the length of their imprisonment. Lord Mustill stated that a prisoner would wish to know why the particular term was selected, 'partly from an obvious human desire to be told the reason for a decision so gravely affecting his future, and partly because he hopes that once the information is obtained he may be able to point out errors of fact or reasoning and thereby persuade the Secretary of State to change his mind, or if he fails in this to challenge the decision in the courts'.

The non-instrumental and instrumental justifications for procedural protection are readily apparent in this quotation. It is perfectly possible to support natural justice for both instrumental and non-instrumental reasons, but it should be recognized that the content of natural justice in a particular area may well vary depending upon whether one accords primacy to instrumental or non-instrumental considerations.

---

35 P. Craig, *Administrative Law* (Sweet & Maxwell 2012) Ch 12.

36 J. Resnick, 'Due Process and Procedural Justice', in J. Pennock and J. Chapman (eds) *Due Process* (Nomos 1977) 217.

37 H. L. A. Hart, *Concept of Law* (Clarendon Press 1961) 156, 202; J. Rawls, *A Theory of Justice* (Oxford University Press 1973) 235.

38 F. Michelman, 'Formal and Associational Aims in Procedural Due Process', in Pennock and Chapman (n 36) Ch 4; J. Mashaw *Due Process in the Administrative State* (Yale University Press 1985) Chs 4-7.

39 *R v Secretary of State for the Home Department, ex p Doody* [1994] 1 AC 531, 551.

B. Mini-Codes: Tribunal Rules of Procedure

It is important to understand that while the common law laid the foundation for due process in the UK, and continues to do so, there is now input from ECHR and EU law, and there is considerable statutory input. It is with the latter that we are concerned here and it is particularly evident in relation to UK tribunals, which, in quantitative terms, deal with a very large number of administrative law disputes.

The regime for tribunals was altered significantly in 2007. Prior to that date tribunals were established pursuant to a particular statute, but there was no overarching tribunal service, and no formal connection between the tribunals that operated in particular areas, other than the fact that post-1958 all were overseen by the Council on Tribunals, which was established by the Tribunals and Inquiries Act 1958. The reality was therefore that we did not have anything that could be called a tribunal 'system', notwithstanding the fact that they shared some procedural rules, and some organizational features.

In May 2000 the Lord Chancellor appointed Sir Andrew Leggatt to undertake a review of tribunals. The Leggatt Report, *Tribunals for Users – One System, One Service*[40] recommended the creation of a Tribunals Service, which should be an executive agency of the Lord Chancellor's Department.[41] It should be a national organization with a strong local presence, structured along regional lines. The Leggatt Report proposed that the Tribunals System should be divided into subject-matter divisions, with new tribunals allocated to Divisions by Practice Direction.

The recommendations of the Leggatt Report provided the foundation for the Tribunals, Courts and Enforcement Act 2007. The government's response to the Leggatt recommendation for a single tribunal system was to create two new, generic tribunals, the First-tier Tribunal and the Upper Tribunal, into which existing tribunal jurisdictions could be transferred. The 2007 legislation provides for the creation of a First-tier Tribunal and an Upper Tribunal, each consisting of judges and other members, and presided over by the Senior President of Tribunals. The Upper Tribunal is primarily, but not exclusively, an appellate tribunal from the First-tier Tribunal.

The 2007 Act provides for appointment of judges and other members of the First-tier Tribunal and Upper Tribunal. It also makes provision for the establishment of 'chambers within the two tribunals so that the many jurisdictions transferred into the new system can be grouped together appropriately. Each chamber is headed by a Chamber President.[42] There are now twelve chambers within the First-tier Tribunal, which are: Asylum Support; Care Standards; Crimi-

[40] Report of the Review of Tribunals by Sir Andrew Leggatt, *Tribunals for Users – One System, One Service*, August 16 2001, http://webarchive.nationalarchives.gov.uk/+/http://www.tribunals-review.org.uk/.

[41] Report of the Review of Tribunals by Sir Andrew Leggatt, *Tribunals for Users – One System, One Service*, paras 5.3-5.4.

[42] TCE Act 2007 s.7 and Sch.4.

nal Injuries Compensation; General Regulatory Chamber; Immigration and Asylum Chamber; Mental Health; Primary Health Lists; Property Chamber; Social Security and Child Support; Special Educational Needs and Disability; Tax Chamber; and War Pensions and Armed Forces Compensation. There are four chambers within the Upper Tribunal: Administrative Appeals Chamber; Immigration and Asylum Chamber; Lands Chamber; and the Tax and Chancery Chamber.

Prior to 2007, tribunals had their own procedural rules, and rule-making normally vested in the Lord Chancellor or secretary of state, subject to consultation with the Council on Tribunals,[43] which sought to balance uniformity with the need to design procedures for a particular tribunal.[44] There were procedural codes for different subject matter areas, which drew on the guide produced by the Council on Tribunals. These procedural codes were formally binding and enshrined in statutory instruments. They applied to diverse areas from regulation of estate agents to mental health, from tax to social welfare, from lands disputes to asylum and from employment to financial services.[45] Procedural protection prior to the TCE Act 2007 was thus an admixture of the tribunal procedural rules, statutory rules requiring the provision of reasons,[46] and the common law rules of natural justice.

The Tribunals, Courts and Enforcement Act 2007, section 22, was designed to produce greater consistency in the development of procedure. Tribunal Procedure Rules are made by the Tribunal Procedure Committee.[47] It is to exercise this power with a view to securing the objectives specified in the TCE Act section 22(4), that: justice is done; the tribunal system is accessible and fair; proceedings are handled quickly and efficiently; the rules are both simple and simply expressed; and that the rules where appropriate confer on members of the First-tier Tribunal, or Upper Tribunal, responsibility for ensuring that proceedings before the tribunal are handled quickly and efficiently. The Senior President of Tribunals is also empowered to make Practice Directions concerning practice and procedure of the First-tier Tribunal and the Upper Tribunal.[48]

The details concerning the making of procedural rules are set out in the Tribunals, Courts and Enforcement Act 2007, Schedule 5. Part 1 makes provision for what the tribunal procedural rules may contain; time limits; the extent to which matters may be decided without a hearing; whether a hearing may be public or private; proceedings without prior notice; representation; evidence and witnesses; use of information; and arbitration. Schedule 5 Part 2 is concerned

---

[43] Tribunals and Inquiries Act 1992 s.8.

[44] Council on Tribunals, *Model Rules of Procedure for Tribunals* (1991) Cm.1434. The Model Rules of Procedure were revised in 1999 to take account of the Human Rights Act 1998; N. Brown, 'Tribunal Adjudication in Britain: Model Rules of Procedure' (1993) *Special Number ERPL* 287.

[45] P. Craig, 'Perspectives on Process: Common Law, Statutory and Political' (2010) *PL* 275, 288-289.

[46] Tribunals and Inquiries Act 1992 s.10.

[47] See https://www.gov.uk/government/organisations/tribunal-procedure-committee.

[48] TCE Act 2007 s.23.

with the creation of the Tribunal Procedure Committee, and Part 3 with the process by which the procedural rules are made. The Committee is required to consult before rules are made. The Lord Chancellor's powers are limited. He can allow or disallow the rules, and can specify a purpose that the rules must attain.

The Tribunal Procedure Committee has produced greater consistency in procedural rules, more especially because the number of separate tribunals has been reduced as a result of the 2007 Act. Insofar as there is a need for different procedural rules for different subject matter areas this is accommodated by tailoring procedural rules to the specific chambers. The procedural rules devised by the Tribunal Procedure Committee can be tested for conformity with the guiding principles set out in the Tribunals, Courts and Enforcement Act 2007, section 22(4), and with the principles of natural justice, although a claimant would have to show some clear breach before a reviewing court would strike down the tribunal procedural rules on such grounds.

Detailed procedural rules have now been made pursuant to the powers in section 22.[49] The rules are tailored to the needs of the specific subject matter dealt with by the Chamber. They constitute what are in effect procedural codes for the relevant area and the quality is high. They reveal a willingness to draw on both adversary and inquisitorial models of procedure when devising the procedural rules. The procedural rules are enshrined in formal secondary legislation as statutory instruments, and they address in detail many of the issues dealt with by Book III of the Model Rules.

The procedural rules of the health, education and social chamber can be taken by way of example.[50] The overriding objective of the Rules is to enable the Tribunal to deal with cases fairly and justly, which includes:[51] dealing with the case in ways which are proportionate to its importance, the complexity of the issues, the anticipated costs and the resources of the parties; avoiding unnecessary formality and seeking flexibility in the proceedings; ensuring, so far as practicable, that the parties are able to participate fully in the proceedings; using any special expertise of the Tribunal effectively; and avoiding delay, so far as compatible with proper consideration of the issues. The Tribunal must seek to give effect to the overriding objective when it exercises any power under the Rules, or interprets any rule or practice direction. Parties must help the Tribunal to further the overriding objective, and generally co-operate with the Tribunal.

There are detailed rules concerning a plethora of important procedural issues, including:[52] delegation to staff; case management powers; procedure for applying for and giving directions; failure to comply with rules; striking out a

49 See https://www.gov.uk/government/organisations/tribunal-procedure-committee; Craig (n 45) 290-292.

50 The Tribunal Procedure (First-tier Tribunal) (Health, Education and Social Care Chamber) Rules 2008, SI 2008 No. 2699 (L 16).

51 *Ibid.*, rule 2.

52 *Ibid.*, Part 2.

party's case; substitution and addition of parties; orders for costs; representatives; calculating time; sending and delivery of documents; use of documents and information; evidence and submissions; summoning of witnesses and orders to answer questions or produce documents; and withdrawal.

There are also detailed rules concerning the hearing itself,[53] which include rules relating to the application notice, and the response required from the public body whose decision is being challenged. The default position is that the tribunal must hold a hearing before reaching a decision, but this presumption can be displaced if each party gives consent to the case being decided without a hearing, and the tribunal feels that it can decide it in this manner.[54] The tribunal must give reasonable notice of the time and place of the hearing, the default period being at least 14 days.[55] The general legal presumption is that the hearing will be in public, although the tribunal has power to displace this in cases dealing with, for example, disability and special educational needs.[56] The Rules make provision for cases to be decided by consent orders and formal decisions. There is a separate section dealing with applications and hearings in mental health cases.[57]

The detailed rules concerning the hearing include provisions relating to the type of evidence and submissions that the tribunal will receive.[58] Thus the Tribunal may give directions as to the issues on which it requires evidence or submissions; the nature of the evidence or submissions it requires; whether the parties are permitted or required to provide expert evidence, and if so whether the parties must jointly appoint a single expert to provide such evidence; any limit on the number of witnesses whose evidence a party may put forward; the manner in which any evidence or submissions are to be provided; and the time at which any evidence or submissions are to be provided. The Tribunal can admit evidence whether or not it would be admissible in an ordinary civil trial, and irrespective of whether the evidence was available to a previous decision maker. It can also exclude evidence that would otherwise be admissible where the evidence was not provided within the time allowed by a direction or practice direction; the evidence was otherwise provided in a manner that did not comply with a direction or a practice direction; or it would otherwise be unfair to admit the evidence. The tribunal may consent to a witness giving, or require any witness to give, evidence on oath, and may administer an oath for that purpose.

There are in addition provisions concerning the correction, setting aside, review and appeal of tribunal decisions. The relevant provisions include power to correct clerical error, accidental slips and omissions.

---

53 *Ibid.*, Part 3.

54 *Ibid.*, rule 23(1).

55 *Ibid.*, rule 25.

56 *Ibid.*, rule 26.

57 *Ibid.*, Part 4.

58 *Ibid.*, rule 15.

C. ReNEUAL Book III: A Common Law Perspective

ReNEUAL Book III deals with single case decisions. There are two points that should be made concerning it from a common law perspective in the light of the preceding discussion.

First, the coverage of Book III, as judged by the type of topics addressed, is not different in significant respects from those covered in the subject matter procedural codes that exist in the UK, as exemplified by the tribunal procedural rules adumbrated above. These topics include the procedural norms that regulate the way in which applications should be made; the duties of the administration when in receipt of an application; the way in which complaints should be made; the duties of the administration when managing an administrative procedure; the administration's powers of investigation and inspection; the rules that govern who can be a party to a hearing; and the nature of the hearing that must be afforded.

Secondly, while there may be some differences in terms of detailed content as between the relevant UK rules and those contained in Book III the differences do not signal issues that are particularly difficult in terms of principle. Thus while differences of procedural detail are inevitable, this does not betoken any fundamental difference in principle as between the domestic rules and those in the ReNEUAL project.

D. ReNEUAL Book III: Application to Member State Action that Falls Within the Scope of EU Law

There would be advantages if the model rules were applicable to Member States when they act in the sphere of EU law. It would provide those affected by such national decisions with a clear set of procedural rights and render it easier for national administration to understand the procedural obligations incumbent on them. They would not have to determine afresh on each occasion whether procedural rules in national court decisions, national codes of procedure or an admixture of the two, sufficed to meet the requirements of EU law. The exclusion of national administration from the reach of such rules will make life more complex for claimants, national administration and EU administration, more especially when they act in context of shared administration. They will have to piece together the appropriate procedural obligations from the model rules as they apply to the EU administration, with the addition of national procedural norms, insofar as they are consonant with EU general principles of law, being applicable to the national element of the determination. If decisions are made to which EU and national administrations contribute via shared administration, then to confine the procedural rules to one part of the shared schema is not optimal, since it presumes that their respective contributions to the decision can be hermetically sealed or differentiated in a way that is often belied by the legal and administrative structure of such schema. The rationale for inclusion of Member State administration when it acts in the sphere of EU law is therefore grounded on the legal and political reality of shared administration, a reality repeatedly sanctioned by and through EU legislation agreed to by the Member States.

There were nonetheless reasons why the model rules were confined to EU administration, subject to the caveat that sector-specific legislation could render them applicable to Member States, or that the Member State might choose to adopt them. It was in part because of doubts as to EU competence to enact such model rules. While a plausible argument for application of such rules to Member States can be made, it is contestable, as recognized by the ReNEUAL steering committee. The choice as to the scope of application of the model rules was also in part the result of consultation exercises undertaken during the drafting of the model rules. The steering committee received much valuable assistance from meetings with judges, practitioners and academics knowledgeable with regard to administrative procedure. It became apparent that there was considerable opposition to the application of the model rules to Member States, more especially from national administrative courts. The rationale for this opposition varied, but the general tenor was that it would intrude too greatly on the terrain covered by national administrative procedure acts or the equivalent. The soundness of this concern may be debated, but the bottom line was that the issue threatened to derail the project as a whole. The existence of EU legal competence and political acceptance of a legislative initiative drafted pursuant to such competence are self-evidently distinct. Thus even if it was decided that there was competence to enact a set of model rules, the writing on the wall was clear, viz that national judicial opposition would translate into political rejection in the Council. The steering committee therefore decided to limit the scope of application of the model rules in the manner adumbrated above.

The rest as they say is history. The objection that the rules would intrude too greatly on Member State action and therefore diminish desirable plurality of view is therefore moot. I do not however believe that this concern was warranted, in relation to the core proposals concerning single case decision-making. There was nothing in the content of the proposals that should have caused alarm in this respect. The rules were drafted fully cognizant of the analogous provisions on applications, complaints, inspections, hearings and the like contained in existing EU legislation and in national procedural codes. There may well be particular detailed provisions that differ from those in relevant national legislation. But while national diversity is an important value, it should surely be kept in perspective. In an EU of 28 Member States, it is commonly the case that there have to be compromises in relation to substantive issues related to trade, goods, services and the like. There is no a priori reason to place national rules of administrative procedure on a higher plane in this regard.

E. Conclusion

The European Parliament has undertaken new initiatives in relation to procedural rules for single case decision-making. The proposals draw on Book III of the ReNEUAL Model Rules, although there are differences between them. The fate of such proposals remains to be seen. The UK has not embraced a general code of procedure in the manner increasingly common in continental Europe. The UK has nonetheless protected process rights for four hundred years and it has seen the virtue of more detailed procedural codes applicable to particular subject matter areas. There is in reality nothing for the UK to fear from the EU initiative on process rights, more especially given that it is limited in its application to EU institutions.

Unilateral Single Case Decision Making: Some Comparative Remarks

Comment by Athanasios Gromitsaris

A. Paths to Administrative Procedure

Starting from varying historical foundations, in the beginning of the 19th Century major legal systems developed different forms of control over bureaucracy. In the United States of America the protection of the individual against government activity and the proliferation of administrative power was found in procedural due process, which was supported by provisions of a written constitution that served to limit governmental but not private actions.[59] In the United Kingdom natural justice was developed by the courts during the 17th Century. The courts often relied on natural law to justify decisions when no statute or precedent was available to guide them and attributed the fundamental principles of *"audi alteram partem"* and *"nemo jude in re sua"* to the law of nature.[60]

In France, suspicion of the courts ("parlements") produced institutions for achieving control over the government. The administrative law of continental Europe was focused on the substantive correctness of administrative decisions in deciding whether to let them stand. In 1950, the French Conseil d´Etat made a significant amendment to established jurisprudence under which, in the absence of a legal text requiring it, the decisions of administrative authorities need not be reasoned ones. The obligation to give reasons was imposed in order to enable the reviewing court to be able to determine the validity of a challenged decision, i.e. to determine if the law had been followed.[61] The Conseil d´Etat held that administrative procedure must not violate the "general principles of law", which include the right to be heard. "Believing", however, "itself the servant of these principles", the Conseil d´Etat "is, in fact, their creator".[62]

In Prussia a merit-based bureaucracy was established under absolutist governments. The bureaucracy "ruled through law" and was "the guardian of the public interest".[63] Even with limited parliamentary control, "the mores of an incorruptible administration implanted by Frederick the Great, combined with

59 E. Borchard, 'French Administrative Law' (1933) *Faculty Scholarship Series*. Paper 3445. http://digitalcommons.law.yale.edu/fss_papers/3445.

60 F. F. Shauer, 'English Natural Justice and American Due Process: An Analytical Comparison' 18 *Wm & Mary L Rev* 47 (1976) 50 (discussing relevant decisions in their historical context).

61 B. Schwartz, 'Administrative Procedure and Natural Law' 28 *Notre Dame L Rev* 169 (1953) 175, 180, 182-183, 186 (commenting on CE Trompier-Gravier, May 5, 1944), 190 (commenting on CE Bilard, January 27, 1950).

62 J. Rivero, 'Le Juge Administratif Francais: Un Juge Qui Gouverne?' *Daloz chronique* 21, 22 (1951).

63 F. Fukuyama, 'Good Government, Bad Government' *The American Interest*, Vol. X, No 2, November/December 2014, pp. 7-16, 10.

the development of the theory of the *Rechtsstaat*",[64] had assured the calculability of an administrative system designed to insure the public interest, while protecting the freedom of the individual. This protection was then assured through judicial courts in several of the states or through the administrative courts in other states. The establishment of a federal administrative court turned the protective machinery into the administrative channel, albeit not in the field of public contracting or in the field of damages. The case law of the Federal Constitution Court brought the proceduralisation of individual decision-making under the influence of constitutional law.

The so called "Greek/southern Italian path" was based neither on State building in a context of military competition (like in Prussia) nor on middle class groups formed by early industrialisation (like in the UK and the US) which could have led a drive for civil service reform and public sector modernisation and combatting political clientelism after the advent of democracy (as in the US). Rather, the "weakness and lack of opportunity in the capitalist economy made the state an object of capture, first by elite social groups and then by mass political parties as democracy deepened".[65]

B. What Is a Unilateral Single Case Decision?

I. Declaration of intent, administrative act, individualised decision, adjudication

Unilateral single case decisions are considered in many jurisdictions of continental Europe as "administrative acts". They are a strongly formalised type of administrative decision making that achieves a combination of legal certainty and flexibility. In this sense administrative "form is the sworn enemy of arbitrariness, the twin sister of liberty."[66] Administrative procedure codes usually limit themselves to 'procedural' rules, avoiding definitions of concepts. The Greek administrative procedure code, for example, has a whole chapter covering the adoption and validity of "administrative acts" but contains no definition of the term. By contrast, the German Administrative Procedure Act (section 35) defines the concept of administrative act as any order, decision or other sovereign measure taken by an authority to regulate an individual case in the sphere of public law and which is intended to have a direct external legal effect.

The notion of an administrative act straddles the distinction between process and substance. It lies at the intersection of administrative court proceedings, administrative procedure and substantive administrative law. While the "pathol-

---

64 Borchard (n 1) 134.

65 For a description of the different paths see Fukuyama (n 5) 7-16, 10 (quotations).

66 R. von Ihering, *Geist des römischen Rechts auf den verschiedene Stufen seiner Entwicklung II 2*, (5th ed., Breitkopf und Härtel Leipzig 1898) 471.

ogy" of administrative acts is important for judicial protection, this does not mean that this pathology is exclusively part of administrative court proceedings. Rather, it is an important part of substantive administrative law and administrative procedure.

The term "act" is different from a "declaration of intent" which binds only the declarant and depends on the mental and physical welfare of a declaring person. An administrative act is binding not only the authority but also the addressee. Its validity does not depend on the civil servant´s subjective state and position but on its objective legality. What is more, the "act" is enforceable by means of administrative enforcement without necessarily having recourse to a writ of execution issued by a court. For these reasons the term "administrative declaration of intent" cannot replace the term "administrative act" and several jurisdictions prefer the term "act" rather than the term "administrative decision". The main difference between them is that the term "act" has a wider scope and meaning, that it allows for far more information to be requested from a far greater number of persons in a far greater variety of organisational contexts and administrative operations. Unlike French and German law, UK law does not distinguish between "acte administratif" or "Verwaltungsakt"[67] and other administrative actions. In French administrative law the word "acte" in the notion "acte administratif" refers to formal administrative decisions whereas actions of the administration have a different character. "Given the ambiguity of the word `act´ in English in relation to these two ideas", distinguishing between "decisions" and "actions"[68] is more precise. Finally, in US administrative law,[69] the term "adjudication" means exercise of judicial powers by an administrative agency and it is "any and every decision-making process other than rule-making".[70] Against this background, the term "single-case decision-making" reflects adequately the type of administrative action that is traditionally connected with the concept of "unilateral individual administrative act".

II. Classification of unilateral single case decisions

Classifications are usually made by using the following distinctions: unilateral acts and administrative contracts; individual acts and regulatory acts; enforceable acts and non-enforceable acts. According to the legal limits on the public authority taking the single case unilateral decision, decisions are

67 E. Schmidt-Aßmann, *Das allgemeine Verwaltungsrecht als Ordnungsidee* (Springer Verlag GmbH Berlin 2006) Chapter 1 para 4, Chapter 6, para 34.

68 L. Neville Brown, J. Bell and J.-M. Galabert, *French Administrative Law* (5th ed., Oxford University Press 2003) 157-158.

69 Pursuant to US APA § 551 (7) "adjudication" means agency process for the formulation of an order; pursuant to § 551 (7) "order" means the whole or a part of a final disposition, whether affirmative, negative, injunctive, or declaratory in form, of an agency in a matter other than rulemaking but including licensing.

70 P. Cane, *Administrative Tribunals and Adjudication* (Hart Publishing 2009) 73.

discretionary, non-discretionary, or "free" decisions. This is a way of defining how far a court can go in examining an administrative action and whether the judiciary should persuade or force administrative authorities to develop rules rather than to adopt single case decisions. This is due to the fact that the debate over rules versus discretion is linked with the question of the judicial control of discretionary power. Very often discretionary action has been linked with individual single case decisions.[71] The distinction between single case decisions and abstract and general rules is drawn on the basis of the persons and the facts which a decision takes into account. If it deals with an indefinite number of persons or facts it is abstract and general. There can be a (in-) determinate number of persons and a (in-) determinate state of affairs. According to their consequences, unilateral single case decisions have beneficial or encumbering consequences on the addressee and/or third parties. There are also decisions with double effects. According to the subject matter, there can be commanding, structuring, declaratory, positive or negative decisions. From the viewpoint of its temporal application a unilateral single case decision can produce permanent effects, continuously updating itself: for example, retirement pension rulings. As far as the administrative proceedings that lead to the adoption of a unilateral single case decision are concerned, they can be instigated ex officio or upon application. Participation of other authorities (from the same or different jurisdictions) is another criterion of classification: there are single-level or multi-level unilateral single case administrative decisions (for example issuance of the decision with the prior approval of another authority). An independent (stand-alone) unilateral single case administrative decision is based directly on the constitution, on a statute or a regulation; a dependent administrative act is adopted on the instruction or prior authorisation of another public authority. Further, a unilateral single case decision can be taken with specific or no requirements as to form (written, verbal, electronic or any other form).

III. Separation of powers

A unilateral individual administrative act or a single case decision must not be an act of legislation or act of government and must be distinguished from a judicial decision. Many of the theories about how an administrative decision should look derive from established doctrines of the separation of powers. A general implication of these doctrines is that administrative decisions and actions serve to implement in concrete cases the abstract rules laid down by the legislator.

IV. Judicial model and administrative action

Since it was recognized that the executive could have rulemaking powers and that administrative decisions are often a sort of adjudication,

[71] P. Craig, *Administrative Law* (4th ed., Sweet & Maxwell 1999) 521.

there are difficulties in separating the administration from legislative and judicial power. Classically, an individual administrative decision is distinguished from a general one because of its similarity to judicial determinations and the need to apply basic fairness principles. Common law countries tended to equate important categories of administrative action with the adjudication of courts and to require analogous procedural safeguards.[72] They have institutionalized the "judicial model" within the administrative process to a greater extent than other legal systems. Administrative procedures "typically emerge as a shared responsibility of executive and judiciary".[73] The development of the tribunal system in the UK went hand in hand with a debate on whether such institutions should be regarded as part of the machinery of the administration (with a more inquisitorial role) or as part of the machinery of adjudication. Whatever a tribunal is, "it is certainly not the name".[74] If the process rights before a public authority are supposed "to mirror those of the ordinary courts", then some types of administrative decision-making take, "even if in a modified way", the "form of judging".[75] "Lis inter partes" and "a duty to act judicially" were said to be "false constraints" and the idea was expressed that the applicability of natural justice finally depends on "the nature of the power exercised and its effects upon the individual concerned".[76] The epithet 'quasi-judicial' has also become familiar in English administrative law. Generally speaking, "it is applied to powers which can be exercised only when certain facts have been found to exist, and it indicates that these facts must be found in conformity with a code of rules called 'natural justice'."[77] In the late 1960s natural justice expanded to new fields of decision-making under the name of "fairness".[78]

In France, the "administrative" character of the "judicial model" is reflected in the French expression: "to judge the administration is still to administer". Nevertheless, different concepts of procedures have become necessary that highlight the separation of powers: Rules governing the adoption and the legal regime of administrative acts belong to the "non-contentious" administrative procedure. Administrative appeals before the authority that issued a contested act or before a higher administrative authority are equally administrative, albeit contentious, proceedings. They are non-jurisdictional because they lead to the adoption of another administrative act, the other basic difference between a court and an administrative organ being that a court entrusted with the review

72 J. Willis, 'Three Approaches to Administrative Law: The Judicial, the Conceptual, and the Functional' (1935) *University of Toronto L J* 1, pp. 53-81.

73 C. Harlow and R. Rawlings, 'National Administrative Procedures in a European Perspective: Pathways to a Slow Convergence' (2010) *Italian Journal of Administrative Law* 2, pp. 218-58, 222.

74 Craig (n 13) 250.

75 Craig (n 13) 10, 11.

76 Craig (n 13) 406.

77 H. W. R. Wade,'" Quasi-Judicial" and its Background' (1949) *Cambridge Law Journal* 10, pp. 216-240, 216.

78 Craig (n 13) 402-425, 412.

of administrative action is not in a hierarchically superior position to the administration. Administrative appeals in the French system blur the line between administrative and judicial functions: although appeals are addressed to administrative authorities, they have a judicial aspect as they determine the validity and appropriateness of an administrative act.[79]

In Germany, administrative proceedings only comprise those activities that have an external effect and are directed to the examination of the requirements, the preparation and the adoption of a unilateral single case administrative act ("Verwaltungsakt") or to the conclusion of a public law contract ("öffentlich-rechtlicher Vertrag" under the sections 54-62 of the Administrative Procedure Act "Verwaltungsverfahrensgesetz"). The role of an administrative authority in an administrative procedure is to examine the conditions, preparation and adoption of an administrative act or the conclusion of an agreement under public law (section 9 of the German Administrative Procedure Act).

V. Judicial intervention

In France, judicial review by the ordinary courts represented, historically, an encroachment upon the executive power and therefore oversight had to be entrusted to a specialized body connected with the executive branch. While the Conseil d´Etat was granted the power to annul administrative acts, administrative litigation was perceived as serving mainly "objective" purposes, linked to the correct working of administrative agencies. It did not have the procedural tools necessary to force the administration to comply with its decisions. Since the 1980s however, the Council of State has gradually acquired more effective means of enforcement. It was given the power to fine non-compliant administration actions ("astreinte") and to issue injunctions ("injunction"). Although one of the main features of the "administrative acts" in France, the privilege of being valid and binding ("exécutoire") as long as they have not been annulled by a court is comparable to the German theory of validity of the administrative act ("Bestandskraft"), a strict concept of the separation of powers has for a long time resisted the possibility of suspending the harmful effect of a challenged act by a court and, hence, the creation of a fully-fledged interim relief ("référé").[80]

VI. Administrative refusals and omissions

A strict separation of powers doctrine has further had an impact on the status of negative or omitted administrative decisions and on the function of interlocutory procedures. The refusal to take a decision is a decision itself. In Greece, the suspension of the enforcement of a negative or an omitted

[79] R. Bousta and A. Sagar, 'Alternative Dispute Resolution in French Administrative Proceedings', in D. C. Dragos and B. Neamtu (eds.) *Alternative Dispute Resolution in European Administrative Law* (Springer 2014) 63.

[80] Loi no 2000-597 du 30 juin 2000 relative au référé devant les juridictions administratives.

decision was traditionally not allowed. The reason for this was that the temporary enforcement of a negative decision would amount to temporarily accepting and enforcing an application that has already been rejected.[81] Suspension of the enforcement of a negative decision is deemed permissible, however, when the decision is aimed at avoiding irreversible legal effects (for example, rejection of the renewal of approvals or authorizations, or the decision entails the rejection of a student's admission, registration, re-registration, and de-registration, rejection of the application for release from the obligation of demolishing an illegal building, rejection of the application for admission to an examination). The suspension of the rejection of the application for admission to an exam simply makes the participation in the exam possible. However, this does not lead to attesting that a definitive certificate has been legally issued or validated. The influence of the German code of administrative procedure has been decisive in this. In German law, where there is an action of enforcement ("Verpflichtungsklage"), it is known that the suspensive effect does not work when the plaintiff seeks a legal remedy against a rejection of a favourable individual administrative act. In these cases the enforcement action, and not the "rescissory action" ("Anfechtungsklage") is suitable because the plaintiff wants an individual administrative act to be issued. An interim order can be made by the court when the danger exists that the enforcement of a right of the plaintiff could be prevented or impeded by means of an alteration of the existing state of affairs or when the order is necessary to avert major disadvantages or to prevent the imminent use of force or for other reasons.[82] Separation of powers doctrines influence the conception of negative unilateral single decisions and their judicial review.

VII. Consequences of the classification of a decision as a "Unilateral Single Case Decision"

1. Validity

An administrative authority cannot make a valid decision that is inconsistent with the Constitution, statute law, or decrees.[83] There are legally non-existent, invalid or void, and voidable single case unilateral administrative acts. It will be inexistent if it does not even have the appearance of a legal act. Its withdrawal, annulment or otherwise cancellation is neither legally possible nor practically necessary. An invalid act is one that is vitiated by essential and manifest legal errors and produces no legal effects. Invalid acts do not produce legal effects, they do not bind the administration, the courts or citizens, irrespective

[81] See, on the interconnections between interim relief and the concept of administative act under French and German influence, the monograph of E. Dimitropoulou, *Vorläufiger Verwaltungsrechtsschutz in Griechenland* (Duncker & Humblot 2006).

[82] U. Stelkens, 'Administrative Appeals in Germany' in Dragos and Neamtu (n 21) 3-56, 14-15.

[83] B. Schwartz and A. T. Vanderbilt, *French Administrative Law and the Common-Law World* (The Lawbook Exchange 1954) 111.

of withdrawal, annulment, revocation or otherwise cancellation. Unlike inexistent acts, invalid acts allow the claim of a legitimate interest in lodging a remedy for an explicit declaration of the nullity of the act. The French doctrine draws a distinction between (next to inexistence of an "act") "nullité relative" and "nullité absolue". An administrative act can be subject to a cause of non-existence, absolute nullity, relative nullity or declaration of nullity. Relative nullity can only be alleged by the public authority.

A private law transaction that is wrong in fact and law is usually invalid, and shall be deemed not to have been taken. There are different validity rules for single case administrative decisions. One older, outdated, explanation for this difference is the supposed increased authority and credibility of the public sector compared to the credibility of private persons. Another reason is the enhanced confidence of the citizen in the public administration as the representative of the common interest; the single case administrative decision is supposed to contribute to the achievement of a number of general interest objectives and to implement the public, not a particular or private, interest. The rationale for the validity theory of single case decisions, however, is not respect towards State authority but, rather, a matter of confidence and legal security. In Greece, the adoption of the concept of the 'void' administrative act has been long resisted on the grounds that it was against the so called "presumption of legality" or "presumption for the benefit of validity of administrative acts". The use of the term "presumption" is not correct in this context because the validity of the act is neither a rule on the burden of proof nor a legal fiction.[84]

Another crucial difference from private law transactions is that coercive administrative acts may be executed by the administrative authority. Unlike private persons, the authority does not require the help of the courts but may act by itself. The administrative act thus replaces the writ of execution issued by a court needed by a citizen to start an enforcement proceeding.

The theory of validity is further important in the case of failure to observe process rights. Given the high "transaction costs" of the "production" of an administrative decision, failure to comply with a particular process right usually renders the decision voidable in most jurisdictions and not void. There are instrumental and non-instrumental justifications for procedural rights. One technique is to distinguish between mandatory and directory provisions. A breach of mandatory procedural requirements will lead to a decision being set aside for procedural impropriety.[85] Another technique is to inquire whether "it is obvious" that "the infringement of regulations governing procedure, form or

84 In Germany, where section 43(2) of the Administrative Procedure Act (Verwaltungsverfahrensgesetz, VwVfG) stipulates: "An administrative act shall remain effective for as long as it is not withdrawn, annulled, otherwise cancelled or expires for reasons of time or for any other reason", the term "Vermutung der Gültigkeit" was probably used for the last time by the Federal Administrative Court in BVerwGE 1, 67 (69): "Die von staatlichen Organe erlassenen Akte tragen die Vermutung der Gültigkeit in sich". Cf. R. Schmidt-De Caluwe, *Der Verwaltungsakt in der Lehre Otto Mayers* (Mohr Siebeck 1999) 240.

85 Craig (n 13) 373, 402.

territorial competence" "has not influenced the decision in the matter".[86] Pursuant to section 45 of the German Administrative Procedure Act, infringements of regulations governing form or procedure can be "cured" as long as they do not render the individual administrative act void by doing what is necessary (i.e. by filing applications, stating grounds, hearing the participants or obtaining decisions and collaboration of other authorities) subsequently. This may even be done in the course of administrative appeals and judicial review. However, this instrumental logic is accompanied by an intense review on substantive grounds.

2. Coupling and de-coupling the concept of unilateral single case decision with/from the types of legal remedies

The question raised here is whether and to what extent the adoption of a unilateral single case decision pre-empts or anticipates the choice of specific legal remedies and specific rules for reviewability and standing. The name given to a decision is not important. Only objective compliance with the criteria for an administrative act differentiates it from other types of administrative action.

In Germany, the concept of administrative act is important for the selection of the correct time-limited court remedies against either the unilateral single case decision imposing an obligation, or the unilateral single case decision to reject the adoption of a beneficial administrative act. Prior to lodging a rescissory action or an enforcement action, which are the correct court actions against the adoption, rejection or omission of a unilateral single case decision (administrative act) in German law, the lawfulness and expedience of the unilateral single-case decision or its rejection shall be reviewed in preliminary proceedings. If such a review did not take place, the rescissory or enforcement action is inadmissible. Forms of administrative action that are not classified as administrative acts are controlled by other types of legal remedies. The two major categories are the action for affirmative relief or performance ("Leistungsklage") and the declaratory action ("Feststellungsklage"). Administrative decisions concerning contractual disputes, public procurement and state liability matters are, in Germany, not considered as administrative acts.[87] In French administrative law, an ultra vires administrative act can be the subject of both an action to annul and an action for damages. In both, the action is decided on the basis of the court's answer to the question of the legality of the act. In the action to annul the challenged act is set aside if the court determines that it is ultra vires. In the action for damages against the State the determination of the illegality of the act causing the injury leads to a judgment against the State on the basis of the fault it has committed.

In English law, courts have been generally reluctant to interfere when a public authority makes a rule of a generalised nature rather than "engaging in

---

[86] Section 46 German Administrative Procedure Act.

[87] See Stelkens (n 24) 9.

individualised adjudication".[88] At EU level, the system of remedies, as interpreted by EU courts, makes it easier to bring an action against a single case decision, as distinct from a measure of general application. However, the ECJ has decoupled legal review from a precise concept of "administrative act". "The choice of form cannot change the nature of the measure."[89] An institution cannot deny or restrainn or change the possibilities of legal protection merely by the choice of the form of the adopted act. An act's general applicability does not *eo ipso* foreclose reviewability,[90] which is independent from the contested act's nature. European institutions have the possibility to choose, within the limits foreseen by the Treaty, the type of act they want to adopt but they cannot decide, by choosing the act, to what extent reviewability is possible.[91]

88 Craig (n 13) 10.

89 Case 101/76, *Koniklijke Scholten Honig* v *Council*, [1977] ECR 797, paras. 5/7; Joined Cases 789/79 & 790/79, *Calpak et al* v *Commission*, [1980] ECR 1949, para. 7; Case 307/81, *Alusuisse Italia* v *Commission and Council*, [1982] ECR 3463, para. 7.

90 Case C-309/89, *Codorniu* v *Council*, [1994] ECR I-1853, para. 19; Case C-358/89, *Extramet* v *Council*, [1991] ECR I-2501, para. 16.

91 J. Bast, 'On the Grammar of EU Law: Legal Instruments', Max-Planck-Institut für Ausländisches Öffentliches Recht und Völkerrecht (Jean Monnet Center for International and Regional Economic Law & Justice Verlag, NYU School of Law 2003) 1-72.

VIII. Features of a unilateral single-case decision

Administrative Public authority	Sovereign Measure	Unilateral Character	Regulatory Character: Production of Legal Effects	Direct External Legal Effects	Due Procedure for Issuing a Decision	Individual Case
			Antonyms and Distinctions			
- Legislative and judicial acts - Administration active/ administration contentieuse	- Actes d'autorité/ actes de gestion - Public Authority and Fiscus - Administration acting in private law - Acts of government in the fields of constitutional and international public law not amenable to judicial review - Prerogative and statutory powers	- Décision exécutoire/non exécutoire - Public contracting	- Administrative factual operations, physical acts - Preliminary actions in preparation of a final act - Actions following the issuance and preparing the administrative execution of an administrative act	- Administrative instructions regulating internal matters of the administration - Indirect decisions: The making of a decision requires several steps taken by several authorities: optional or obligatory delivering of the opinion of another authority, approval or authorisation of a decision by another authority	Decision as the outcome of the administrative procedure	- Abstract and General Rules - Plurality of those affected by the decision

Legal comparative work is met with difficulties where homonyms and synonyms are used or introduced without their relevant antonyms that often change implicitly over time. What is more, terminology inspired by foreign jurisdictions reflects a foreign institutional framework. Otto Mayer translated the terms "acte du contentieux" and "actes de nature contentieuse" with the term "streitiger Verwaltungsakt" und "actes de pure administration" with the term "freie Verwaltungsakte". He connected the terminology he "coined" with the German "Pandektistik" and the debate about public law rights.[92] Nowadays, the meaning shared by synonyms like the central terms "acte administratif" and "Verwaltungsakt" is encapsulated in the modern concept of "unilateral single case decision" which has been adopted by the model rules on European Administrative Procedure. The concepts depicted in the chart above reflect the experience of different national routes to merit-based bureaucracy and administrative law. In some countries[93] (e.g. Germany and France), what was initially considered as most important in administrative law was not the procedure through which a general or individual act was produced, but the outcome of the procedure, the "administrative act" itself, based on the principle of legality. In the UK, the distinction between individual and general decisions is historically less important because the main emphasis used to be on the procedure. Nowadays, a unilateral single case decision or a unilateral individual administrative act must be produced in a procedure in line with natural justice principles: the right to a fair treatment, the right to be heard, the right to impartiality, the right to information and advice accompanied by the obligation for the administration to give reasons. Procedural and substantive rights of those dealing with the administration in a democratic society are equally guaranteed. In the following, the antithetical labels mentioned in the chart link to some debates at national and EU-level.

1. Public authority

Since the conceptual shift from government to governance and the trend towards "agencification", the public/private divide is no longer a clear cut one. English law developed without "any need to exploit the distinction between private law and public law, because of the unitary jurisdiction of the ordinary courts".[94] The term "public authority" is used in section 6(3) of the Human Rights Act 1998 in the United Kingdom to include any person or body certain of whose functions are functions of a public nature. From the perspective of the courts the question is whether a body is sufficiently public to be amenable to judicial review. The existence of monopolistic power will not, for instance, suffice to bring a body within the rules of judicial review.[95] The extension of the definition of public authority to include all kinds of social power broadens the scope of application of procedural principles, such as those of fair

---

92 A. Gromitsaris, ‚Das deutsche System des französischen Verwaltungsrechts, Introduction', in O. Mayer, *Theorie des französischen Verwaltungsrechts* (Keip Verlag Goldbach 1998) VII-LXXVII, XVI et seq., XX et seq.

93 W. Rusch, 'Administrative Procedures in EU Member States', Conference on Public Administration Reform and European Integration Budva, Montenegro 26-27 March 2009, pp. 1-10, http://www.sigmaweb.org/publications/42754772.pdf.

94 S. Flogaitis, *The Evolution of Law and State in Europe* (Hart Publishing 2015) 33.

95 Craig (n 13) 25, 41.

hearings and the like, usually used in the context of administrative procedure. Should they, for example, also apply to "public" bodies such as trade associations or unions?[96] Another point is that the nature of the task to be fulfilled by the "public authority" will have an impact on the choice between adversarial and inquisitorial procedures: if decisions on competition are to be effective the authority must be granted adequate investigative powers.[97]

2. Sovereign act: prerogatives of public authority

In the UK, there is case law on the question whether the nature or the source of governmental power should be decisive for justiciability and control. The *Government Communications Headquarters (GCHQ)* case broke from previous English law, which held that prerogative powers were not in any way subject to judicial review. The House of Lords found that the application of judicial review would be dependent on the nature of the government's powers, not their source. The Lords saw no "logical reason why the fact that the source of the power is the prerogative and not statute should today deprive the citizen of that right of challenge to the manner of its exercise which he would possess were the source of the power statutory".[98]

Private law, not statutory powers, is in French law the antonym for "prerogative". In French law, prerogatives of public authority may be also granted to private persons. However, the French Constitutional Council has ruled out delegation to the private sector of "missions of sovereignty" (e.g. power of eminent domain, tax of judicial power).[99] Prerogatives of public authority affect the rights of private persons without their consent, unilaterally and immediately, without a prior hearing before a court ("exécution d´office").[100] In French law, the two categories of acts of government ("actes de gouvernement"), i.e. acts of the executive in its relations with Parliament and in its international relations, are sovereign acts but they are not reviewable, unless a part of them is viewed as a "detachable" administrative act.[101] Further, the Conseil d´Etat recognized back in the 19th Century that apart from administrative decisions

96 Craig (n 13) 16.

97 Craig (n 13) 260-261.

98 *Council of Civil Service Unions v Minister for the Civil Service* [1985] AC 374, 417-418.

99 CC Dec. 2003-473 DC-June 26, 2003 Loi habilitant le gouvernement à simplifier le droit, cons. 19, Rec. 386. E. Zoller, *Introduction to Public Law. A Comparative Study* (Leiden 2008) 257.

100 This view is reflected in Recommendation CM/Rec(2007)7 of the Committee of Ministers to Member States on good administration: "the administration exercises its prerogative of public power to carry out the tasks required of it". Pursuant to Article 11 –Definitions "1.For the purposes of this code, `administrative decisions´ shall mean regulatory or non-regulatory decisions taken by public authorities when exercising the prerogatives of public power."

101 Article 45 V of the Presidential Decree 18/1989 on the Greek Council of State stipulates that "acts of state and orders pertaining to the exercise of political power shall not be challenged by an application for annulment".

of authority ("actes d´autorité"), which fell exclusively under the competence of the administrative courts, there were also "actes de gestion", adopted by the so-called administration domaniale. At the same time litigation involving local government authorities was dissociated from the litigation involving central state authorities. Eduard Laferrière wrote in the 19th Century that the distinction between administrative and ordinary courts is based on the nature of the act being challenged. He wrote that the "actes de gestion" were motivated by the public interest, nonetheless public power did not intervene.[102] Therefore, they fell under the competence of the ordinary courts. In the context of contracts this distinction took the form of distinguishing between "gestion publique" and "gestion privée" through the decision of the Tribunal des Conflits, *Compagnie d´assurances le Soleil* of 1910[103] which inspired the case law of the Conseil d´Etat.[104] The latter found that the administration can enter into contracts just like an ordinary private person. The Tribunal des Conflits accepted, in the decision *Mademoiselle Blanco* (8 February 1873), that jurisdiction is granted to the administrative courts on the basis of the exercise of "public service". Following this decision and a series of decisions in the 20th Century any litigation dealing with the organization, interruption or other malfunctioning of the public service falls within the competence of the administrative courts.[105] However, the distinction between "gestion privée" and "gestion publique" was finally established in public contracting where public service, both industrial and commercial ("service public industriel et commercial"-"SPIC") was dissociated from administrative public service ("service public administratif").[106] If the public service is operated under the same conditions as for private firms, it is a "SPIC" and falls under the competence of the ordinary courts: it has an economic objective that might also be pursued by a private investor; funding comes, at least partly, from the users or the main service receivers, and management and labour relations are similar to the ones in a private firm. Unilateral decisions taken within the context of a "SPIC" are private law, unless a prerogative of public authority ("prérogative de puissance publique") is at play[107] or the unilateral decision is related to the actual organisation of the public service itself,[108] in which case the administrative judge retains the competence. Today, the decision on the division of competences between the administrative and ordinary courts has to take

---

[102] P. Gonod, 'Édouard Laferrière, un juriste au service de la République' (1998) *LGDJ* 151 et seq. D. Bailleul, 'L'efficacité des recours pour excès de pouvoir et de plain contentieux objectif en droit public français' (2002) *LGDJ* 277 et seq.

[103] Tribunal des conflits, 4 juin 1910, *Compagnie d'assurance Le soleil*, Rec. C.E. p. 446.

[104] Conseil d'Etat, 31 juillet 1912, arrêt Société des granits porphyroïdes des Vosges (conclusion Blum).

[105] Terrier (CE, 6 February 1903); Thérond (4 March 1910); Tribunal des Conflits (29 February 1908) and De Fons Colombes (11 April 1908).

[106] Tribunal des Conflits, 22 January 1921, *Société commerciale de l'Ouest Africain.*

[107] An act of taxation on water distribution is, pursuant to TC, 26 Juin 1988, *Société de distribution d'eau intercommunale'* an act of public authority.

[108] TC, 15 January 1968, *Société Air France c/Epoux Barbier.*

into consideration a number of factors: the nature of the persons involved (a private[109] person may be granted the operation of a public service by contract or through delegation), the nature of the action (administrative or industrial and commercial) and the nature of the act which has caused the dispute (is this act a unilateral one leaving no room for negotiation or a contract?). The administrative court's jurisdiction has a constitutional value in cases of annulment or modification of administrative decisions taken in connection with the exercise of prerogatives of administrative authority.[110]

A unilateral single case decision is an administrative act, according to German law, if it falls within the domain of administrative, not of constitutional, international, or private law and it is taken with reference to a hierarchical relation of supreme and subordinate.[111] Private law transactions are not administrative acts. Conversely, administrative acts can have repercussions on private law and result in the debarment of certain civil law rights ("privatrechtsgestaltende Verwaltungsakte"). Single case decisions that take private law forms and use private law instruments are administrative private law acts. Unilateral administrative acts can also be issued by a publicly appointed entrepreneur empowered to adopt measures of sovereign character ("Beliehener").[112] When ordinary courts have jurisdiction over a dispute on a measure of a public authority, for example on non-contractual state liability, the act is not an administrative act. It is obvious that the public/private-divide and the separation of ordinary and administrative courts as well as the State theory of "fiscus" that was influential in the period of late absolutism have played a role[113] in shaping the concept of an "administrative act" in Germany.

3. Unilateral act

Decisions concerning the conclusion and execution of public contracts are not considered as administrative acts in Germany. In a system like

[109] In this case the theory of the 'collaborateur occasionnel' applies: CE, 2 November 1946: *Commune de Saint Priest la Plaine*.

[110] DC no 86-224 CC, 23 January 1987, loi tranférant à la jurisdiction judiciaire le contentieux des décisions du Conseil de la concurrence.

[111] M. P. Singh, *German Administrative Law in Common Law Perspective* (Springer 2001) 64-5.

[112] G. Püttner and B. Losch, 'Verwaltung durch Private und in privatrechtlicher Form', in K. G. A. Jeserich (ed.) *Die Bundesrepublik Deutschland* (Deutsche Verlagsanstalt GmbH 1987) 368-84.

[113] As "fiscus" public authorities make contracts or commit torts. D. Ehlers, *Verwaltung in Privatrechtsform* (Duncker & Humblot 1984) 75, distinguishes four concepts of "fiscus". See further F. von Weiler, *Über Verwaltung und Justiz und über die Gränzlinie zwischen beiden* (Schan- und Götz'sche Hofbuchhandlung 1826); O. Bühler, *Die Zuständigkeit der Zivilgerichte gegenüber der Verwaltung im württembergischen Recht und ihre Entwicklung seit Anfang des 19. Jahrhunderts. Ein Beitrag zur Lehre von der Abgrenzung von Justiz und Verwaltung* (Verlag von Ferdinand Enke 1911); O. Mayer, *Deutsches Verwaltungsrecht I* (Duncker & Humblot 1895) 47 et seq.; E. Forsthoff, *Lehrbuch des Verwaltungsrechts I: Allgemeiner Teil* (10th ed., C. H. Beck 1973) 29.

the French one where bilateral or multilateral agreements are also acts of the administration, the concept of "enforceable decision" ("privilège de la décision exécutoire") plays the role of distinguishing between unilateral single case decisions and regulations on the one hand and bilateral or multilateral agreements on the other.

The distinction between a public contract and a unilateral act is not always easy to draw. In French law, the concession of public service encompasses a unilateral act with regulatory character as the part of the contract related to the technical, operative and organizational specification of the public service. Concessions are organized, in French law, as a contract of public law. There are different types of concessions: the concession of public works, the concession of public service, and the concession of the right to occupy the public domain (public land). Otto Mayer translated "concession" as "Verleihung",[114] clearly separating it from a police permission ("Polizeierlaubnis") which is not a contract. "Concession" came to mean in German law a series of different things: granting of an individual right, granting of an administrative authorization (in the sense of an approval, licensing, permission, for ex. § 15 para 2 of Trade, Commerce, and Industry Regulation Act "Gewerbeordnung") andaward of a contract to a private company, where the latter exclusively carries out a public task and is granted a right to charge users of the public service.

4. Individual case

In German law, a single case administrative decision can be specific and individual, specific and general, or abstract and individual. An abstract and general measure is a legislative act. Pursuant to section 35 para. 2 of the Administrative Procedure Act a general order ("Allgemeinverfügung") which is directed at a group of people defined or definable on the basis of general characteristics or relating to the public law aspect of a matter ("öffentlich-rechtliche Eigenschaft einer Sache") or its use by the public at large, is also an administrative act. It is not always easy to draw these distinctions in practice. For example, planning procedures that are legally binding ("Planfeststellungsverfahren" §§ 72 et seq. Administrative Procedure Act) produce effects similar to administrative rules, although they lead to the adoption of a single case unilateral administrative measure. According to French administrative law, regulations and individual decisions are both administrative decisions submitted to a series of common rules concerning the way they are issued, the conditions of their legality, and the techniques under which they can be challenged before a court.[115] However, there are specific rules that are particular to individual decision. Where a decision addresses precise people, it is said to be individual ("décision individuelle") if it has one addressee, and "particular", if it

[114] Mayer (n 34) 294, 302-303.

[115] On the concept of "decision" see A. Panchaud, 'La décision administrative, Etude comparative' (1962) *Revue internationale de droit comparé* Vol. 14 N°4, 677-697.

has several. Where a decision has no precise addressee, where it is "anonymous", in the sense that it pronounces a norm which will apply to any people who find themselves in a certain situation, then it is said to be regulatory ("décision réglementaire"). The notion of "decision" is problematic in EU law. Whereas Article 288 TFEU refers to the individuality of a decision, the notion incorporates different meanings in procedural law, where it mainly serves, in accordance with the French administrative law tradition, as a synonym for "reviewable act"[116], a notion applied in Article 263 TFEU.

5. Legal Regulation

A unilateral single case decision establishes or declares or asserts rights and obligations or immediately affects rights, liberties or legal interests of persons or organizations. Apart from issuing formal (binding) decisions, public authorities also carry out informal actions often specified by verbal or written guidelines, instructions, interpretative circulars etc., and consisting, for instance, in the organization of their internal function or in the material provision of services. According to section 9 of the German Administrative Procedure Act all proceedings that are directed to prepare factual or non-binding administrative activities that are not regarded as "administrative acts" are not administrative proceedings in the sense of this provision. Purely factual administrative measures, such as advice, information, investigation, preparatory or part measures that are usually considered as devoid of any regulatory character, are not, formally, "administrative acts". This does not mean that there is no legal protection possible against them. As long as factual acts create legal consequences the rules of standing for adequate remedies are applicable. It is obvious that a warning notice not to buy a certain type of product interferes drastically with the rights of the producers. Physical acts are also part of administrative activity. The concept of 'administrative procedure' is interpreted in such a way as to include these actions too. Sometimes, initial or intermediate measures of a factual nature interfere with the rights of a person in such a drastic way that they are considered as reviewable because they are capable of developing an adverse effect independently of the final act. This was the case, for example, in *AKZO Nobel*, where the Court held that, in on-the-spot investigations in competition cases, the physical act of seizing the documents and placing them in the investigation file, which is a purely factual act, can constitute a reviewable decision under Article 263 TFEU, because it may violate the applicant's right to confidentiality irrespective of the possible violation of competition rules. The Court held that the physical act could be considered to entail a "tacit decision" that "should be open to challenge by an action for annulment".[117] "Decision" means here a reviewable act intended to produce legal effects in the sense of Article 263 TFEU.

[116] H. C. Röhl, 'Die anfechtbare Entscheidung nach Art. 230 Abs. 4 EGV' (2000) *Zeitschrift für ausländisches öffentliches Recht und Völkerrecht* 60, 331.

[117] CFI Joined Cases T-125/03 and T-253/03 of 17 September 2007, para 49.

6. Direct external legal effects

External effects of a unilateral single case decision play a role in determining a series of issues: the impact on the legal sphere of addressees and third parties, the status of the participant in an administrative proceeding, the distinction between affected and non-affected participants, or the rules of standing. An administrative act produces direct legal effects, when its adoption by a public authority does not require several additional steps to be taken by other authorities. Common examples of acts with indirect effects are the optional or obligatory delivering of the opinion of another authority, or the approval or authorisation of an act by another authority.

Sometimes administrative decisions have solely internal effects. In French administrative law, only regulatory circulars, unlike interpretative ones, have adverse effects.[118] According to more recent case law of the Conseil d´Etat, an imperative circular has, unlike a non-imperative one, a decisionary and, hence, an adversely affecting character.[119] Directives are a type of internal acts that have no adverse effects.[120] However, individual measures of implementation of a directive adversely affecting a person are reviewable. Measures of an interior nature, finally, are designed to regulate the organisation and operation of the civil service and they have no binding effect on the citizens' life. Their legal control is not the business of the judiciary. In Germany, administrative directives, guidelines, or circulars ("Verwaltungsvorschriften") are binding only on the public authorities that are required to implement them, not on citizens and regulated industries.[121] However, the courts treat administrative guidelines with regulatory ("normkonkretisierend"), not interpretative, character, as binding when administrative decisions based on them are challenged as a violation of the plaintiff´s individual rights. Guidelines are used as functional equivalents to regulations, rather than to unilateral single case decisions.

a) Impact on individual rights

External effects are produced on the citizen's legal sphere. They can also be produced on the legal sphere of a public body other than the public body that issued the administrative act. In Germany, public entities exercising public authority can be the addressee of an administrative act under the same general

---

118 Conseil d'Etat, 29 January 1954 *Notre-Dame du Kreisker.*

119 Conseil d´Etat, 18 December 2002, *Duvignères.*

120 Conseil d'Etat, section, 11 December 1970, *Crédit foncier de France.*

121 The ECJ held, in a conflict between the EU and Germany over the nonbinding character and reviewability of guidelines, that guidelines are not measures with "unquestionable binding force" to satisfy "the requirement of legal certainty" and to constitute an adequate tool of implementation of EU law. "It cannot be claimed, therefore, that individuals are in a position to know with certainty the full extent of their rights in order to rely on them, where appropriate, before the national courts or that those whose activities are liable to give rise to nuisances are adequately informed of the extent of their obligations." Judgment of the Court of 30 May 1991, C-361/88, *Commission/Germany*, para 20.

rules that are applicable as with individual acts addressed to private persons. Therefore, a local government can be the addressee of order issued by the municipal supervisory authorities, to modify an illegal local regulation or to withdraw an illegal individual decision.[122] Public authorities have to go through the same procedure to challenge this supervisory act.

Under the influence of the need to effectively protect basic liberties against government action administrative law has become "constitutionalised". It is in this connection that, in Germany, one speaks of administrative law as "concretised constitutional law". Administrative authorities have to reach a decision through a consideration of its impact on individual rights, equality, legitimate expectations, and proportionality. A duty on public authorities to conduct a (Strategic) Environmental Impact Assessment is mostly provided for in specific statutes. There is a trend and an increasing necessity[123] for the public authorities to take into consideration during the single case decision making process the results of a social impact assessment.[124] Social impact assessment is defined as "the process of identifying the future consequences of a current or proposed action which are related to individuals, organizations and social macro-systems".[125] It is important that decision-makers understand the impact of their decisions before they act. This goes beyond an obligation to communicate the existence of a procedure to the holders of rights that might be affected. The Italian Administrative Procedure Act extends this obligation of communication to all "easily identifiable parties",[126] which practically presupposes an assessment of identifiable impacts. Where a "minimum level of research and analysis into the effects" of administrative measures "that is necessary to assess in a meaningful manner their full impact on vulnerable groups in society"[127] is missing, the courts are under pressure to introduce a social impact assessment themselves, even though this happens under the heading of the proportionality principle. The Greek Council of State saw itself confronted with the question of whether it "should continue to be confined to the separate assessment of the current stage of every single new measure, or, rather, whether it should start assessing the cumulative effect of certain types of conduct of the Greek legislature and admin-

[122] Stelkens (n 24) 8.

[123] M. Brewer, 'Social Impact Assessment with a Focus on Methodology, Tools and Data Sources', European Commission, Peer Review in Social Protection and Social Inclusion, Brussels 17-18 November 2011.

[124] M. E. Salomon, 'Of Austerity, Human Rights and International Institutions', LSE Law, Society and Economy Working Papers 2/2015, www.lse.ac.uk/collections/law/wps/wps.htm; A Fischer-Lescano, 'Human Rights in Times of Austerity Policy', Bremen, 2014 February 17, p. 30 http://ak-europa.eu/_includes/mods/akeu/docs/main_report_en_331.pdf.

[125] H. Becker, *Social Impact Assessment* (UCL Press 1997) 243.

[126] O. Mir Puigpelat, 'Participation in Administrative Procedures: Lessons from the Spanish Experience' (2010) *Italian Journal of Public Law* 2, 328-338, 332.

[127] *Pensioners' Union of the Agricultural Bank of Greece (ATE) v Greece*, European Committee of Social Rights, Complaint, Complaint No. 80/2012 16 Jan. 2012, para. 75.

istration in order to be able to evaluate the full extent of the impact of recurrent measures on the same category of adversely affected persons".[128]

b) Measures of preparatory character and complex administrative operations

The function of external adverse effect is to point out that there is a phase of investigation and preparation of administrative action which is not reviewable. According to section 9 of the German Administrative Procedure Act administrative proceedings include the issuing of an administrative single case decision but they exclude all proceedings that take place internally within the public authority, although they are connected to their preparation of an administrative act.

The courts will not intervene while the administrative authority is still in the stage of investigation and preparation. While measures of preparatory character may not themselves be the subject of an application for annulment, any legal defects affecting them may be relied upon in proceedings against the final measure of which they represent a preparatory stage. A basic categorization of the composite procedures in European administrative law focuses on the activities which are preparatory to the decision-making process. A final act, which is adopted by an EU organ or a Member State, is based on procedures involving inputs of different actors from different jurisdictions. Initial and intermediate (positive and negative) EU measures could be challenged in national proceedings directed at the challenge of the final national measure.

Complex administrative operations ("opérations administrative complexes")[129] involve a series of successive decision-making steps aimed at reaching a final result; the intermediary decisions are only important because of their relevance to the final decision; the validity of each step is conditioned on the validity of the former steps, they are all integrated procedurally in the final act. In this case it is accepted that the final decision must be awaited in order to challenge the legality of the intermediary decisions. The final decision is the result of a sequence of several other decisions. In this case it is possible to rely upon the illegality of the intermediary decisions that have since then become definitive on the occasion of remedy directed against the final decision. In France, the public utility declaration ("déclaration d'utilité publique") – the

[128] S. Al Rizos, 'Die "Kraft des Faktischen" in der jüngsten Rechtsprechung des Staatsrats', in A. Hatje, C. Iliopoulos, J. Iliopoulos-Strangas and J. A. Kämmerer (eds.) *Verantwortung, Solidarität und Kooperation in der Europäischen Union: Ein deutsch-griechischer Rechtsdialog* (Baden Baden 2015) 149-158, 157. Another judge of a national constitutional court, Jan Zobec, also speaks of "the normative power of the crisis", a "(p)araphrase of Gurvitch's and Jellinek's idea of a normative power of facticity", at the International Conference on "The role of constitutional justice in protecting the values of the rule of law", pp. 1-15, at p. 1. Event dedicated to the 20th Anniversary of the Constitution of the Republic of Moldova Chi in u, 8-9 September 2014. http://www.constcourt.md/public/files/file/conferinta_20ani/programul_conferintei/Jan_Zobec.pdf.

[129] CE 20 mars 2015 *Société Urbanis aménagement*, req. n° 371895. H. Charles, '"Actes rattachables" et "actes détachables" en droit administratif français. Contribution à une théorie de l'opération administrative', *Bibliothèque de droit publict*. LXXX, Paris, *Librairie générale de droit et de jurisprudence*, 1968.

last act of the expropriation procedure taken after a public enquiry – declares the public utility of a project and therefore the requirement of an expropriation. According to the theory of complex administrative operations it is possible to file a plea of illegality of a public utility declaration having become definitive and to obtain its annulment on the occasion of a remedy brought primarily against the official approval of expropriation ("arrêté de cessibilité"). Another example: a candidate that has not been admitted to a competition can challenge the decision that has established the list of persons eligible to participate in the competition, the choice of tests on specific subjects in the relevant field, or the list of the participants in the competition although these decisions have become definitive. A complex administrative operation constitutes a single procedure. Substantive and procedural consequences arise out of this unity. The first relates to the fact that the validity of the individual sequential acts depends on the validity of all the preceding preparatory acts. The latter concerns specifically the conditions of admissibility of the action of annulment: only the final administrative act can be challenged, while the legality of the preparatory acts is challenged at the same time.[130] The assessment of the admissibility of the remedy against the whole complex administrative operation reflects the state of law at the date on which the final administrative act was issued.

c) Affected persons and their right to be heard

External legal effects are a criterion for the right to good administration. This right includes the right of every person to be heard, before any individual measure which would affect him adversely is taken (Article 41(2)(a) Charter of Fundamental Rights of the EU). The right to be heard applies because the measure significantly affects the applicant's interests. It is applicable against Member State institutions when they act in the scope of EU law.[131] In EU composite procedures, when the assessment of the relevant EU Institution deviates from the decision of the national administration, the General Court held that the EU Institution "had a duty to arrange for the applicant to be heard" by the national authorities,[132] or to ensure the right of the applicant to be heard before the EU Institution itself, even in the absence of any rules governing the procedure in question.[133] It is all the more important that observance of the right to be heard be guaranteed in composite procedures before an EU Institution when that Institution proposes not to follow the opinion of the national authority, e.g. as to whether any obvious negligence can be attributed to the person concerned.[134] A distinction is drawn "between fields such as competition law

[130] P. Dagtoglou, *General Administrative Law* (7th ed., Sakkoulas Publications 2015) para 578 (in Greek).

[131] Case T-170/06, *Alrosa Company Ltd v Commission* [2007] ECR II-2601, paragraph 91; Case T-189/02, *Ente per le Ville vesuviane v Commission* [2007] ECR II-89, para 88.

[132] Case T-346/94, *France Aviation v Commission* [1995] ECR II-284, para 36.

[133] Case T-42/96, *Eyckeler & Malt AG v Commission* [1998] ECR II-401, para 77, 84-86; Case T-50/96, *Primex Produkte ImporT-Export GmbH & Co and others v Commission* [1998] ECR II-377, para 59, 65-67.

[134] Joined Cases T-186/97, T-187/97, T-190/97 to T-192/97, T-210/97, T-211/97, T-216/97, T-217/97, T-218/97, T-279/97, T-280/97, T-293/97 and T-147/99, *Kaufring AG and Others v Commission* paras 151-153, 155.

or the collection of anti-dumping duties, where it is the Community institutions which decide to institute the procedure which may lead to the punishment of an economic agent who has contravened the provisions of the Treaty, and other situations".[135] The autonomous EU sanctioning regime is another specific field.[136] It agrees with the logic of the distinction of different specific fields of administrative action with adverse effects which may vary in intensity at different procedural stages, that before any decision which produces its own distinct – and in the context of a composite procedure – additional adverse effects an opportunity for a hearing should be granted.

C. Conclusion

In the French and German traditions the legal instrument of the "administrative act" constitutes, with significant differences, a conceptual framework governed by the principles of legality, proportionality and legal security coupled with legal certainty and flexibility. "Unilateral single case decisions" are part of this conceptual framework. In Common law countries, the main features of what is considered a unilateral single case decision have not been developed in connection with an organising conceptual principle such as the "administrative act". Rather, the operative term is "decision making process" in connection with natural justice and procedural fairness. Therefore, the term "unilateral single case decision" cannot be considered as a Europe-wide familiar name for a familiar thing. Some of its features are more familiar to lawyers from some jurisdictions than lawyers from other jurisdictions. Nevertheless, the Model Rules on EU Administrative Procedure can build on the different separate conceptual elements attributed to a unilateral single case decision in national legal orders, under the condition that homonyms and relevant (historical and present) antonyms are made explicit. Some aspects of the Civil law administrative act doctrine is, for example, helpful for the understanding of European composite procedures. This approach is compatible with the (at least) four[137] major traditions of administrative law in Europe: the administration-centred tradition (which views administrative law as a tool for governments to run an efficient administration); a more individual-oriented view of community administrative procedures (which tends to treat administrative law as an instrument for controlling government and protect individuals from infringements of

[135] Opinion of AG Mischo, delivered on 25 November 1999, Case C-462/98 *P Mediocurso – Estabelecimento de Ensino Particular SA v Commission of the European Communities*, para 17. Judgment of the Court of 21 September 2000, Case C-462/98 *P- Mediocurso – Estabelecimento de Ensino Particular Ld.ª v Commission of the European Communities*, para 43.

[136] C. Eckes and J. Mendes, 'The Right to Be Heard in Composite Administrative Procedures: Lost in between Protection?', *European Law Review* (2011) Vol. 36, No. 5, 651-670.

[137] See the Swedish Statskontoret, 'Principles of Good Administration In the Member States of the European Union' 2005, p. 74.

their rights); the legislator-centred tradition (which relies on a detailed administrative procedure act and on constitutional provisions); and the ombudsman-centred tradition. The Model Rules on EU Administrative Procedure present the opportunity to simplify and stabilise administrative proceedings and foster integration without levelling out national differences. National debates about the categories and single aspects of unilateral administrative decision making are expected to meet each other in the interpretation and implementation of these common rules.

CHAPTER 4

The Book III of the ReNEUAL Model Rules from a Spanish Perspective

When Procedural Law Becomes Substantive

Oriol Mir

A. Introduction

In this chapter I will analyse Book III of the ReNEUAL Model Rules (Model Rules)[1] from the perspective of Spanish Administrative law.

Adopting a national perspective to analyse an academic code mainly addressed to the EU institutions may be questionable. Within the Member States, it is certainly not usual to examine the law applicable to the national central Administration from the perspective of the regional Administrative law.

This approach is however justified at least for the following reasons.

First, although European Administrative law – in its narrow sense[2] – has experienced a strong development particularly in the last two decades, it still isn't as mature as national Administrative law. It presents many gaps and has achieved so far a lower degree of academic systematisation. With the only exception of the non-binding European Code of Good Administrative Behaviour,[3] there is no other similar code at EU level or at an equivalent supranational level that the Model Rules can be compared with. Book III of the Model Rules has been therefore strongly inspired by the existing national codifications[4].

* Update during correction of the proofs in April 2016: The two bills mentioned in footnote 13 were finally passed by the Spanish Parliament and published in Spain's Official Journal on 1 October 2015 without any substantial changes: Act 39/2015 of 1 October 2015 on the Common Administrative Procedure (*Ley 39/2015, de 1 de octubre, del Procedimiento Administrativo Común de las Administraciones Públicas* – LPAC) and Act 40/2015 of 1 October 2015 on the Legal Regime of the Public Sector (*Ley 40/2015, de 1 de octubre, de Régimen Jurídico del Sector Público*). They will enter into force and repeal and replace the current LRJPAC on 2 October 2016. The new LPAC includes only – many – minor changes with respect to the LRJPAC, the most important being the regulation of the electronic procedure and the inclusion of a final part on administrative rulemaking. Electronic administrative procedures where until now regulated in a separate piece of legislation and are now supposed to be the standard administrative procedure to be followed by all Spanish public administrations. As it is explained in footnote 13, administrative rulemaking was not regulated in the LRJPAC, but in the national and regional Acts on the respective Governments and other pieces of legislation, and now the APA contains some general provisions applicable to all of them. Almost all Articles of the LRJPAC cited in this chapter are included unchanged – or with minor changes – in the LPAC, with a different numbering.

1 H. C. H. Hofmann, J.-P. Schneider, J. Ziller, J.-B. Auby, P. Craig, D. Curtin, G. della Cananea, D.-U. Galetta, J. Mendes, O. Mir, U. Stelkens, M. Wierzbowski (eds.) *ReNEUAL Model Rules on EU Administrative Procedure*, version for online publication, 2014, available at http://www.reneual.eu/publications/ReNEUAL%20Model%20Rules%202014/ReNEUAL-%20Model%20Rules-Compilation%20Books%20I_VI_2014-09-03.pdf.

2 As the law applicable to the EU Administration ("*Eigenverwaltungsrecht der EU-Administration*" according to E. Schmidt-Assmann, *Das allgemeine Verwaltungsrecht als Ordnungsidee* (2nd ed., Springer 2006) 385 ff.)

3 European Ombudsman, *The European Code of Good Administrative Behaviour*, Luxembourg, Office for Official Publications of the European Communities, 2005.

4 See paragraphs 28 to 33 of the introduction to the ReNEUAL Model Rules included in Book I Model Rules and the explanations of Book III Model Rules.

Second, even if – mainly for strategic reasons – Book III of the Model Rules is only applicable to the EU institutions (unless sector-specific EU law or the respective Member State law renders it applicable to Member State authorities[5]), it is also expected to inspire national legislators, judges, officials and scholars.[6]

Third, from a theoretical point of view, a comparison between the law applicable to EU institutions and the national law is interesting to identify regulatory models and influences and see how they circulate within the European legal (and administrative) space.[7]

Last but not least, national experts usually know their own national Administrative law far better than European Administrative law. Hence, comparing the Model Rules with the different national codifications allows them to be visible and understandable for a broader audience.

In this chapter I will therefore briefly compare Book III with the Spanish regulation on single case decision-making. First I will present some of the many similarities existing between them (B.) and then I will focus on the main differences (C.), the most important being the more substantive approach of the Model Rules to administrative procedure. The chapter will show that even if Spanish administrative procedure law has a very long and influential tradition, it may be notably enriched by other European experiences reflected in Book III of the Model Rules.

A further preliminary remark has to be made before beginning this comparison: for two reasons my analysis may be biased. First, I cannot be fully impartial, even if I try, because I participated in the working group that elaborated Book III of the Model Rules.[8]

Second, as a scholar interested in European and comparative Administrative law, I will probably tend to overestimate solutions coming from abroad and be too critical with regard to Spanish law; it is an empirically verifiable fact that when scholars know other legal systems better than their compatriots they tend unconsciously to present them as a model to follow by the national law and science.

---

5 Art. III-1(1) Model Rules.

6 See paragraphs 6 and 11 of the explanations of Book I Model Rules.

7 On the notion of European legal space see A. von Bogdandy and P. M. Huber, '§ 42 – Staat, Verwaltung und Verwaltungsrecht: Deutschland', in A. von Bogdandy, S. Cassese and P. M. Huber (eds.) *Handbuch Ius Publicum Europaeum*, vol. III (C. F Müller 2010) paragraphs 1 ff. (with Spanish translation: A. von Bogdandy and P. M. Huber, 'Estado, Administración y Derecho administrativo en Alemania', in A. von Bogdandy and O. Mir (eds.) *Ius Publicum Europaeum. El Derecho administrativo en el espacio jurídico europeo* (Tirant lo Blanch 2013) paragraphs 1 ff.).

8 Along with Paul Craig, Giacinto della Cananea, Jens-Peter Schneider, Vanessa M. Tünsmeyer and Marek Wierzbowski.

B. Main Similarities Between Book III of the ReNEUAL Model Rules and the Spanish Administrative Procedure Law

There are many more similarities than differences between Book III of the Model Rules and Spanish administrative procedure law. Such similarities make this Book perfectly understandable for a Spanish reader, who will find its structure and main concepts very familiar,[9] as was evidenced during the presentation and discussion of the Model Rules in Spain.[10]

I. The importance given to the codification of administrative procedure and the relationship with specific procedural legislation

The similarities begin with the importance given to the codification of administrative procedure itself. Spain has a very long codifying tradition. The first Spanish general codification on administrative procedure was passed in 1889,[11] the same year in which the Spanish Civil Code was adopted. That was almost forty years before Austria enacted its famous *Allgemeines Verwaltungsverfahrensgesetz* of 1925.

The later Spanish Administrative Procedure Act (*Ley de Procedimiento Administrativo*) of 17 July 1958, which was technically much better and much more effective than the Act of 1889, had a remarkable influence in other countries – particularly in Latin America[12] – and established an advanced regulation of the matter that is still present in its key elements in the current Spanish

9 The same can be said about Book II of the ReNEUAL Model Rules on administrative rulemaking and on Book V on mutual assistance (even if the regulation of the latter is much more detailed than that contained in Article 4 of the Spanish APA). Book IV on contracts and Book VI on administrative information management may instead be more difficult to understand for a Spanish reader. In the case of Book IV, this happens because it is based on the current legal situation of EU contracts, which are normally subject to private law (while in Spain public contracts are normally subject to Administrative law); Book VI is particularly innovative and addresses issues that haven't been much regulated yet by Spanish Administrative law. These difficulties arose during the translation process of the Model Rules into Spanish, which I coordinated (the Spanish translation has already been published: *Código ReNEUAL de procedimiento administrativo de la Unión Europea* (INAP, 2015) available at http://www.reneual.eu/publications/ReNEUAL%20Model%20Rules%202014/codigoreneualdeprocedimientoadministrativodelaue.pdf).

10 Conference "Jornada: El Código ReNEUAL de procedimiento administrativo de la Unión Europea", held at the Faculty of Law of the University of Barcelona, 30 January 2015, Barcelona (programme available at http://www.reneual.eu (section "Events"); the video recording of the Conference is available at http://uboc.ub.edu/portal/Play/41422a83413e41cb895827246fbaadcb1d).

11 *Ley de bases del procedimiento administrativo* of 19 October 1889.

12 E. García de Enterría, 'Introducción: un punto de vista sobre la nueva Ley de Régimen Jurídico de las Administraciones Públicas y del Procedimiento Administrativo Común de 1992', in J. Leguina Villa and

Administrative Procedure Act, the Act 30/1992 of 26 November 1992 (*Ley 30/1992, de 26 de noviembre, de Régimen Jurídico de las Administraciones Públicas y del Procedimiento Administrativo Común* – LRJPAC –[13]).

The LRJPAC plays a central role in Spanish Administrative law and there is a wide consensus among Spanish scholars on the convenience of having such a general codification.

In this context, it is no surprise that Administrative law scholars have strongly supported the idea of enacting an administrative procedure act for the EU institutions.[14] The very fact that the term "Code" (*Código*) has been used in

M. Sánchez Morón (eds.) *La nueva Ley de Régimen Jurídico de las Administraciones Públicas y del Procedimiento Administrativo Común* (Tecnos 1993) 11.

13 Last amended by Act (*Ley*) 15/2014 of 16 September 2014. The LRJPAC has 146 articles and 26 final provisions. It not only regulates administrative procedure *stricto sensu* and related questions, such as the validity, effects, enforcement and withdrawal of administrative acts, but also some general aspects on administrative organization, administrative appeals, administrative sanctions and state liability. Contracts and administrative rulemaking are regulated in other pieces of legislation (the Spanish Act on public procurement – *Real Decreto Legislativo 3/2011, de 14 de noviembre, por el que se aprueba el texto refundido de la Ley de Contratos del Sector Público* of 4 November 2011 – and the national and regional Acts on the respective Governments). The LRJPAC is applicable to all Spanish administrative authorities, also those at regional and local level. On 18 May 2015 two bills intended to repeal and replace the LRJPAC (and other Acts) came up for discussion at the Spanish Parliament: the bill on the Common Administrative Procedure (*Proyecto de Ley del Procedimiento Administrativo Común de las Administraciones Públicas*, Ref. 121/000155, available at http://www.congreso.es/public_oficiales/L10/CONG/BOCG/A/BOCG-10-A-155-1.PDF) and the bill on the Legal Regime of the Public Sector (*Proyecto de Ley de Régimen Jurídico del Sector Público*, Ref. 121/000155, available at http://www.congreso.es/public_oficiales/L10/CONG/BOCG/A/BOCG-10-A-154-1.PDF). The regulation of administrative procedure and of the aforementioned related questions (validity, effects, enforcement and withdrawal of administrative acts, as well as administrative appeals and a new part on administrative rulemaking) is included in the first bill, without presenting substantial changes with respect to the LRJPAC. The discussion in this chapter will therefore remain valid even if this bill is finally passed by the Parliament.

14 See e.g. E. Nieto Garrido and I. Martín Delgado, *European Administrative Law in the Constitutional Treaty* (Hart Publishing 2007) 115 ff. and 137 ff.; O. Mir, 'La codificación del procedimiento administrativo en la unión administrativa europea', in F. Velasco and J. -P. Schneider (eds.) *La unión administrativa europea* (Marcial Pons 2008) 73-85 (with German translation: 'Die Kodifikation des Verwaltungsverfahrensrechts im Europäischen Verwaltungsverbund', in J.-P. Schneider and F. Velasco (eds.) *Strukturen des Europäischen Verwaltungsverbunds* (Duncker & Humblot 2009) 198-210); O. Mir, 'Arguments in favour of a general codification of the procedure applicable to EU administration', in European Parliament, *Workshop on EU administrative law: state of play and future prospects*, PE453.215, Brussels, European Parliament, 2011, pp. 67-74; M. Fuertes, 'The importance of keeping it simple: Reflections on a Law on Administrative Procedure for EU Institutions', PE462.419, Brussels, European Parliament, 2011, pp. 4-10; J. E. Soriano (ed.) *Procedimiento Administrativo Europeo* (Civitas-Thomson Reuters 2012) *passim*.

the title of the Spanish version of the Model Rules[15] shows the positive connotation it has in this country.

The existing parallels regarding the relations between the different legal sources at EU level and in Spain lead also to a similar relationship between the Model Rules/LRJPAC and specific procedural rules envisaged by other pieces of legislation (Article I-2 Model Rules).

II. The general conception, structure and functions of administrative procedure

The general conception of the administrative procedure as the process by which a public authority prepares and formulates a decision (Article I-4(2) Model Rules), its sequential structure (initiation ex-officio or by an application, gathering of all information needed to take a sound and lawful decision, including the hearing and consultation of the public and of other public authorities, conclusion of the administrative procedure) and its investigatory, non-adversarial nature are similar too.

Administrative procedure also fulfils in Spain the twofold function of fostering the effective discharge of public duties and protecting the rights of individuals[16] and has acquired a central position within Spanish Administrative law as a key steering instrument of Administrative action.[17]

III. The main procedural rights

The main procedural rights are also the same in Book III Model Rules and in the LRJPAC: the right to be represented by a lawyer or some other person (Article III-8(1)(e) Model Rules /Articles 32 and 85(2) LRJPAC), the right to use any of the official languages (Article III-8(1)(c) Model Rules /Articles 35(d) and 36 LRJPAC), the right to request the exclusion of non-impartial officials (Article III-3(4) Model Rules /Article 29 LRJPAC), the right to propose witnesses and experts (Article III-15(2) Model Rules /Articles 80 and 81 LRJPAC), the right to access their own file (Article III-22 Model Rules /Articles. 35(a) and 84(1) LRJPAC), the right to be heard (Article III-23 and III-24 Model Rules /Articles 35(e), 79, 84 and 89(1) LRJPAC), the right to be given reasons for the final decision (Article III-29 Model Rules /Articles 54 and 89(3) LRJPAC), the right to be informed of the available remedies (Article III-30 Model Rules /Articles 58 and 89(3) LRJPAC) or the right to be notified of the final decision (Article III-33 Model Rules /Articles 58 and 59 LRJPAC) within a maximum time-limit

15 See n 9.

16 Paragraph 11 of the introduction included in Book I Model Rules.

17 O. Mir, '§ 84 Grundzüge des Verwaltungsrechts in gemeineuropäischer Perspektive: Spanien', in von Bogdandy, Cassese and Huber, paragraphs 49 and 50 (with Spanish translation: O. Mir, 'El Derecho administrativo español en el actual espacio jurídico europeo', in von Bogdandy and Mir (n 7) paragraphs 49 and 50).

(Article III-9 Model Rules, establishing a default time-limit of three months, as in Article 42(3) LRJPAC).

The general list of rights contained in Article 35 LRJPAC served particularly as a source of inspiration for Article III-8(1) Model Rules.

There are however relevant differences regarding the content of some of these rights, as will be seen below.

IV. The high degree of convergence achieved within the European Administrative Space

Considering that Book III of the Model Rules was not drafted only by a Spaniard, in view of Spanish Administrative law, but by a group of scholars coming from five different legal traditions,[18] in light of a wide range of legal sources (mainly primary and secondary EU law, jurisprudence of the CJEU, EU and Council of Europe soft law and Administrative Procedure Acts of the different Member States),[19] the aforementioned similarities show that a remarkable degree of convergence regarding the administrative procedure has been already achieved within the European Administrative Space.

Such convergence goes far beyond the minimum requirements of Article 41 of the Charter of Fundamental Rights of the EU. It makes clear that a sufficient level of maturity has been reached in order to codify the regulation of administrative procedure at EU level.

C. Main Differences Between Book III of the ReNEUAL Model Rules and the Spanish Administrative Procedure Law

Despite the substantial coincidence described in the previous paragraphs, there exist a number of important differences between Book III of the Model Rules and the Spanish LRJPAC. Some of them constitute best practices that in my view should be adopted by the Spanish legislator.

The following fifteen differences are the most relevant.

I. The definition of the central notions of "decision", "party" and "public authority"

The definition of the central notions of "decision", "party" and "public authority" diverge. The concept of decision that derives from the definition contained in Article III-2(1) Model Rules, imported with some differences

18 Working Group II of ReNEUAL was composed of six members coming from Germany (Jens-Peter Schneider and Vanessa M. Tünsmeyer), Italy (Giacinto della Cananea), Poland (Marek Wierzbowski), Spain (Oriol Mir) and the UK (Paul Craig). It was surprisingly easy to agree on the general conception and on the concrete features of Book III.

19 As the explanations of Book III Model Rules show.

from the German definition of "administrative act" (§ 35 of the German APA,[20], which was to be found in Article 4(5) of the Community Customs Code of 1992[21]), is much narrower than the concept of administrative act used – but not defined – by the Spanish legislation and jurisprudence.

The concept of administrative act mainly used in Spain, inspired by the Italian *atto amministrativo,*[22] also includes non-binding acts such as opinions and recommendations, preparatory measures and acts having purely internal effects.

The narrow notion of the Model Rules resembles nevertheless the dogmatically less developed concept of *"resolución (que pone fin al procedimiento administrativo)"* contained in Article 89 LRJPAC, which also is the administrative act *par excellence* in Spain.[23]

The definition of the other key notion of "party" (Article III-2(3) Model Rules) also differs. While the Model Rules concept includes "the addressee of the intended decision and other persons who are adversely affected by it and who request to be involved in the procedure", the Spanish central notion of *"interesado"* (Article 31 LRJPAC) is based on the traditional and less clear distinction between subjective rights and – individual or collective – legitimate interests.

In practice, according to the Spanish jurisprudence all persons who might benefit or be adversely affected by the decision may request to be involved in the procedure and acquire the status of *interesado.*[24] This includes NGOs and other legal persons acting in defence of collective interests. But even if the Spanish courts have interpreted the notion of *interesado* in very broad terms, the distinction between the addressee and other persons who are adversely affected seems to be clearer and to offer a better basis for developing an adequate protection of third parties within administrative procedures.

Similarly to Article 31(1)(c) LRJPAC, for efficiency reasons Article III-2(3) Model Rules does not impose on the public authority the duty to identify all those persons who might be adversely affected by the intended decision. It is up

---

20 Verwaltungsverfahrensgesetz ([2003] I Bundesgesetzblatt 102), last amendment of 27 July 2013 ([2013] I Bundesgesetzblatt 2749).

21 Council Regulation (EEC) No 2913/92 of 12 October 1992 establishing the Community Customs Code.

22 As formulated by G. Zanobini, *Corso di Diritto Amministrativo*, vol. 1 (8th ed., Giuffrè 1958) 243.

23 Some relevant Spanish scholars have suggested in recent years to import the German narrow concept of administrative act: R. Bocanegra, *Lecciones sobre el acto administrativo* (4th ed., Civitas-Thomson Reuters 2012) 27 ff., 33 ff.; J. García Luengo, *La nulidad de pleno derecho de los actos administrativos* (Civitas 2002) 31 ff. In favour of a broad concept of administrative act for the EU Administration, in the Spanish literature, X. Arzoz, *Concepto y régimen jurídico del acto administrativo comunitario* (IVAP 1998) 66 ff., 193 ff.; X. Arzoz, 'Acto y procedimiento administrativo en el Derecho de la Unión Europea: un catálogo de problemas', in J. E. Soriano (n 14) 204-215.

24 See e.g. the judgements of the Spanish Supreme Court (Third Chamber; *Tribunal Supremo, Sala de lo Contencioso-Administrativo*) of 19.5.2000 (appeal Nr. 4605/1994, Court Consideration Nr. 4) and of 2.6.2014 (appeal Nr. 41/2013, Court Consideration Nr. 6), with regard to the closely related question of the standing of parties before the courts, based on the same concept of *interesado* and of legitimate interest.

to them to make themselves known and to request to be involved in the procedure. But if they do so, they are entitled to become parties with the same procedural rights as the addressee. The authority has no discretion in this regard.

Unlike the LRJPAC, Article III-8(3) Model Rules empowers the public authority to appoint ex-officio a joint representative for all those parties affected in a similar way in procedures where the number of persons adversely affected is large. This provision, inspired by § 18 of the German APA, is also aimed at granting administrative efficiency.

A third relevant conceptual difference regards the notion of "public authority" subject to the Model Rules. Such notion is broader than that of "public Administration" used by the LRJPAC (Article 2) and includes not only public law bodies, but also private persons "when they are entrusted with administrative action on behalf of the EU" (Article I-4(5) Model Rules). This is coherent with the functional approach of the entire Model Rules and of EU law in general that will be addressed below.

In recent years a number of scholars have called for an extension of the rules on administrative procedure to private persons entrusted with public tasks in order to grant an adequate protection of the citizens they relate to.[25]

EU law has already forced to broaden the concept of contracting authorities traditionally used by the Spanish legislation, a concept restricted to public law bodies, in order to meet the functional requirements of the Directives on public procurement.[26]

II. The duty to appoint a responsible official

The duty to appoint a responsible official for managing the procedure (Article III-7 Model Rules) is another significant difference. This duty, taken from the Italian experience,[27] seems particularly important to avoid the dilution of responsibilities and to promote better management of the procedure.

In this regard, Article 41 LRJPAC has been criticized for being too vague and not giving an obligation to appoint a concrete responsible official.[28] This duty is starting to be introduced in Spain at regional level.[29]

---

[25] See Mir (n 17) paragraphs 39-41.

[26] Case C-214/00 *Commission v Spain* [2003] ECR I-4667; Case C-283/00 *Commission v Spain* [2003] ECR I-11697; Case C-84/03 *Commission v Spain* [2005] ECR I-139.

[27] Arts. 4-6 of the Italian APA (*Legge 7 agosto 1990 n. 241, Nuove norme in materia di procedimento amministrativo e di diritto di accesso ai documenti amministrativi (pubblicata nella Gazzetta Ufficiale del 18 agosto 1990 n. 192)*).

[28] M. Sánchez Morón, *Derecho Administrativo. Parte General* (10th ed., Tecnos 2014) 493.

[29] Arts. 48(3) and 50 of the Catalan APA (*Llei 26/2010, del 3 d'agost, de règim jurídic i de procediment de les administracions públiques de Catalunya*), with a wording that could be improved.

III. Reinforced information rights of the parties

Book III of the Model Rules reinforces information rights of the (potential future) parties even before the administrative procedure is initiated. In this regard, Article III-4 Model Rules establishes the duty to promote the provision of general updated online information on the existing administrative procedures, going far beyond Article 42(4) LRJPAC and taking advantage of information technologies. This information should allow potential applicants to know in advance what the applicable legislation is and the procedural and substantive legal requirements that have to be fulfilled to obtain permits, subsidies, etc., avoiding the public authority the costs of informing them individually and of processing defective applications.

Once the procedure is initiated, Article III-5(2) and (3) and Article III-6(3) Model Rules contain a clearer regulation of the notification of ex-officio initiation and of the acknowledgement of receipt of applications, providing the party with more information than Articles 42(4), 70 and 71 LRJPAC. It seems particularly important that the notification of ex-officio initiation contains the rationale for the initiation of the procedure.

When the final decision is adopted, it has not only to indicate the possibilities of administrative appeal and of judicial challenge (as Articles 58(2) and 89(3) LRJPAC also require), but also of recourse to an Ombudsman (Article III-30(2) Model Rules). Ombudsmen also exist in Spain at the national and at the regional level, although they still haven't acquired the social and political relevance of their counterparts at the EU level and in other countries.

IV. Explicit consideration of competitive award procedures

Administrative procedures leading to the allocation of scarce resources have their own particular features and have received a special attention in recent academic literature.[30] Book III of the Model Rules is aware of it and refers *mutatis mutandis* to the competitive award procedure regulated in Book IV Chapter 2 Section 3 Model Rules – with regard to the conclusion of EU contracts – where the number of applications to be granted is limited and such a competitive procedure is to be used (Article III-6(4) Model Rules).

Hence, a minimum common regulation is given to this important type of procedure, that goes far beyond the few provisions on it in the LRJPAC (Articles 54(2), 59(6)(b) and 71 LRJPAC). Sector-specific legislation may of course regulate such procedures in more detail, taking into account sector-specific requirements.

---

30 In Spanish literature recently L. Arroyo and D. Utrilla (eds.) *La administración de la escasez* (Marcial Pons 2015) *passim*, taking into account the German discussion on the *Verteilungsverfahren*.

V. Deeper regulation of the gathering of information by the public authority

Chapter 3 of Book III Model Rules, along with Books V and VI on mutual assistance and administrative information management,[31] also contains a much deeper regulation of the gathering of information by public authorities.

Inspections are not regulated in the LRJPAC,[32] but only in sector-specific legislation and in the Catalan APA,[33] and they have become particularly important after the transposition of the Services Directive,[34] since it has led to the abolition of a large number of authorisation procedures and to a greater relevance of *ex post* control instruments. Articles III-18 to III-21 Model Rules are probably more necessary at EU than at national level, because national inspections not related to EU law only exceptionally count with inspectors from other jurisdictions, but Articles III-16 and III-17 Model Rules could serve as a starting point for a future general regulation of inspections within the Spanish APA.

In particular the duty of careful investigation, a central requirement of the CJEU incorporated into Article III-10(1) Model Rules (and also present in the other Books of the Model Rules) is not adequately considered by the LRJPAC nor the Spanish jurisprudence.[35] This is closely related to the traditional formalistic approach of the Spanish administrative procedure law, as will be seen below.

VI. More detailed and substantive regulation of the right to access the file, to be heard and of the duty to give reasons

Chapter 4 of Book III Model Rules contains a more detailed regulation of the right of access to the file (Article III-22 Model Rules) and of the right to be heard (Article III-23 Model Rules), especially with regard to compos-

---

31 On Books V and VI see above n 9.

32 A number of Spanish authors have suggested the inclusion of a minimum general regulation of the inspections in the LRJPAC that goes beyond the few references contained in Arts. 39, 39.bis and 137(3). See e.g. J. M. Pemán, 'La función inspectora. Conclusiones', in J. J. Díez Sánchez (ed.) *La función inspectora. Actas del VIII Congreso de la Asociación Española de Profesores de Derecho Administrativo* (INAP 2013) 246 and 249.

33 Arts. 88-101 of the Catalan APA (see *supra* n 29). On these provisions V. Aguado, 'La primera regulación general de la función de inspección: luces y sombras', in J. Tornos (ed.), *Comentarios a la Ley 26/2010 de régimen jurídico y de procedimiento de las administraciones públicas de Cataluña* (Iustel 2012) 563 ff., welcoming the existence of a general regulation of inspections and criticising that these provisions don't go further.

34 Art. 9(1)(c) of the Directive 2006/123/EC of the European Parliament and of the Council of 12 December 2006 on services in the internal market.

35 J. Ponce, 'El derecho a una buena administración: Derecho administrativo y lucha en pos de una buena gestión pública', in Tornos (n 33) 238 ff., criticising that this duty has not been included either in the recent Catalan APA.

ite procedures (Article III-24 Model Rules), not considered at all by the older LRJPAC.

Article III-25 Model Rules also includes new consultation mechanisms other than the traditional submission of written comments, such as public hearings and online consultations, which may be better suited to fostering real and effective participation.

In Chapter 5 on the conclusion of the procedure, Article III-29 Model Rules establishes the duty to give reasons for all decisions and not only for those included in a list (compare it with Article 54 LRJPAC). It must, however, be said that the list of Article 54 LRJPAC includes almost all kinds of decisions and even relevant procedural steps other than the final decision. Article III-29 Model Rules adopts nevertheless a much more substantive approach, as will be seen below.

VII. Reluctance regarding implied decisions

From a Spanish perspective it seems particularly relevant that Article III-9 Model Rules, unlike Article 43 LRJPAC, does not expressly refer to implied decisions as the general solution for all those application procedures in which the public authority does not adopt the decision within the established time-limit.

Implied decisions have a long tradition in Spanish Administrative law and have been long questioned by many Spanish scholars, as they may entail important risks for the public interest and for third parties and do not provide sufficient legal certainty for the applicants.[36] The CJEU has also been reluctant to admit implied decisions as an alternative to explicit, reasoned decisions in certain fields.[37]

VIII. A better regulation of the rectification and withdrawal of decisions

Chapter 6 of Book III Model Rules contains a much better regulation of the rectification and withdrawal of decisions (Articles III-35 and III-36 Model Rules).

The Spanish regulation of this important issue laid down in Articles 102-106 LRJPAC is very confusing, incomplete and unbalanced, raising many problems. These provisions do not regulate the rectification and withdrawal of lawful decisions that are beneficial to a party (this is foreseen in sector-specific legis-

[36] L. Parejo, *Transformación y ¿reforma? del Derecho Administrativo en España* (INAP/Global Law Press 2012) 147-164; Mir (n 17) paragraph 65, with further references.

[37] Case C-360/87 *Commission v Italy* [1991] ECR I-812, paragraphs 30-31; Case C-131/88 *Commission v Germany* [1991] ECR I-865, paragraph 38; Case C-230/00 *Commission v Belgium* [2001] ECR I-4595, paragraphs 14 ff. On this jurisprudence and the LRJPAC, A. García Ureta, *Procedimiento administrativo y Derecho comunitario*, (IVAP 2002) pp. 43 ff.

lation in an unsystematic way). The fact that they allow parties to request the rectification or withdrawal of unlawful decisions outside the time-limits for legal challenge, without conceiving it as a discretionary power of the public authority, makes it difficult to distinguish this instrument from legal remedies. No rules are envisaged regarding the effects of the rectification and withdrawal (retroactive or prospective and on third parties).

Above all, they are too restrictive regarding the rectification and withdrawal of unlawful decisions that are beneficial to a party, admitting it only where they are null and void (*"nulidad de pleno Derecho"*, absolute nullity, *Nichtigkeit, nullità*) (Article 102 LRJPAC)[38]. Where decisions are merely annullable (*"anulabilidad"*, relative nullity, *Anfechtbarkeit, annullabilità*), the public authority may only challenge them before the courts within a time-limit of four years since the decision was adopted (Article 103 LRJPAC). This rigid approach leads in practice to an expansive interpretation of the grounds for absolute nullity, may infringe the EU principle of effectiveness in certain cases and in fact only shifts the problem to the courts. Instead, Article III-36(2) Model Rules adopts a more flexible and substantive solution for all kinds of unlawful decisions based on the principle of legitimate expectations, in line with the jurisprudence of the CJEU and of other national Administrative law systems.

Apart from these fifteen relevant concrete differences that have been outlined, there is a general feature of Book III of the Model Rules (and of the entire Model Rules) that distinguishes it from the Spanish administrative procedure law: its more substantive approach. This deserves a separate paragraph.

D. The Substantive Approach of the ReNEUAL Model Rules to Administrative Procedure

Administrative procedure is often characterised in Spain by a highly formalistic approach. Public authorities often still conceive administrative procedures as a merely formal duty they have to comply with ("checklist approach"), or as a barrier to protect themselves against time-consuming applications by citizens, and not as an efficient instrument to gather the information they need in order to duly exercise their powers and adopt the best possible decisions.

This happens not only with regard to single case decisions, but also to rulemaking: the reinforced duties to give reasons and to make consultations before adopting new rules introduced in recent years in light of the Better Regulation

[38] Art. 62(1) LRJPAC lists the circumstances that render an administrative act null and void. Unlike the German or Italian APAs, according to the LRJPAC absolute nullity does not imply that the act has no legal effects. It will have legal effects until the public authority or the courts declare the nullity. The differences between absolute and relative nullity are therefore in Spanish Administrative law much less relevant than in Spanish civil law or in other national Administrative law systems. See on this Mir (n 17) paragraphs 77 and 87-90.

movement (to comply with the higher international standards established by the OECD or the EU) lead usually to very poor regulatory impact assessments and to merely formal consultation exercises.

This formalistic conception is also present in the Spanish jurisprudence. Spanish administrative courts tend to exercise a superficial control on procedural aspects (such as the duty to give reasons), not requiring public authorities to comply with the duty of careful investigation and not examining whether the scope of the different procedural requirements has been fulfilled. Often procedural defects are also used as an excuse for the courts to annul decisions and administrative regulations without entering into the merits of the case. This kind of "blind control" leads both to overestimation and underestimation of procedural defects.

This formalistic approach is in contrast with the more substantive, functional approach of EU law and jurisprudence.

Book III of the Model Rules offers in my opinion many examples of this function-oriented approach, including elements in different provisions that guide the interpretation to be done by public authorities and courts.

Some of them include:

- Article III-3(3), with regard to the conflicts of interest: instead of including a list of possible conflicts of interest (as Article 28(2) LRJPAC does), this provision obliges the superior to exclude the affected official "where the impartial and objective exercise of the official´s function is compromised";
- Article III-8(1)(a), granting the right of the parties to be given information on all questions related to the procedure "in a fast, clear and understandable manner";
- Article III-10(1): "When taking decisions, the public authority shall investigate the case *carefully and impartially*. It shall take into consideration the *relevant* factors, including those favourable to the parties, and *give each of them its proper weight in the decision, whilst excluding any irrelevant element from consideration*";
- Article III-13(1): "The parties shall assist in ascertaining the facts of the case. In particular they shall state such facts and evidence as are known to them and *which can reasonably expected to be presented by them*";
- Article III-22, with regard to the right to access the file:

  "Every party shall have the opportunity to examine all documents in his or her file, *which may be relevant for its defence*, including incriminating and exculpatory evidence, before the decision is taken.

  The way in which access to the file is provided is for the public authority to determine, and may be regulated through sector-specific EU law, *provided that it does not undermine the substance of the right*. Subject to this caveat, access to the file may be provided either through copies of documentation, or the opportunity to study the file in the office of the public authority, or a combination of both";
- Article III-23, with regard to the right to be heard:

"Every party has the right to notice of the *central issues that are to be decided by the public authority and the core arguments that inform its reasoning, in order that the party can effectively make known its views on the matter and can exercise its rights of defence.*

Every party *must have adequate time in which to respond* after notice in accord with paragraph 3 has been provided. The public authority should set clear time-limits within which the response is to occur.

The public authority has discretion as to the form and content of the hearing. This includes the choice as to whether the hearing should be written or oral, whether to allow cross-examination. *In choosing how to exercise this discretion the public authority should take into account the objectives of the legislation, the legislative provisions, the importance of the person's interests, the importance of the additional procedural safeguards for protection of the person's interest, and the costs of granting such specific procedural safeguards*";

- Article III-24, with regard to the right to be heard in composite procedures:

  "The right to be heard must be respected at all stages of a composite procedure between the EU and the Member States leading to a decision in the manner set out in this article. *The application of the right to be heard will depend on the division of responsibility in the decision-making process.*

  In a case of composite procedure, the form and content of the hearing provided pursuant to Article III-23(5) by the public authority that makes the decision *will be affected by the extent to which the rights of the defence were adequately protected at a prior stage in the administrative proceedings by another public authority*";
- Article III-28: "A decision made by the public authority shall be clearly specified *in order to enable the parties to understand their rights or duties*";
- Article III-29, with regard to the duty to give reasons:

  "The public authority shall state the reasons for its decisions *in a clear, simple and understandable manner.* The statement of reasons *must be appropriate to the decision and must disclose in a clear and unequivocal fashion the reasoning followed by the public authority which adopted the decision in such a way as to enable the parties to ascertain the reasons for the decision and to enable the competent court to exercise its powers of review.*

  The duty to provide reasons in cases of composite procedures *will be shaped by the respective roles of the EU and the Member State in making the decision*, as set out in Article III-24".

None of these "functional safeguards" are included in the Spanish LRJPAC. They should be considered by the Spanish legislator, along with the best practices of Book III Model Rules enumerated in the previous paragraph, where it aims to carry out a deep reform of the administrative procedure that allows the full potential of this central steering instrument of administrative action to be reached. This is certainly not the case of the ongoing reform of the LRJPAC.[39]

---

39 See above n 13.

CHAPTER 5

Inspection and Evidence in Preparation of Unilateral Decisions

Roberto Caranta

A. Introduction

EU administration fully belongs to the Western legal tradition of legal-rational type of authority as described by Max Weber in the 19th Century.[1] This means that decisions are taken based on the relevant facts which have been duly ascertained following pre-established procedural rules.[2] This in turn links with the logical distinction between *quaestiones facti* and *quaestiones juris*. The decision maker needs to find the facts to apply the law.[3]

Fully in line with this tradition Book III of the ReNEUAL Model Rules devotes one of its chapters to fact finding or, as its title goes, gathering of information.[4] This is often translated as 'investigation' in Book III. Point 11 of the Introduction indicates that "Chapter 3 is concerned with the *investigation as a major preparatory step in each administrative procedure* and selected issues concerning the law of evidence".[5]

The basic principle of investigation is set out in Article III-10; Articles III-11 and III-12 lay down the procedural norms applicable respectively when investigations are conducted by request and when an investigation is mandated by the relevant EU rules; Article III-13 sets out duties to cooperate between EU and national authorities. Article III-14 deals with privilege against self-incrimination and legal professional privilege. Article III-15 regulates witnesses and experts. Finally, Articles III-16 to III-21 set out the rules relating to inspections which are conceived as a specific instrument of administrative investigations.

As with the other parts of the Model Rules, Chapter 3 of Book III greatly improves on the sectoral approach followed in EU law thus far. However it is submitted that the present text is still somewhat too close to a specific instance of administrative proceedings – those in competition cases – to be plainly applicable to all proceedings. In this chapter, the most relevant model rules on investigation and evidence will be first analysed in the light of the explanations provided by the drafters of the Model Rules. A critical appraisal will follow.

B. The Model Rules

The Chapter on the 'gathering of information' is divided into two sections, one laying down general rules and the other specific to inspec-

1 C. Harlow and R. Rawlings, *Process and Procedure in EU Administration* (Hart 2014) 15 and 39 f.

2 'Administrative procedure' is defined in Article I-4(2) of the Model Rules.

3 The law itself needs to be investigated to find the rules applicable, solving conflicts, including those between EU and national law: J. H. Jans, 'The Consequential Effect of European Law in Respect of the Requirement of Due Care' (2007) *Rev Eur Adm Law* 63, and establish their interpretation. These aspects are however not dealt with in the rules administrative procedures, but in the general rules and principle on statutory construction.

4 See also Explanation 44 to Book III.

5 Emphasis in the original.

tions. The supplementary relationship between investigation and inspection is clarified in the Explanations by considering the latter an "especially important instrument of investigation". Basically, "inspections are not conceived as an alternative to investigations, but as an important subcategory of the instruments needed for performing effective investigations".[6]

I. The general rules

The general rules open with a provision dedicated to the 'Principle of investigation'. Article III-10(1) sets the tone by setting the duties binding on the public authority when managing the fact finding phase of the single case decision making procedure. More specifically it shall (a) investigate the case carefully and impartially; (b) take into consideration the relevant factors, including those favourable to the parties; (c) give each factor its proper weight in the decision; (d) exclude any irrelevant element from consideration, and (e) "use such evidence as, after due consideration, it deems necessary in order to ascertain the facts of the case".

As the explanations make clear, the main source of inspiration for Article III-10(1) is Article 9 of the European Code of Good Administration published by the European Ombudsman which refers to a duty of 'objectivity' of public officials.[7] This derivation is especially strong in the insistence on the distinction between relevant and irrelevant factors.[8] The distinction itself is very much indebted to English administrative law.[9] Reference to the general principles of (fairness and) impartiality – as spelt out in Article III-3 – can also be derived from the European Code of Good Administration, which in turn develops some of the principles enshrined in Article 41 of the European Charter of Fundamental Rights (again on the Right to Good Administration).[10] The duty of careful consideration spelt out in the same provision may indeed be seen as required from the fairness principle.[11] The Model Rules are here the truest to the aim of ensuring that the constitutional values of the Union are present and complied with.[12]

---

6 Explanation 45.

7 Explanation 45.

8 See the analysis by J. Wakefield, *The Right to Good Administration* (Kluwer Law International 2007) 140 ff.

9 E.g. *R* v *Secretary of State for the Home Department*, ex parte *Venables* [1998] A.C. 407; see P. Cane, *Administrative Law* (5th ed., Oxford University Press 2011) 65 f.

10 See Article 11 and 8 of the Code respectively; on the specific relevance of the principle of good administration for the work of the European Ombudsman see E. Chevalier, *Bonne administration et Union européenne* (Bruylant 2014) 157 ff; Wakefield (n 8) 93 ff.

11 See also Explanations 46 and f, and references to the case law therein.

12 Generally J. Ziller, 'The ReNEUAL Model Rules on EU Administrative Procedure: Method, Contents and Prospects', in B. Gerencsér, L. Berkes and A. Z. Varga (eds) *Current Issues of the National and EU Administrative Procedures (the ReNEUAL Model Rules)* (Pázmány Press 2015) 247.

The provision has however to be coordinated with Article III-13(1) which seems to be characterised by a different approach as it will be discussed later.

Article III-10(2) rather lists the tools which may be employed to get factual information. Under the conditions laid down in Article III-11 and Article III-12 and/or in other provisions of EU law the public authority may: "(a) gather information of all kinds, (b) hear the evidence of the parties, witnesses and experts or gather statements in writing or electronically from parties, experts and witnesses, (c) obtain documents and records, and (d) under the conditions of Article III-16 visit and inspect the premises involved".[13]

Finally Article III-10(3) refers to the provisions in Book VI on exchange of information when this is provided by a public authority to another public authority.

Articles III-11 and III-12 respectively regulate 'Investigation by request' and 'III-12 Investigation by mandatory decision'. The two provisions are completed by III-13 on the duty to cooperate of the parties and by III-14 on the privilege against self incrimination.[14]

'Request' is to be understood as 'simple request' meaning that, unlike Article III-12, no specific sector-specific rule gives the public authority the power to enact a mandatory decision binding on the addressee and if applicable on its representative. The same is the case when such a power is not used.[15]

Under Article III-11(1) a public authority "may request a party to be interviewed or to provide all necessary information". Under Article III-2(3) `Party´ means the addressee of the intended decision and other persons who are adversely affected by it and who request to be involved in the procedure [...]".

Under Article III-11(3) the public authority asking for information "shall state the legal basis and the purpose of the request, specify what information is required and fix the time-limit within which the information is to be provided, and indicate the penalties provided for in the relevant EU law for supplying incorrect or misleading information".

Given that it deals with binding requests for information, Article III-12(2) simply adds that the competent authority shall also "indicate the legal consequences for not responding to a mandatory decision".

Also relevant is Article III-13(1) which, having laid down a duty on the party "to state such facts and evidence" as are known or reasonably expected to be presented adds that "A more extensive duty to assist in ascertaining the facts, and in particular the duty to appear personally or make a statement, shall exist only where the law specifically requires this".

Article III-13 on the duty of cooperation of the parties reinforces – and to some extent qualifies – the provisions laid down in Articles III-11 and III-12.[16] Article III-13 is made of two sections, the first very general, the second applica-

---

13 My lettering.

14 See the comparative analysis by C. Girard, *Culpabilité et silence en droit comparé* (L'Harmattan 1997).

15 See Explanation 49.

16 See also Explanation 52.

ble only to application procedures according to Article III-6(3). However, Article III-13 goes well beyond the duty of cooperation of the parties, also giving rules on how the public authority is to manage its search for the facts. One could question whether all the rules therein really belong to a provision with such a title.

It is to be remarked here that the choice to have a somewhat restrictive definition of 'party' in Article III-2(3) – parties are the addressee of the intended decision and those other persons who are adversely affected by it and who request to be involved in the procedure – has the side effect of limiting the sphere of application of some of the provisions on fact finding, such as Article III-13 on the duty of cooperation.

Concerning specifically the duty of cooperation of the parties as defined under Article III-2(3), Article III-13(1) provides that they "shall assist in ascertaining the facts of the case. In particular they shall state such facts and evidence as are known to them and which can reasonably expected to be presented by them". The provision adds to the notion of 'incorrect or misleading information' which is used in Article III-11(3), in turn referred to in Article III-12(2). It is doubted however whether the formula 'facts and evidence which can reasonably expected to be presented by them' is really helpful. As already recalled, under Article III-11(3) it is the public authority asking for information which should "specify what information is required". Considering the gravity of the possible sanctions it is submitted that the party should not be responsible under a vague test of reasonableness where the public authority was not specific enough in its requests. Article III-9 on time limits might be very well relevant here.

All the rules on this topic are shorter that those found for instance in Article 23(1) of Regulation (EC) No 1/2003 on the implementation of the rules on competition laid down in Articles 81 and 82 of the Treaty, which is perfectly fine. However, they are also – it is submitted – less clear.

The duty of cooperation in application procedures according to Article III-6(3) is elaborated upon in Article III-13(2) providing that "the applicant supplies in an appropriate form the information specified in EU law". The applicant may also require the public authority to give an opinion on the information to be supplied by the applicant, but the opinion given does not preclude the public authority "from subsequently requiring the applicant to submit further information". This might be questioned under the principle of the protection of legitimate expectations unless the provision is construed as referring to further information which becomes needed to clarify the materials originally requested.

Still on the duty of cooperation Article III-13(2) provides that "Any public authorities holding relevant information must make this information available to the applicant on his or her specific request and on the condition that the applicant cannot reasonably be expected to obtain this information on his or her own". It is uncertain how the last qualification is coordinated with either Article III-22 of the model rules or with the general rules enacted in Regulation (EC)

No 1049/2001 regarding public access to European Parliament, Council and Commission documents. As a matter of good administration public authorities should be ready to make available information in documents to which the right of access applies.

Departing from its title, Article III-13(1) also regulates management of the fact finding powers of the public authority. In a way which is not easy to reconcile with the principle of investigation, it provides that "If a participant fails to state such facts, the final decision shall be taken on the basis of the information available". The question might be 'available on which basis'? Article III-13(1) answers by adding that "the public authority is obliged to conduct additional investigations ex officio only if additional evidence or issues to be investigated are evident". While understanding the desire not to overburden public authorities, one might also have thought that the 'duty of careful investigation' spelt out in Article III-10(1) had set a higher standard.

The Model Rules treatment of persons not being parties because they are neither the addressee nor have requested to be involved is less clear (at least to the author). Article III-11(6) extends the application *mutatis mutandis* of procedural provisions of Article III-11 to these persons "for the case where sector-specific EU law grants to the public authority the power to interview a person who is not party, who consents to be interviewed for the purpose of collecting information relating to the subject-matter of an investigation". It is submitted that when EU law gives the power to interview, consent is immaterial. Indeed, under Article III-15, witnesses (and experts) may be obliged to make a statement by a specific legal provision. Reciprocally, when consent is given there is no need for an explicit legislative authorisation; a public authority hearing parties or witnesses who volunteer information is simply discharging its duty of careful fact finding.[17]

In conclusion, the parties may have a choice not to respond if the request is not binding, or if Article III-14 on the privilege against self-incrimination applies, but if they decide to answer they must tell the truth in a straightforward way.

Given the multi-level structure of the EU, the competent authorities of the Member State concerned must be involved according to the rules laid down in Article III-11(4) and (5) which are also referred to in Article III-12(2).[18]

II. The specific rules on inspections

Unlike 'investigation', 'inspection' is defined in the Model Rules. Under Article III-2 (5) 'Inspection' means an on-the-spot check for the purposes of information gathering.[19]

---

17 See, but only with reference to 'some fields' of EU law, Explanation 49.

18 See also Explanations 50 f.

19 Explanation 10 is more iterative than a real explanation.

Unsurprisingly, given the rather 'invasive' nature of inspections, the model rules give detailed – if at times generic – regulation on this topic. More specifically, Article III-16(1) provides that, in addition to on-the-spot-checks carried out by the authorities of the Member States in accordance with their national law, EU authorities shall have the power to inspect premises when two cumulative conditions are present, that is the power is provided for in the relevant legislation and "this is necessary, to fulfil their duties under EU law".[20] The latter condition, while arguably putting some constraints on the public authority is still somewhat generic, considering that 'necessity' is referred in Article III-10(1) as well with reference to the need "to ascertain the facts of the case". The duty of fairness provided in Article III-3(1) will have to apply here, as well as the better developed general principle of proportionality. A number of rights enshrined in the Charter of Fundamental Rights of the Union, starting with human dignity, will also have to be taken into account.

In keeping with the need to safeguard the rights of those inspected, under Article III-16(2) "Where EU law establishes a power or a duty to inspect for a public authority, it should specify the ways in which the power or duty is exercised". The list in the same paragraph of Article III-16 is therefore simply indicative.

In many ways reiterating the duty of cooperation laid down in Article III-13, Article III-16(3) additionally provides that those affected by the inspection "shall cooperate with the EU officials in their investigation".

Article III-17 lays down duties of the inspecting officials. These officials must act in accordance with EU law, and in particular respect the Charter of Fundamental Rights and comply with EU and national provisions on the protection of personal data. Concerning the latter they must ensure the confidentiality of the information communicated or obtained during an inspection.

As Explanation 60 reminds all of us, "EU inspections occur in Member State territory and are therefore inherently cooperative". The varying degree of cooperation between Member State and EU authorities has led to different provisions, namely Article III-18 on the duties of sincere cooperation during inspections by EU authorities; Article III-19 on the participation of EU authorities in Member State inspections; Article III-20 on joint inspections of Member State authorities, and Article 21, on an EU or Member State authority request to an authority from another Member State to conduct an inspection to be able to fulfil its task (in the latter case Book V of the Model Rules is also specifically relevant).[21]

---

[20] That the conditions are cumulative is made clear in Explanation 64.

[21] See more generally about the different possible imbrications of EU and Member States administrative competences J. Ziller, 'Les concepts d'administration directe, d'administration indirecte et de coadministraiton et les fondements du droit administrative européen', in J.-B. Auby, J. Dutheil de la Rochère and E. Chevalier (eds), *Traité de droit administratif européen* (2nd ed. Bruylant 2014) 327; see also M. A. Glaser, 'Les relations entre administrations pour l'exécution du droit de l'Union', in the same volume, 415.

Inspections not only take place on the territory of the Member States, but the EU needs indeed the cooperation of domestic authorities which only have the power to force entry to premises, land or means of transport.[22] This aspect is of course most delicate, and under Article III-18(5) the Member State on whose territory an inspection takes place shall provide any assistance necessary, including requesting "the assistance of the police or of an equivalent enforcement authority". Authorisation from a judicial authority might be needed, and under Article III-18(6), the national judicial authority shall ensure that the authorization of the inspection is authentic and that the coercive measures envisaged are neither arbitrary nor excessive having regard to the subject matter of the inspection. However domestic courts may not call into question the necessity for the inspection.[23]

C. An Assessment

The drafters of the provisions on investigation have indeed done a lot of work analysing a huge mass of legislation and case law and trying and distilling a number of rules both consolidating and improving the law as it is now.

Besides what appears to be a somewhat complex drafting, a possible criticism of the Chapter on the 'gathering of information' is that it is still much dependent on the model of competition law procedures as laid down in Regulation (EC) No 1/2003 on the implementation of the rules on competition laid down in (then) Articles 81 and 82 of the Treaty.

This is shown by the same choice of words such as 'investigation'. Chapter V of Regulation (EC) No 1/2003 deals indeed with 'powers of investigation'. This is fully appropriate in those proceedings since the Commission is very much acting as a police authority or public prosecutor – depending on which jurisdiction is chosen as the term of comparison – going after undertakings suspected of having breached what are now Articles 101 and 102 TFEU. These proceedings aim at putting an end to the breach and at sanctioning those responsible for the breach. These are at least potentially sanctioning proceedings. This is *Eingriffsverwaltung* if not quasi-criminal administrative action. This is paralleled in the US tradition with the famous Sherman Act 1890 providing for civil and criminal remedies.

Indeed Article 7 of Regulation (EC) No 1/2003 gives the Commission the power to find and terminate infringements. This very much recalls 'seek and destroy' in administrative procedure. To find, the Commission is given the power to investigate under Article 17. Chapter VI of the regulation deals with 'penalties'. Article 23 regulates the power to impose fines which may go up to 1% of the total turnover in the preceding business year. Article 24 instead deals

[22] See also Ziller (n 12) 254.

[23] See also Explanation 71.

with periodic penalty payments not exceeding 5 % of the average daily turnover in the preceding business year per day. These powers are mirrored in those provided by Article 5 for the competition authorities of the Member States which now share with the Commission the jurisdiction to go after breaches of competition rules. These national authorities may also impose "fines, periodic penalty payments or any other penalty provided for in their national law". Unsurprisingly Article 20 of Regulation (EC) No 1/2003 regulates the power of inspection of the Commission. As has been remarked, "the Commission has at its disposal a highly developed toolkit of sanctions in antitrust cases".[24]

Investigations by OLAF, while administrative in principle, have again a quasi-criminal character since their follow up may lead to both decision making under administrative law or criminal prosecution in the member States.[25] Under Article 2 number 4 of Regulation (EU, Euratom) No 883/2013 "'administrative investigations' ('investigations') shall mean any inspection, check or other measure undertaken by the Office in accordance with Articles 3 and 4, with a view to achieving the objectives set out in Article 1 and to establishing, where necessary, the irregular nature of the activities under investigation".[26] While these investigations are not covered under Book III of the Model Rules because they don't end in the adoption of a binding decision and therefore probably had little influence on the drafters of the Model rules, they confirm that the term 'investigation' is more appropriate in the context of administrative proceedings which are specific because they may end up in a sanction being imposed.[27]

While administrative procedures in the area of EU competition law are highly structured and are certainly an unavoidable reference point for codification of EU administrative law, it is indisputable that EU institutions are also very much involved in *Leistungsverwaltug*, that is, according benefits to individuals and undertakings. This does not need a long demonstration, since in exemplifying single case decisions Explanation 3 to the Model Rules names both the decision to grant or to refuse subsidies or loans in the framework of the Common agricultural policy or of the EU structural funds, and the decision concerning funding of a project in the framework of the EU policy aiming at promoting research and development. These are both proceedings possibly leading to a benefit being conferred.

It is therefore submitted that 'investigation' is not the best possible term to be used to refer to fact finding activities in administrative proceedings. 'Investigation' is not the most current word in either English or – besides the area of competition law or other areas where fines may be imposed – European admin-

24 Harlow and Rawlings (n 1) 216.

25 P. Langbroeck and O. Jansen, 'The research project on rights of the defence in fraud investigation', in P. Langbroeck and O. Jansen (eds) *Defence Rights during Administrative Investigations* (Intersentia 2007) 3.

26 See, with reference to the pre-existing – but terminologically identical – legislation P. Langbroeck and O. Jansen, 'The juridical background of OLAF investigations', in Langbroeck and Jansen (n 25) 14 ff.

27 See the reasons for the exclusion of OLAF investigations in Explanation 62.

istrative law. 'Investigation' is not an entry in the *Oxford Dictionary of Law*, which has instead 'investigation of a company' as an inquiry into the potentially illegal conduct of companies and their management. To make an incursion in a possible future as to how law is made and understood, the *Essential 25000 Law Dictionary* entry 12313 is devoted to 'investigate' which is defined as "-gat.ed gat-ing vt: to observe or study by close examination and systematic enquiry ;specif – to make (a criminal suspect) the subject of inquiry and study for the purpose of ...". Entry 12313 reinforces the criminal law flair of 'investigation'.[28]

Apparently 'investigation' (same spelling, different intonation) is used in French administrative law and is linked in French legal writings with the inquisitorial character given to fact finding in that jurisdiction.[29] As such the word may be found with reference to other jurisdictions when the language used is French. For instance, in describing the German law it has been written that "Le principe d'investigation d'office conduit à ce que la procédure soit inquisitoire (§ 24 et § 26 VwVfG)".[30]

This is not simply a terminological dispute. It is suspected that the too heavy reliance on the model provided by Regulation (EC) No 1/2003 is responsible for some of the tensions in the drafting between provisions derived from the European Code of Good Administration which describe in a very proactive way the fact finding powers of the EU public administrations (Article III-10(1) is the obvious instance) and provisions rather stressing the duty of cooperation of the investigated party (Article III-13(1) is an example here).[31] In a way, an adversarial undercurrent is disturbing an otherwise inquisitorial approach to fact finding. Or, to borrow the scheme used by Giacinto della Cananea, some of the rules seems to have been written with the citizen (or undertaking) in mind – *ex parte populi* – others instead moving from the position and interests of the public administration – *ex parte principis*.[32] It is worth noting in passing that when bending on the latter approach the ReNEUAL Model Rules adhere to a characteristically French law approach.[33]

---

28 https://play.google.com/store/books/details/The_Essential_25000_Law_Dictionary_is_a_great_reso?id=lSS7CQAAQBAJ.

29 E.g. E. Chevalier, 'Les méchanismes de la procédure administrative non contentieuse de l'Union', in Auby and Dutheil de la Rochère (n 21) 211.

30 A. Jacquemet-Gauché and U. Stelkens, 'Caractères essentiels du droit allemand de la procédure administrative', in J.-B. Auby and T. Perroud (eds) *Droit comparé de la procédure administrative – Comparative Law of Administrative* (Bruylant 2015 *forthcoming*) 32; when English is used in the same collective work, 'investigation' is again referred to proceedings leading to the imposition of a sanction: O. Jansen, 'A Few Characteristics of the Law of Administrative Procedure in the Netherlands', in Auby and Perroud, *ibid.*, at 109 and 113.

31 See Chevalier (n 29) 211 f.

32 See G. della Cananea, 'A Law on EU Administrative Procedures: Implication for National Legal Orders', in Gerencsér et al (n 12) 285.

33 As discussed by Chevalier (n 29) 201, whose opening remarks would probably not be shared in either Germany or Italy.

This reliance on the competition law model is somewhat of a pattern in Book III. Elsewhere I have criticised the reiterated reference to the burden of proof which characterised the first drafts of the Model Rules.[34] There again one – and arguably ill suited – model had been generalised. It is fair to say that this has been almost fully remedied in the Model Rules as they have been published. The reference is now to the duty to give reasons which is now enshrined in Article III-29.[35]

That duty is quite obviously implied in Article III-10(1) which refers to the public authority's 'consideration' which cannot but be translated into reasons given. It is submitted that 'fact finding' would be a much more appropriate terminological choice than 'investigation'. If with 'investigation' we mean the duty to find facts in a careful and impartial way, I would rather refer to that duty.

D. Conclusions

As with the rest of Book III and of the Model Rules more generally, the drafters of the provisions on investigation must be commended for the huge task of analysing a mass of legislation and case law and distilling a number of rules both consolidating and improving the law. The present fragmentation of EU administrative law in this area is indeed a major source of uncertainty for citizens and undertakings.[36]

However I must personally avow to have found Articles III-11 to III-13 very difficult to navigate, with provisions continuously referring to each other. The quite miscellaneous nature of Article III-13 has already been pointed out. Article III-12 is another good case in point. Section (1) thereof provides that "When sector-specific EU law grants to the public authority the power to investigate by a mandatory decision, the procedural rules in this article are applicable". However the rest of the provision either replicates the provisions found in Article III-11 or refers to them, possibly with the *mutatis mutandis* caveat. More sensibly, the Explanations deal with the two provisions together.[37]

---

34 Please refer to R. Caranta, 'Burden of Proof *vs* Duty to Give Reasons in Administrative Law', in Gerencsér, Berkes and Varga (n 12) 317 ff.

35 See also point 6 of the Introduction to the Model Rules; on the systemic relevance of reason giving see Harlow and Rawlings (n 1) 39 f. and 79 ff.; see also M. Smith, 'Tracing the development of administrative principles in the EU: a possible new approach to legitimacy?', in M. Trybus and L. Rubini (eds) *The treaty of Lisbon and the Future of European Law and Policy* (Edward Elgar 2012) 114.

36 See Ziller (n 12) 250.

37 However Explanation 49 indicates that "The first sentence of Article III-12(2) refers to the procedural rules stipulated in Article III-11 as far as they are adequate in the context of a mandatory decision concerning investigations. It does not refer to all other procedural rules of Book III. As existing sector-specific law like Article 27(1) Regulation 1/2003 shows, the applicability of all these procedural rules would not be an adequate general rule for this sort of decision. Consequently, it is for the sector-specific provisions to render applicable additional model rules". On its face, however, the provision referring to

Finally I submit that the choice to refer to 'investigation' is unfortunate and may generate confusion. Sticking to the more traditional idea of fact finding seems to me a wiser course.[38]

some parts of Article III-11 does not really seem sufficient to exclude the application of all the remaining parts of Book III. On the other hand Book III would be of little use if its application were to be ruled out every time the public authority is given a power to issue binding requests for information. It is submitted that this part of Explanation 49 itself requires more explanations.

38 For the use of 'fact finding' see for instance Harlow and Rawlings (n 1) e.g. 78.

Codifying the Rules in European Administrative Law and National Administrative Law: A Brief Comparison

Comment by Jacques Petit

I would like to start by addressing the issue of the peculiarity of European Administrative Law (which concerns the law that rules the execution of European Union Law (EU) enforced by its own institutions and the States) compared to the administrative law of the EU Member States (i.e. the set of laws that regulates national administrations when they are not acting with the purpose of implementing EU law).[39]

This general matter applies to the specific problem concerning the codification of procedural rules that regulate the way in which administrative inspections can be conducted and the proofs that can be collected accordingly. This leads to a two-fold issue: when laws are codified, both on a European and a national level, do we deal with the same sort of issues, or different ones, and if not, are the solutions the same or different?

There are different ways to approach the issue as the answer can be nuanced: the matters and solutions we are concerned with here are both similar and also different.

A. Similarities

This section examines the problems that arise during the codification of procedural rules, and their potential solutions. In European Administrative Law, as in all national administrative laws, when talking about an inspection that can be conducted, we identify as a fundamental problem, the balance between administrative prerogatives and public interest – the former complying with the latter – and the protection of individual rights, including fundamental rights.

The nature of the problem of balance has not changed, regardless of the national general interest or, as it states in Article 52-1 of the Charter of Fundamental Rights of the European Union (CFREU): "objectives of general interest recognised by the Union".

In this case the distinction is irrelevant, as the fundamental rights involved in the matter are similar in substance, even if they don't have the same origin: the right to respect private life (right to privacy) and, more precisely, the inviolability of the home and the right to due process.

Baically, solving the problem of balance would mean understanding the solutions, as their identity is the same. The question of balance can be resolved in the same manner in both the EU administrative law and national administrative

[39] On this subject see S. Cassese, 'Le droit administratif européen présente-t-il des caractères originaux ?', in F. Moderne, *Mélanges en l'honneur* (Dalloz 2004) 1183 and following.

laws, as both are subject to the European Convention of Human Rights (ECHR) which has a definite unifying role as between States and the EU. This unifying role can be identified as both a direct dependency for the States, as parties to the Convention and as an indirect dependency for the European Union through the application of general principles of EU law and through Article 52-3 of the Charter of Fundamental Rights of the European Union.

As a result part of the codification established by the ReNEUAL Model Rules project, which ties up the balance between administrative prerogatives and fundamental rights (conditions that admit the remedy of the inspection, powers and inspectors' duties), deals with the same questions and provides similar solutions as confronted in national law.

The conditions that have to exist in order to exercise the so-called power of inspection in local companies, set out in Article III-16 (1), represent a good example. According to these conditions, the power of inspection has to rely on the grounds of a European legislative act; its implementation has to be mandatory in order to enable EU authorities to perform their duties.

These two conditions correspond to the requirements for a violation of the right to a home in both Article 8 of the ECHR and Article 7 – 52-1 of the CFREU. This is a consequence of the assimilation of the term local company to the concept of someone's home under the jurisprudence of the ECHR in order to enforce Article 8 of the ECHR (even if the protection is less important when compared to the concept of a home owned by an individual).[40]

This incorporation is followed in national jurisdictions upon application of Article 8 ECHR[41] and it is also endorsed by the ECJ.[42] In this context, *mutatis mutandis*, the national law which aims at codifying the fundamental rules for administrative inspections in local companies have to meet two conditions, that is to say, to be imperative and to be ruled by law (of course, the law could be interpreted considering the tradition of liberal democracies or in a more formal meaning as an act adopted by Parliament in conformity with the legislative procedure).

B. Differences

Despite the similarities, differences persist. The latter are linked to the peculiarity of EU administrative law when compared to administrative national law.

While EU administrative law works on two levels, or more accurately, enables the intervention of two groups of people (EU institutions and EU officers), national administrative law can only enable the intervention of national officers (there is no distinction between national and local).

40 ECHR, *Chapellv Great Britain*, 30 March 1989.

41 See Conseil d'Etat, section, 6 novembre 2009, *Société Inter confort*, n° 304300.

42 CJCE, 22 oct. 2002, *Roquette Frères SA*, aff. C-94/00, pt. 29.

This is particularly true for the case of the inspection. Even if the power of inspection is possessed by an EU body, the intervention of national institutions and officers is necessary because of the nature of the inspection itself. For example, the inspection conducted on the States' territory may include the use of physical coercion, which remains a State's privilege (and has to be authorised by a national judge).

Furthermore it has to be noted that EU administrative law is not part of the national law. Thus, the European Codification focuses on a problem ignored by national administrative law: the collaboration between EU bodies and EU and national law (and among the Member States) regarding inspections.

This coordination is the second main objective of the codification implemented by the ReNEUAL Model Rules (III-18 to 21).

Another stabilising factor governs this context (which is specific to the field of European Administrative Law): a uniform enforcement of EU Law through the application of the principles of effectiveness, equivalence and loyal cooperation on the one hand and subsidiary and autonomy on the other, which are notably institutional and procedural.

This second problem of cooperation between the EU and Member States and the balance which has been struck has the consequence that the balance between administrative powers and fundamental rights presents itself in a very specific manner in European administrative law, and in a far more complex way than in national administrative law.

Schematically, in national administrative law, fundamental human rights are compared to the prerogatives of an administration that puts the national general interest under the judge's control.

On the contrary, in European Administrative Law, whoever has to face an inspection has to face a multiplicity of operators, more or less linked (EU, National States and even other Member States). Furthermore, the control involves multiple jurisdictions (European Union jurisdiction, national judges, even jurisdictions of other State members) and it sets rules to protect fundamental rights which are not wholly the same as the unifying impact of the ECHR.

This unifying impact requires specific limits for two reasons. As long as the States and the European Union have a degree of discretion in the implementation (direct or indirect) of the ECHR, it means that the balance between public interest and fundamental rights can be realised in a different way, if the protections are sufficient, regardless of the Convention's requirements. In any case, the State and the European Union can always exceed the minimum level of protection as required by the Convention.

Two examples can help clarify the difference between EU administrative law and national administrative law despite the unifying application of the Convention. The first concerns the judicial review of conduct during inspections. According to the established case law of the ECtHR, interference with the right to residence, which an inspection necessarily involves, cannot be considered as "necessary in a democratic society" as required by Article 8 of the ECHR, if it is surrounded by adequate and effective safeguards against any abuse. These guarantees are mainly procedural and are specific to the intervention of a judge.

Nevertheless, the States' law can set such a requirement in several different ways. This is exactly what the report on the competent investigative authorities in competition law in the EU Member States published by the European Commission,[43] illustrates. According to the Report, in 14 EU Member States, an inspection conducted on business premises requires prior judicial authorisation; in some other States, such an authorisation is required only if the competition authority faces opposition from the company in question and therefore has used coercion; in other States, no prior court order is required.

The way in which EU administrative law implements the requirement for judicial authorisation (which is set by Articles 7 and 52 of the CFREU) is unique and it follows the specific characteristics previously identified.

We will take as an example the power of inspection held in European Competition Law already largely employed as a model for the ReNEUAL Model Rules. The decision of the Commission on an annual inspection is not, in principle, subject to prior judicial authorisation, but may be subject to an action for annulment before the EU courts. The compatibility of the lack of judicial review ex ante to the requirements of Article7 of the CFREU interpreted according to the case law of the ECtHR on Article 8 of the ECHR was raised but in *Deutsche Bahn* General Prosecutor Nils Wahl concluded it was compatible.[44] In case of opposition from the company, the use of public power can only be a result of an action taken by the concerned Member State, if the law requires it, upon judicial authorisation.

Therefore, the supervision practised by the national court is limited by the necessity to respect the competence among different EU jurisdictions entitled to check that the decision to proceed to the inspection is lawful. Specifically, according to the jurisprudence of the *Roquette*[45] case, and replicated in Article 20 of the Regulation n. 1/2003 and by Article III-19 (6) of the ReNEUAL Model Rules, the national judge "can't question the necessity for inspection or require the communication of information included in the Commission's dossier." This limitation of the diligence of the national judge, which in fact stresses the fundamental importance of non-interference with the right to respect the domicile –and its necessity – may seem questionable.

A further problem involves the use of information coming from an inspection considered to be evidence to justify the application of sanctions. Once again, we can take competition law as an example and more specifically we can consider the provisions of Regulation No 1/2003. In this context, the logic of cooperation within the network entails, in the name of effective protection of competition and of a uniform application of EU law, the dissemination of information among the members of the network, which is actually regulated

[43] Investigative Powers report, 31 October 2012.

[44] See the case c. 583/13 *Deutsche Bahn AG*.

[45] *Roquette Frères* (n 4).

by Article 12 of the Regulation. Unfortunately this is not acceptable, according to the fundamental rights that envisage equal guarantees to protect the way in which information is obtained through the inspections run by the different members of the network. In addition to that, this is clearly stated in the explanatory memorandum of the Regulation as well as in Article 12.

A recent French case can better illustrate the difficulties that may arise in this context.[46] In this case, the French competition authority had asked its British counterpart to conduct inspections of companies established in the UK, on the basis of Article 22 of Regulation No 1/2003.The information thus obtained was then used to impose sanctions on French companies.

The latter then questioned the validity of the British inspection before the French courts.

According to the provisions of Article 65 F of the Competition Act dated 1998, the inspection had taken place without prior judicial review. Therefore, the sanctioned companies argued that a prior authorisation by a judge was required under the provisions of CFREU and ECHR. Correctly, the French judge declared himself incompetent to rule on the matter, since the question focused on the compatibility of the UK law with CFREU and ECHR.

Despite that, he noted that the sanctioned companies were not entitled to seize a British judge; this seems to imply, on the other hand that in the name of the right to an effective remedy, the French jurisdictions could declare themselves competent to rule on specific matters.

---

46 Court of Cassation, Commercial Chamber, 20 January 2015, *Total Company overseas and otherwise*

CHAPTER 6

Inspection and Evidence in European Cooperative Decision-Making Process

Francisco Velasco

A. Introduction[1]

Chapter 3 of Book III of the 'EU ReNEUAL Model Rules on Administrative Procedure' (Model Rules) regulates direct gathering of information, in the course of an administrative decision-making procedure, taking place in the territory of a Member State or regarding a subject located in a particular Member State. The immediate collection of information is carried out either by a European authority or by a national authority not pertaining to the Member State in which the information is obtained. The subject of Chapter 3 (Articles III-10 to III-21 of Book III) is the immediate acquisition of information by an administrative authority in the territory of a Member State.

Such immediacy allows a distinction between the acquisition of information provided for in Chapter 3 from other information-gathering phenomena. This is the case of the collection of structured information or information available in shared data banks, which is a well-known phenomenon in the relevant sector-specific law,[2] and now constitutes the subject of Book VI. This is also the case for the information transmitted between authorities. It also common in sector-specific law.[3] In the Model Rules it is generically designated as 'mutual assistance,' and it is regulated in Book V thereof. The information transmitted may stem from a prior investigation or inspection conducted by a national authority

---

1 This study was developed with funding from the research project DER2012-34855 of the Spanish Ministry of Economy and Competitiveness. Translated from the Spanish original text by Guillermo and Javier Frutos Miranda.

2 For example, regarding the 'Customs Information System', Article 23 of Council Regulation (EC) No 515/97 of 13 March 1997 on mutual assistance between the administrative authorities of the Member States and cooperation between the latter and the Commission to ensure the correct application of the law on customs and agricultural matters (OJ L 82, 22.3.1997, p. 1). For further examples see A. David, 'Inspektionen als Instrument der Vollzugskontrolle', in E. Schmidt-Assmann and B. Schöndorf-Haubold, *Der Europäische Verwaltungsverbund* (Mohr Siebeck 2005) 237-265, 241. In English: A. David, 'Inspections as an instrument of control of implementation in the European composite administration', in O. Jansen and B. Schöndorf-Haubold (eds.), *The European Composite Administration* (Intersentia 2011) 357-381, and F. Velasco Caballero, 'Procedimiento administrativo español para la aplicación de Derecho comunitario' (2008) 28 *Revista Española de Derecho Europeo* 433-476, 462.

3 As to the agricultural market: Article 192 of Council Regulation (EC) No 1234/2007 of 22 October 2007 establishing a common organization of agricultural markets and on specific provisions for certain agricultural products (Single CMO Regulation) (OJ L 299, 16.11.2007, p. 97). For authorizations in the food markets: Articles 33 et seq. of Regulation (EC) No 1107/2009 of the European Parliament and of the Council of 21 October 2009 concerning the placing of plant protection products on the market and repealing Council Directives 79/117/EEC and 91/414/EEC (OJ L 309, 24.11.2009, p.1). See J. A. Chinchilla Peinado, 'The Administration of the food safety in the European Internal Market', in F. Velasco Caballero and F. Pastor Merchante (eds.) *The Public Administration of the European Internal Market* (Europa Law Publishing 2015) 11. In competition law see the diverse ways to exchange information within the 'European Competition Network' in J. Ortega Bernardo, 'The Administration for the enforcement of European Competition Law', in *ibid.*, 12.

in its own territory, which can be carried out either on its own initiative,[4] by authority of EU law,[5] or following the request submitted by an EU authority[6] or by another Member State authority.[7] These inspections conducted by a national authority in its own territory remain outside the scope of Chapter 3. Whereas sector-specific law has traditionally regulated the acquisition of information in a joint or complementary manner, one of the distinct features of the Model Rules project is that it provides for a structural dissociation of the various ways of gathering procedural information.

Nor does Chapter 3 directly address investigation or inspection authority groups or networks. In sector-specific rules and in practice, there are investigation groups or networks governed by 'guidelines' or homogeneous provisions which lay down certain criteria regarding intervention and transfer of information. These national authority groups or networks are sometimes coordinated by a European agency, such as the European Medicines Agency. National authorities take part in this agency's governance. These groups and networks act in accordance with investigation standards and patterns with a high degree of technical homogenization.[8] Versus these structured forms of investigation

---

4 For instance, the information gathered by the National competition authority is forwarded to the other Member States authorities and to the Commission in accordance to Article 12 of Council Regulation (EC) No 1/2003 of 16 December 2002 on the implementation of the rules on competition laid down in Articles 81 and 82 of the Treaty (OJ L 1, 4.1.2003, p. 1).

5 Regarding the agricultural market, see the mandatory inspections (to be carried out by the Member States and whose reports are to be conveyed to the Commission) which are regulated in Articles 103, 106, and 107 as well as in the Annex V of Commission Implementing Regulation (EU) No 543/2011 of 7 June 2011 laying down detailed rules for the application of Council Regulation (EC) No 1234/2007 in respect of the fruit and vegetables and processed fruit and vegetables sectors (OJ L 157, 15.6.2011, p.1). As to the food inspections, see also Article 3 of Regulation (EC) No 882/2004 of the European Parliament and of the Council of 29 April 2004 on official controls performed to ensure the verification of compliance with feed and food law, animal health and animal welfare rules (OJ L 165, 30.4.2004, p.1). Related to the fisheries policy, see Article 17 (2) of Council Regulation (EC) No 1005/2008 of 29 September 2008 establishing a Community system to prevent, deter and eliminate illegal, unreported and unregulated fishing, amending Regulations (EEC) No 2847/93, (EC) No 1936/2001 and (EC) No 601/2004 and repealing Regulations (EC) No 1093/94 and (EC) No 1447/1999 (OJ L 286, 29.10.2008, p.1).

6 That is the case of the requests of checks on-the-spot, according to Article 48 (1) of Regulation (EU) No 1306/2013 of the European Parliament and of the Council of 17 December 2013 on the financing, management and monitoring of the common agricultural policy and repealing Council Regulations (EEC) No 352/78, (EC) No 165/94, (EC) No 2799/98, (EC) No 814/2000, (EC) No 1290/2005 and (EC) No 485/2008 (OJ L 347, 20.12.2013, p. 549).

7 For example, Article 4 of Council Regulation (EC) No 515/97. Regarding the banking system see also Article 38 of Directive 2006/49/EC of the European Parliament and of the Council of 14 June 2006 on the capital adequacy of investment firms and credit institutions (recast) (OJ L 177, 30.6.2006, p. 201). This type of European coordination agency is considered in E. Chiti, 'European Agencies' Rulemaking: Powers, Procedures and Assessment' (2013) 19-1 *European Law Journal* 93-110, 96.

8 Related to the clinical trials and the 'Good Clinical Practices (GCP) Inspection Services Group,' see: C. Göbel, D. Baier, B. Ruhfus and F. Hundt, 'GCP Inspections in Germany and in Europe following the

or inspection, Chapter 3 focuses on single case decision-making procedures, initiated and managed by an administrative authority in which other authorities (either domestic or EU authorities) may 'participate.'

Immediate search for information may take three basic forms: the simple request for information, an interview of people who are aware of certain facts, or an on-the-spot check.[9] The collection of information, in any of its forms, normally affects the legal sphere of natural or legal persons who have the information inquired about.[10] This can be either because the investigations themselves may restrict certain rights, or because the information obtained therefrom may be used in the decision-making procedure. This natural impact on the legal status of the subjects being investigated explains why Article III-17(1) of Book III provides for an explicit subjection of the inspection activities to the European Union Charter of Fundamental Rights and to the EU and national provisions on the protection of personal data. It also provides an explanation as to why Articles III-16 through III-19 set forth relevant limits and requirements in order to protect the subjects being inspected. Apart from the immediate effect on the rights and freedoms of the persons concerned, the immediate acquisition of information shows another relevant legal aspect: the relationship between the investigation authority and the authorities of the Member State where the person or the premises holding the information searched for are located. This Chapter focuses on this inter-administrative aspect of the immediate acquisition of information.

Strictly speaking, there are two forms of inter-administrative interaction: the first occurs when the investigation refers to individuals, and the latter takes place when the inquiries target a Member State. Although Chapter 3 (as in Book III in general) draws no structural distinction whatsoever between decision-making procedures concerning individuals and those referred to Member States, such a distinction makes perfect sense,[11] and in fact it underlies several modulations expressly provided for in Articles III-11 to III-20. As has been stated, the gathering of information in the territory of a given Member State is governed on a twofold basis, namely the subjective perspective (protection of natural and legal persons' rights) and the inter-administrative perspective (prerogatives and limits of the investigation or inspection authority). However, this twofold regulatory dimension contained in Chapter 3 becomes blurred when the investigation or the inspection is projected onto a national authority. Firstly, this is due to the fact that certain safeguards and limits (Charter rights, for instance) only make sense when applied to individuals and not to public authorities. Secondly, it is because there are certain charges or limits stemming from the principle of

implentation of the Directive 2001/20/EC' (2009) 7 *GMS German Medical Science* 3.

9 The primary distinction between these two forms of investigation, in M. Rebollo Puig, 'La actividad inspectora', in J. J. Díez Sánchez (ed), *La función inspectora* (INAP 2013) 55-116, 60.

10 J.-B. Auby, 'Les pouvoirs d´inspection de l´Union européenne' (2006) 1 *Revue Trimestrielle de Droit Européen* 131 et seq., 132.

11 David (n 2) 247.

sincere cooperation, which do not apply to investigatory duties, such as the right of the national authority to participate in an EU authority's inspection in its territory. Such right is excluded when the subject being inspected is the national authority itself (Article III-18(1)). This is also the case of the duty incumbent on EU authorities to inform the concerned Member State authorities in good time of an inspection to be conducted in the Member State's territory. The relevant authority shall only be freed from this duty to inform when the inspected subject is the national authority itself (Article III-18(2)).

The highly complex interaction amongst authorities governed by Chapter 3 can be explained in the light of three fundamental statements:

a) In the first place, Article III-11(2) grants general investigatory powers to every administrative authority – both EU authorities and those Member State authorities which apply EU law – within the territory of the relevant Member States. This general principle of law does not prevent the most stringent forms of investigation, such as mandatory interviews and on-the-spot checks, from having to be expressly permitted by sector-specific provisions (Articles III-12(2) and III-16(1), respectively). Therefore, the general principle establishes that in order for EU law to be complied with, administrative authorities may carry out investigation or inspection activities either acting unilaterally, or participating in an information-gathering procedure conducted by another authority (below § 38). However, this legal principle, which can be induced from Chapter 3, shows two intensity levels. Its most intense wording targets the investigations of EU authorities. Its application is very strict in this regard, and except for what may be provided by sector-specific law, the EU is granted broad investigatory powers, based on Articles 337 and 352 TFEU.[12] In a second tier, Chapter 3 also provides for horizontal investigations, i.e. the chance for a national authority to investigate in another Member State's territory or to inquire about subjects based in its own territory. These transnational investigation possibilities are much narrower and depend on the prior agreement of the Member State concerned (host authority), or on the explicit provision of an EU legislative act.

b) Secondly, the general investigation or inspection duties, in the somewhat broad terms provided for in sector-specific law and the agreements between various authorities, lead to a general duty to tolerate the inspection conducted by an outside authority which is incumbent on the Member State concerned (host authority).

c) In the third place, once the investigatory powers to be exercised in the territory of a Member State have been established, along with the subsequent duty to tolerate or duty of submission to the investigations conducted by other authorities (either national or European) incumbent on the host authority, Chapter 3 sets forth many limits and instrumental duties aimed at channelling and balancing out 'trans-territorial' investigation and inspection duties. These limits are mostly duties or charges incumbent on the inspection authority, such as the duty to inform the Member State authorities before carrying out an inspec-

[12] *Ibid.*, 245.

tion, the duties to comply with the inspection instructions issued by the host Member State authority when the remaining authorities simply 'participate' in the domestic procedure, or the duties to inform the Member State authorities of the outcome of such inspections. Notwithstanding, there are also certain duties incumbent on national authorities so as to enable EU authorities to conduct the relevant inspection in their territory, such as the duty to provide judicial or police assistance to an outside inspection.

This interaction between the inspection authority and the authorities of the host Member State concerned can be broadly labelled as 'sincere cooperation' (Article III-18), which directly ties the various powers and cooperation duties to Article 4(3) TEU. Ultimately, every form of inter-administrative assistance can be traced back to the general duty of 'loyalty' set out in Article 4(3) TEU.[13] Such 'sincere cooperation' regarding investigations and inspections crystallises in a set of powers, controls, and duties placed on the various authorities concerned in the information gathering process. This set of powers, controls, and duties is enshrined in Articles III-10 through III-20. However, given the existence of a general principle of 'sincere cooperation' in Article 4(3) TEU,[14] in practice some other complementary cooperation duties could be pointed out,[15] which are not expressly provided by Book III or by sector-specific law.

The fact that the duties of 'sincere cooperation' are expressly foreseen in Articles III-10 through III-20 does not imply that the authorities enabling the investigation or helping therein have an ancillary role, since the very provisions contained in Articles III-10 through III-20 – which set out cooperation duties – also confer on the host national authority a monitoring role, either direct or indirect, over the outside authority's activities. Such monitoring role is exercised over the activity of both EU authorities and Member State authorities. Hence, whilst Article III-18(5) sets out the duty, incumbent on national authorities, to assist the inspection authority (regardless if it is an EU authority or a Member State authority) such form of assistance is set up as a sort of control over the inspection in question. By means of such 'assistance,' control over the outside inspection is exercised, regardless of whether the inspection is conducted by an EU or a Member State inspection authority.

B. Reference Framework: the Administrative European Union

Investigation and inspection activities in the EU account for an administrative reality inherent to the European Union itself. This regulation

[13] C. Harlow and R. Rawlings, *Process and Procedure in EU Administration* (Hart Publishing 2014) 41.

[14] Among others: Case C-14/83 *Von Colson and Kamann* [1984] ECR 1891, para. 12; Case C-230/81 *Luxembourg v Parliament* [1983] ECR 255, para. 38.

[15] M. Klamert, *The Principle of Loyalty in EC Law* (Oxford University Press 2014) 238.

began in the early years of the EEC. At first, legislation focused on the possible findings or inspections of the EU in the Member States, either checking on national administrations or investigating or inspecting private parties within a Member State. A good example of the former is provided by the Common Agricultural Policy (CAP),[16] whereas a good example of the latter is displayed by secondary legislation on competition.[17] From the very start, this legislation involved national authorities in the EU investigation activities in various ways and with varying degrees of intensity. These shared or joint activities could be designated as 'shared administration' or 'mixed administration.' The subsequent evolution of secondary law has furthered the complexity of the relevant connections and interactions among EU investigation and inspection bodies and national authorities. This is mainly because horizontal interaction has been added to the already existing vertical interaction, relating to which the notions of 'shared administration' or 'mixed administration' have been coined. Hence, and taking banking law as an example, a national authority can investigate facts and obtain information in another Member State's territory with greater or lesser control or participation on the part of the Commission.[18] Vertical and horizontal interactions, which may occur simultaneously, go beyond the historically narrower notion of 'shared' or 'mixed' administration. Thus, for a good part of the inspection activity carried out within the EU it would be more fit, from an epistemological perspective, to talk about a 'European Administrative Union.'[19] Along these lines, the codification of law on investigations and inspections in Chapter 3 of Book III would allow an 'Administrative Union of Investigation and Inspection' to be spoken of.

Reference made to an 'Administrative Union of Investigation and Inspection' is not only valuable from an epistemological or theoretical standpoint; there is a clear heuristic dimension to it. It offers a reference analytical framework which allows for solving the issues posed by investigations and inspections, such as the following: the procedural status of persons affected by procedures managed by 'outside' authorities (an EU authority or another national authority); or the very difficult distinction within a sole investigation procedure between national and EU activities, for the purpose of determining the rules applicable in each case, the national court competent for judicial review, where appropriate, and the possibility of holding liable for damages one national authority or another.

---

16 Regarding Regulation 729/70/EEC, see P. Craig, *EU Administrative Law* (6th ed., Oxford University Press 2012) 83 et seq. In current law, inspections ('on-the-spot checks') on the funds of the CAP are regulated in Article 47 of Regulation (EU) No 1306/2013.

17 Council Regulation (EEC) No 17/62 of 6 February 1962 implementing Articles 85 and 86 of the Treaty (OJ l 13, 21.2.1962, p. 204).

18 Article 29(1) of Directive 2000/12/EC of the European Parliament and of the Council of 20 March 2000 relating to the taking up and pursuit of the business of credit institutions (OJ L 126, 26.5.2000, p.1).

19 E. Schmidt-Assmann, 'Der Europäische Verwaltungsverbund und die Rolle des Europäischen Verwaltungsrechts', in Schmidt-Assmann and Schöndorf-Haubold (n 2) 1-24, 2.

The defining feature of the 'Administrative Union of Investigation and Inspection' is the close connection between the activities carried out by EU and national authorities participating or cooperating in the information-gathering process. Each authority's officials act in an integrated manner, not only connected or networked with other authorities (either domestic or European). For instance, there is a high degree of integration when, in statement-taking activities conducted by an EU authority there is some sort of participation by the Member State authority, by means of its own officials, where the investigated subject lives or is based. This integration accounts for more than mere assistance or cooperation. It may also be perceived when an EU authority requests from a national judicial authority a warrant for a coercive entry into the premises of the subject being inspected. From a formal perspective, such authorization issued by a judicial authority is a distinct legal act, which can be clearly differentiated from the inspection decision as well as from the request of entry issued by the EU authority. However, they are strongly integrated acts, which have the same meaning and the same purpose, and to that extent they should not be assessed in isolation.

According to this approach, the separation principle – which calls for an analytical distinction of each authority's actions, regardless if it is a national authority or an EU authority, as well as for the subsequent definition of the applicable rules and of the judicial authority competent for a potential judicial review -[20] has logical gaps. This is due to the fact that it breaks down in a plurality of acts (each of them with its own regulatory framework and its own grounds for judicial review) what is actually a heavily integrated action. There is no doubt that the so-called separation principle fosters legal certainty, since it prevents both regulatory and control overlaps. By means of the breakdown of the investigation or inspection activities, each act or measure is reassigned to an authority, and thus to a legal and control framework, yet at the expense of deforming the integrated administrative reality inherent to the 'Administrative Union of Investigation and Inspection.' This work acknowledges from the outset the need to have regard to the separation principle or differentiation. However, certain complementary pathways are suggested herein. These proposed pathways are meant to allow for a comprehensive legal understanding of the investigation and inspection activities. This is done by admitting the existence of a plurality of rules (both national and EU rules) applicable to the set of integrated actions within investigation or inspection procedures as a whole; as well as by admitting the possibility that Member States are able to immediately assess the legality of inspections and investigations conducted by an EU authority in a Member State.

[20] David (n 2) 260; J.-P. Schneider, 'Estructuras de la Unión Administrativa Europea. Observaciones introductorias', in F. Velasco Caballero and J.-P. Schneider, *La Unión Administrativa Europea* (Marcial Pons 2008) 25-49, 40. The 'separation principle' is clearly settled in European case-law, for example in Case C-97/91 *Oleificio Borelli* [1992] ECR I-631, para. 9 and in Case C-275/00 *First and Franex* [2002] ECR I-10943. Specially regarding EU inspections see Case C-94/00 *Roquette Frères* [2002] ECR I-9011, paras. 49, 51 and 52.

These two forms of flexibilisation of the separation principle, for the purpose of adapting the legal analysis to the actual integrated inspections and investigations, may lead to overlaps of rules and controls. This is an unavoidable outcome, yet it puts forward what the aim of the theoretical focus should be: it should move towards the drafting and perfection of 'nomodynamic criteria' (realizations of the principle of primacy of EU law) as well as towards a fine distinction, within the legal controls exercised over integrated administrative action, between the validity assessment of a particular legal act (which obviously can only be on a judicial authority) and the verification of the compliance of a given act with the relevant rules, which may be in various judicial bodies at the same time (in the ECJ and the national courts, for instance).

C. Duties to Inform in Good Time

As has been pointed out before, notwithstanding the provisions of sector-specific legislation, Book III of the Model Rules provides for broad investigation and inspection powers of the administrative authorities applying EU law. In turn, within each national territory, Member States tolerate and facilitate such investigations or inspections. The actual scope of these broad powers and duties is defined by means of certain instrumental charges or duties expressly provided by Book III. These instrumental duties make up the 'sincere cooperation' system inherent to the 'European Union of Investigation and Inspection.' The first set of duties under examination herein consist in informing Member State authorities in good time of an inspection which is to take place in the territory of the Member State in question. This duty to inform prior to the inspection applies both in relation to a request for information addressed to a party located in a Member State (Article III-11(4) and (5), as much as anticipating an EU inspection in the territory of a Member State (Article III-18(2)).

I. By request or mandatory order for information and interview

Articles III-11 and III-12 provide for the request or mandatory decision addressed to a party to be interviewed or to provide all necessary information as a basic way of collecting information. The wording of these articles has been clearly inspired by competition law.[21] Such a request has two legal effects. One for the party concerned, and another one between the EU and the relevant national authorities. As to the effects on the party, the request, as opposed to the mandatory decision, is not compulsory for its addressee. From the perspective of inter-administrative cooperation, Articles III-11 and III-12 impose cooperation charges or duties amongst the various authorities concerned. In this sense, Articles III-11 and III-12 draw a distinction between the

[21] Articles 18 and 19 of Council Regulation 1/2003.

request or mandatory order of an EU authority, and the request or order from a Member State authority to another national authority. The duty of inter-administrative cooperation becomes more intense when the request comes from the EU authority (Article III-11(4) and III-12(2)) than when it comes from a Member State authority (Article III-11(5) and III-12(2)).

In the first case, pursuant to Article III-11(4), it is on the EU authority to communicate its request or mandatory order, 'without delay,' to the competent authority of the Member State in whose territory the seat of the party requested is located, as well as to other national authorities 'whose territory is affected.' The explicit distinction between the State where the seat of the party is located and the State whose territory is affected makes perfect sense, particularly for undertakings with a legal seat in a Member State yet with economic activity and employees or managers in other Member State(s). This duty to inform brings with it a procedural duty of accuracy regarding which national authority is competent for the request. Article III-11 identifies two kinds of request, namely, the request to provide all necessary information and the request of interview.

a) As for the request or mandatory order of information, it can be considered that the duty to inform incumbent on the EU authority is somewhat flexible. It is enough for the EU authority to submit it following the request and 'without delay,' since no national authority's activity is dependent on the compliance with the duty to inform.

b) A very different case is that of the request or mandatory order for an interview. Regarding the mere request for an interview (i.e. not a compulsory request), because a possible domestic action depends on the effective communication of the request (by the Member State where the interview is to be carried out): it is a request that its officials assist the officials of the EU authority to conduct the interview. Such assistance is only possible if the national authority is aware of the request for an interview in good time. That is why an interpretation of Article III-11(4) in accordance with the principle of 'sincere cooperation' leads to conclude that the forwarding of the request to the national authority must be dispatched simultaneously with that dispatched to the party concerned; and the date set for the interview may not be immediate but sufficiently delayed to allow a response from the national authority.

c) As for the requests of information or interview from a Member State authority, Article III-11(5) also foresees the forwarding of a copy of the request to the national authority of the country in which the addressee is located. As with the situation described above, the forwarding of the copy could be flexible when related to a request or duty to inform, as no relevant legal consequence stems from such obligation. Conversely, the copy must be submitted far enough in advance of the foreseen interview date, as the Member State has the power to refuse it.

II. Duty to inform in good time of an inspection

Following the pattern of previous rules,[22] Article III-18(2) imposes on the inspection EU authority the duty to inform the respective Member State authorities of the planned inspection to be conducted therein. This duty has an instrumental nature with respect to the general mandate enshrined in Article III-17(4), according to which public authorities shall ensure that similar inspections are not being conducted at the same time in respect of the same facts.[23]

III. Duty to assist incumbent on a Member State during inspections conducted by EU authorities

1. Introduction

The powers of inspection of the EU authorities, as well as the relevant duty to facilitate the inspection in one's own territory, call for additional limits and duties when the inspection has a coercive nature, i.e. it is against the inspected subject's will. Book III does not authorize EU authorities to forcibly enter any private premises. As a result, such an entry can only take place following the single case authorization of the relevant Member State. In this connection, Article III-18(5) and (6) provides for a duty of assistance incumbent on national authorities regarding the coercive investigation conducted by an EU authority. Such assistance may be of a police or a judicial nature, pursuant to the legislation of the Member State where the inspection is carried out.[24] On the other hand, owing to its nature, the assistance by the national authority can only be provided by means of those actions which cannot be performed by the EU authority by itself. For instance, where the EU authority may impose penalty payments in order to overcome a given subject's reluctance towards being inspected, the said EU authority may not request assistance from a Member State.[25] Although Article III-18(5) refers to legal assistance to be provided to the EU inspection authority by national authorities, the action of national authorities is neither strict nor merely cooperative, at the service of the EU authority. Through its assistance, the given Member State controls or monitors the EU

---

22 In this sense, Article 47 (2) of Regulation (EU) No 1306/2013 on the CAP.

23 The prohibition of parallel inspections can be previously found i.a. in Article 3 of Council Regulation (EURATOM, EC) No 2185/96 of 11 November 1996 concerning on-the-spot checks and inspections carried out by the Commission in order to protect the European Communities' financial interests against fraud and other irregularities (OJ L 292, 15.11.1996, p. 2).

24 Case C-94/00 *Roquette Frères* [2002] ECR I-9011, par. 34.

25 This opinion with regard to Article 20 of Regulation 1/2003, in S. Hirsbrunner, 'Kommentierung zu Artikel 20', in H. Schröter, T. Jakob, R. Klotz and W. Mederer (eds.), *Europäisches Wettbewerbsrecht* (2nd ed., Nomos Verlag 2014) 1176-1183, 1182, § 15.

inspection authority's activities, in order to safeguard the right to privacy among other rights to which the subjects being inspected in its territory are entitled.[26]

The regulation provided by Article III-18(5) and (6) is closely related to various sector-specific rules which had been previously enacted[27] and particularly with current Article 20 of Regulation 1/2003. Competition law is the area of law which has had the greatest influence on the wording of Article III-18(5) and (6). Pursuant to Council Regulation 1/2003 and the all-important case-law stemming therefrom, the assistance of national authorities provided to outside inspections is founded on three rules:

a) In the first place, secondary legislation on competition authorises the Commission to conduct all necessary inspections of undertakings in Member States (Article 20(1) of Council Regulation 1/2003).

b) Secondly, there is a general principle of EU law according to which the inspections carried out by the Commission, when they are not allowed by the undertakings, should only be conducted following a judicial authorization issued by the concerned Member State, in order to avoid 'arbitrary and disproportionate interventions by public authorities in the private sphere.'[28]

c) Thirdly, the potential judicial review performed by the competent national courts over the Commission's inspections is fairly narrow. Its sole purpose is to verify that the Commission's decision is authentic and that the coercive measures envisaged are neither arbitrary (not lacking in legal foundation) nor disproportionate to the subject-matter of the inspection (proportionality control). These limits, initially stated by the ECJ,[29] are now expressly laid down in Article 20(8) of Council Regulation 1/2003. Accordingly, the EU inspection authority is not obliged to submit to the national judicial authority all of the information and evidence gathered by the time the inspection was ordered. It shall only make available to the competent national court enough information (even prepared on an 'ad hoc' basis) with which the relevant judicial authority can make sure on an adequate basis that the inspection measure is neither arbitrary nor disproportionate.[30]

The relevant case law on coercive inspections in the competition domain has had a decisive impact on the general regulation provided by Article III-18(5) and (6). As a result, in practice, even in the absence of a sector-specific law ruling on the application of the Model Rules to particular kinds of inspections, the substantive rules contained in Article III-18(5) and (6) shall be equally applicable, since they contain general principles of EU law.

---

[26] Case C-410/98 *Hoechst* [2001] ECR I-1727, para 35; Case C-94/00 Roquette Frères [2002] ECR I-9011, para. 35.

[27] See Article 9 of Council Regulation (EURATOM, EC) No 2185/96.

[28] Case C-410/98 Hoechst [2001] ECR I-1727, para. 33; Case C-94/00 Roquette Frères [2002] ECR I-9011, para. 35; Case T-289/11 REC *Deutsche Bahn AG and Others v Commission*, para. 92.

[29] Case C-94/00 *Roquette Frères* [2002] ECR I-9011, para. 40.

[30] Hirsbrunner (n 25) 1179 § 5.

2. The scope of the duty of assistance: a plurality of regulatory standards

National judicial assistance provided to EU inspection authorities has often been included within the so-called 'separation principle.'[31] Thus, regarding judicial assistance there are two clearly differentiated actions, each of them subject to totally or partially different regulatory standards and assigned to different authorities (national and European). Accordingly, the inspection decision lies within the EU authority, it is subject to EU law, and a possible review of legality lies with the Court of Justice (by no means shall this review lie in a national court).[32] On the other hand, the warrant of search and seizure, as for the enforcement of an EU inspection decision, would fall within the national scope: connected with each Member State law and exclusively attributed to the national judicial authority. Notwithstanding, despite its apparent simplicity and attainability, the reality of judicial assistance provided to the inspection decided on by an EU authority is much more complex. This is due to the fact that strictly speaking, 'judicial assistance' brings with it a set of intermingled acts, which can hardly be taken account of through the notion of 'separation.' First we are confronted with the EU inspection decision; secondly we encounter the EU request of a warrant of entry, search and seizure; and thirdly we are faced with the national judicial decision. In this sequence, various European and domestic rules intermingle with varying intensities and different meanings.

In the first place, the inspection decision is fully subject to EU law. Thus, it is subject to both sector-specific rules and general mandates enshrined in Articles III-16 through III-20. Pursuant to Article 263 TFEU, it is on the Court of Justice to ensure compliance with the abovementioned rules. However, since the inspection decision is the legal act on which the subsequent (or simultaneous) request for judicial assistance as well as the very settlement of the request for judicial assistance are grounded (pursuant to Article III-18(6)), the powers of national courts for analysing or indirectly assessing the lawfulness of the inspection decision should not be denied. Since it is on the national judicial authority to ensure that the authorization of the inspection is authentic and that the coercive measures envisaged are neither arbitrary nor excessive (in accordance with Article III-18(6)) such task cannot be carried out without having regard to the content of the inspection decision (made by the EU authority) and its compliance with EU law. European case law on the right to inviolability of the home, both from the ECHR[33] and the ECJ,[34] has pointed out that the legal assessment of an inspection measure (which could violate fundamental rights)

---

[31] David (n 2) 260.

[32] Case C-94/00 *Roquette Frères* [2002] ECR I-9011, para. 96.

[33] *Harju v Finland*, no. 56716/09, §§ 40 and 44. See I Simonsson, 'Digital evidence gathering during inspections', *20th St. Gallen International Competition Law Forum ICF*, available at: http://papers.ssrn.com/sol3/papers.cfm?abstract_id=2327122.

[34] Case T-289/11 REC *Deutsche Bahn AG and Others v Commission*, paras. 66 y 74.

depends to a great extent on how the judicial review over its enforcement is performed. An inspection measure which severely restricts the fundamental right to privacy may be admitted where its enforcement is strictly controlled ex ante by a judge. In turn, where there is no prior judicial control over the intervention measure, the judicial review of the inspection decision should necessarily be stricter. This approach, even though it has been elaborated for those cases in which the same Member State authorities make the decision ordering the inspection and authorise the implementation of the necessary measures for the enforcement thereof, can be generally applicable to the scope of the 'Administrative Union of Investigation and Inspection.' In addition, it may be asserted that the assessment of the legitimacy of an inspection decision is not foreign to the domestic court in charge of authorizing intervention measures (to enter premises, to take samples, copies, etc.) for the enforcement of the decision ordering the inspection. In fact, the very scope of the judicial review is dependent on the inspection decision to be enforced. The same conclusion can be drawn from the reference made to the EU case law when it states that in the context of judicial assistance provided to an EU inspection, the national court may refer a question for a preliminary ruling to the Court of Justice in relation to the EU provision on which the inspection decision is founded.[35] This possibility would make no sense if in the judicial assistance procedure the judicial authority was not able to assess the adequacy of the inspection decision under EU law. Obviously this does not mean that judicial assistance gives national courts the opportunity to rule on (and let alone annul) an EU inspection decision.[36] However, it is possible, in the terms of the *Foto-Frost* doctrine,[37] for judicial assessment of compliance of the inspection decision to be assessed, at least summarily, with the applicable law.

Secondly, the EU request for judicial assistance (addressed to a Member State) is subject to the requirements and limits provided by EU law. These requirements and limits might stem both from primary law (fundamental rights) and secondary legislation (sector-specific procedural rules and general standards provided for in Article III-18(5) and (6)). The request for a warrant conferring powers of entry, search and seizure, although lacking any binding force, necessarily has to comply with the applicable EU law provisions, both from a substantive and a formal perspective. In other words, the request cannot call for a judicial authorization without duly justifying its necessity, nor can a disproportionate or excessive judicial authorization be requested, having regard to the information available to the inspection authority. A different issue altogether is that such regulatory standards, which may be immediately projected onto the EU application for authorization, are subject to judicial review by the ECJ by way

[35] Case T-289/11 REC *Deutsche Bahn AG and Others v Commission*, para. 94.

[36] In general terms, not directly referred to inspection procedures: M. Ruffert, 'Von der Europäisierung des Verwaltungsrechts zum Europäischen Verwaltungsverbund' (2007) 18 *Die Öffentliche Verwaltung* 761 et seq., 769.

[37] Case C-314/85 *Foto Frost* [1987] ECR 4199).

of the action for annulment (Article 263 TFEU). Even though it is true that the ECJ has admitted to actions brought against inspection measures enforcing the initial decision, where those measures 'produce binding legal effects such as to affect the interests of an applicant by bringing about a distinct change in his legal position,'[38] such 'binding effect' does not directly apply to the mere request for a warrant conferring powers of entry, search and seizure.

Finally, coercive assistance (warrant of entry, search and seizure) is subject to regulatory standards, both EU and domestic standards. Hence, the judicial authority competent to authorise the entry, search and seizure in a premise is bound by EU law (fundamental rights, sector-specific rules regulating each kind of inspection, and the general provisions contained in Article III-18(5) and (6)), as well as by the ECHR fundamental rights and national rules, mainly by national fundamental rights and the applicable procedural legislation. The foregoing prompts the following remarks:

a) In the first place, the national judicial authority is immediately subject to Articles III-16 through III-20, which lay down the general guidelines applicable to the warrant of entry into a home. In fact, the application of these provisions does not stem from a prior reference contained in a legislative text (EU sector-specific law) in the terms of Article III.1(2). This is due to the fact that what is actually regulated by Articles III-16 through III-20 is not national administrative authority action (which according to Article III.1(2) is not directly governed by the provisions of Book III unless expressly agreed by the Member State concerned or explicitly provided by EU sector-specific law), but rather EU inspections to which assistance is provided by the police or judicial authorities of the relevant Member State. Notwithstanding, and although it may seem contradictory at first, the immediate applicability of Articles III-16 through III-20 does not imply that EU authorities are already authorized, in virtue of such provisions, to apply for judicial authorization when so required by the relevant domestic law. This is because Article III-16, despite the fact that it has direct effect, requires that every power related to coercive inspections (such as entry into private premises) should be expressly foreseen in the applicable EU sector-specific law. Consequently, an EU authority will be able to apply for, and the national court to authorize, the warrant of entry, search and seizure regulated (with direct effect) by Article III-18(5) and (6) only if the said express legal authorisation exists. In this connection, the domestic court must ensure that a warrant of entry, search and seizure not only complies with the requirements set forth by Article III-18(5) and (6), but that it is also grounded on a particular sector-specific rule which entitles the EU authority to conduct the said entry, search and seizure. This might imply that, depending on the specific sector of activity within which the inspection is conducted, the authorizing powers of the national court will be more or less intense. For instance, the authorizing powers of the national court will be much more intense regarding competition inspections (pursuant to Article 20 of Regulation 1/2003) than in agricultural subsi-

[38] Case C-85/87 *Dow Benelux* [1989] ECR 3137, para. 49.

dies, where only the Commission is granted (and thus the national court can only authorise) 'access to the books and all other documents, including documents and metadata drawn up or received and recorded on an electronic means, relating to expenditure financed by the EAGF or the EAFRD,' having regard to the following remark: 'persons delegated by the Commission shall not take part, inter alia, in home visits or the formal questioning of persons within the framework of the domestic legislation of the Member State concerned.' In any event, what is truly relevant for the domestic court are the EU legislative acts, not the numerous sector-specific inspection protocols ('guidelines' and alike) that the Commission (or any of its agencies or committees) has bound itself to apply.[39] The foregoing does not detract from the fact that by means of such 'protocols,' the national judicial authority can assess on a more accurate basis, the arbitrary or disproportionate nature of a given inspection intervention measure.

b) Since the national judicial authority is bound by EU sector-specific law, it may authorize intrusions into privacy different from those expressly established in Article III-16(2). Given the open-ended reference to sector-specific law made by this provision, more intense entry, search and seizure, or intervention measures than those provided for in Article III-16(2) are possible. This may be the case of the entry into private homes of managers and other members of staff, which accounts for a more intense measure than the mere entry into 'premises, land, and means of transport' (to which Article III-16(2)(a) refers) and which is currently set out in EU competition law provisions.[40] In that case, the national judicial authority should authorize the intervention measure within the limits posed by fundamental rights commented on below.

In accordance with the foregoing, a hypothetical national rule imposing more severe limits or requirements on the warrant of entry, search and seizure granted to an EU authority, more restrictive than those contained in Articles III-16 through III-18 or in sector-specific legislation, would not be in compliance with EU law. Consequently, those parts which are non-compliant would not have to be applied by national judicial authorities.

It seems like a possible piece of national legislation which did not provide for any sort of judicial review before the coercive entry of a given authority (either a domestic or an EU authority) would be in compliance with Article III-18. In fact, Article III-18, following the pattern of previous sector-specific law, does not necessarily provide for national judicial review prior to the entry into business premises.[41] It simply foresees the possibility that domestic legislation could require such a judicial authorization. Notwithstanding the fore-

39 References to these guidelines can be found in Case T-289/11 REC *Deutsche Bahn AG and Others v Commission*, para. 83.

40 Article 21 of Regulation 1/2003. See AI Santamaría Dacal, 'Poderes reforzados de la Comisión "versus" derechos de las empresas en los procedimientos de Derecho de la competencia: la búsqueda de un necesario equilibrio', in JE Soriano García (ed.), *Procedimiento administrativo europeo*, (Thomson-Reuters Civitas 2012) 849 et seq., 868.

41 *Deutsche Bahn AG*, para. 94.

going, the requirement for a previous warrant of coercive entry, search and seizure accounts for a general principle of EU law, in spite of the fact that it is not expressly provided for in Article III-18(5). Therefore it is binding on any EU inspection authority. As a result, no national legislative act will be able to free the competent court from carrying out the said judicial review prior to the entry, search and seizure conducted by an EU authority. However, the required judicial review does not have to be identical to that provided for in Article III-18(6).

IV. How fundamental rights are binding on coercive Member State assistance

The way fundamental rights have a binding effect on inspections when a coercive entry into private premises is carried out is particularly complex. There are two fundamental rights examined herein: the right to home privacy and the fundamental right to an effective legal remedy.

1. The right to home privacy

The right to privacy at home has two or three applicable wordings. The first is that provided by Article 7 CFREU. The second is contained in Article 8 ECHR. The third wording is, where appropriate, that which stems from domestic constitutional law e.g. Article 18(2) of the Spanish Constitution, Article 13 of the German *Grundgesetz* or Article 14 of the Italian Constitution. It seems like the scope and intensity of the protection granted to the right to the inviolability of the home in its various European and national wordings should be similar, since the right to the inviolability of the home is part of the European constitutional tradition. However, this is not exactly the case. The ECJ has put forward a restricted understanding of the right to home privacy (taken as a general principle of EU law) when addressed to legal persons and not individuals.[42] In turn, the right to the inviolability of the home has been more far-reaching in the case law of the ECHR.[43] In this regard, although Article 52(3) CFREU and the 'explanations' to which Article 52(7) CFREU[44] refers to clarify that Charter rights shall have the same 'meaning and scope' as ECHR rights, when the same right is recognised in both legal instruments, the truth is that the ECJ case law on the 'general principle' of inviolability of the home (which outlines the content of current Article 7 CFREU), differs in certain points from the case law delivered by the ECHR on Article 8 ECHR. In addition, it is definitely unclear that the ECJ has to adapt its jurisprudence to that of the ECHR on the basis of Article 52(3) CFREU. Finally, national constitutional case law does not show identical features either. The possible diversity within the content of the various fundamental rights to privacy, vis-à-vis invasions of home privacy, can make it hard on

[42] Case C-94/00 *Roquette Frères* [2002] ECR I-9011, para. 29.

[43] *Societé Colas Est and Others v. France*, no 37971/97.

[44] 'Explanations relating to the Charter of Fundamental Rights' (OJ C 303, 14.12.2007, p. 17).

the courts (pursuant to Article III-18(6)) regarding the authorization of coercive inspections in business premises. We will now examine analytically how each fundamental right standard operates vis-à-vis the national authority applying for a warrant of entry, search and seizure and vis-à-vis the national judicial authority competent – in terms of Article III-18 – for authorizing such coercive entry into the relevant business premises:

In the first place, neither the application of the EU authority nor the subsequent Member State warrant of entry, search and seizure, as provided by Article III-18(5) and (6), are hampered by Article 7 CFREU. It must be clarified that to the extent that the domestic court applies EU law (Article III-18), it is bound by the fundamental right to the inviolability of the home (Article 7 CFREU) when it comes to issuing an authorization for a coercive entry. This fundamental right, as it is worded in the Charter, does not hinder the issuance of an authorization for a coercive entry by the national court as provided by Article III-18(6). In principle, it must be understood that Article 7 CFREU contains the ECJ case law delivered up until 2007, worded as a 'general principle' regarding the inviolability of the home. This case law, as was mentioned above, provides for a narrow legal understanding, because it does not require the EU inspection authority to provide the national judicial authority with the whole file (including the already existing evidence held by the EU authority) on which the need for conducting an inspection in situ is grounded.[45] As a result, from Article 7 CFREU's perspective, the warrant of entry, search and seizure shall be issued pursuant to Article III-18(6), i.e. without having been provided with the file assembled by the EU authority.

In addition, it must be considered whether the EU authority interested in entering into private premises, on the one hand, and the national judicial authority competent to authorise such entry, search and seizure, on the other hand, are governed by the highest privacy protection standard in terms of Article 8 ECHR. This greater degree of protection is remarkable with regards to the 'information providing reasonable grounds' which has to be made available to the judicial authority by the inspection authority. At this moment, a distinction has to be drawn between the applicability of the right to home privacy to the EU authority requesting the entry, search and seizure, and to the national judicial authority competent to authorise it.

Regarding the EU authority, it is true that Article 52(3) CFREU establishes that the 'meaning and scope' of the fundamental right enshrined in Article 7 CFREU 'shall be the same' as that of the right to respect home privacy laid down in Article 8 ECHR. Notwithstanding the foregoing, this does not entail – as it does for EU inspection authorities – that Article 8 ECHR overrides Article 7 CFREU. This would result from Article 53 CFREU if the EU became a party to the ECHR. However, since the EU accession to the ECHR is still pending (and has now become probably impracticable after Opinion 2/2013 lodged by the Court of Justice), fundamental rights guaranteed by the ECHR only constitute

[45] Case C-94/00 *Roquette Frères* [2002] ECR I-9011, paras 61 and 62.

part of the 'general principles of the Union's law' (Article 6(3) TEU),[46] and are not immediately applicable individual rights. Although the ECJ has declared expressly and in the abstract that the scope of Article 7 CFREU coincides with the scope of Article 8 ECHR,[47] it is ultimately on the ECJ to outline the interpretation of Article 7 CFREU on the basis of the 'general principle' of respect for privacy induced from Article 8 ECHR. When performing this interpretation, the ECJ may very well differ from the broader understanding offered by the ECtHR.[48] In this connection, the requirement for submission of the assembled file to the national judicial authority – so that such judicial authority can fully assess the opportunity of a coercive inspection – shall not be immediately demanded from the EU inspection authority when the latter calls on national judicial assistance. A different issue altogether is that the high standard of inviolability of the home embedded in the ECHR case law would have to be embraced by the Court of Justice within its interpretation of Article 7 CFREU. This outcome is hypothetically possible, especially if we take into account that a good part of the ECJ case law on the CFREU has chosen to award fundamental rights an intense and comprehensive recognition.[49] However, this option, although it is possible, does not seem probable. This is due to the fact the current ECJ case law on inspections has led to a well-crafted balance between home privacy (which to this day has been understood as a general principle of law) and the effectiveness of EU law by means of inspection activities. This twofold stance of the ECJ, halfway between respect for fundamental rights and the indispensable effectiveness of EU law as a whole, differs from the ECHR approach. This may very well account for the existing case law divergences. In any event, having regard to the long-standing habit of the ECJ to assert the effectiveness of EU law, by means of the 'useful effect' interpretative standard, an interpretation of Article 7 CFREU which ends up balancing out the scope of Article 7 CFREU and Article 8 ECHR is far from foreseeable.

The situation faced by the national judicial authority which has to rule on the application for entry, search and seizure is completely different. It must be taken into account that national judicial assistance does not only account for instrumental activity for the EU inspection but also for Member State action. This implies that, in principle, the warrant of entry, search and seizure should be governed by the inviolability of the home standards applicable in each Member State. The first of these is in fact Article 8 ECHR, which through individual

[46] Among others, Case C-617/10 *Akerberg Fransson* (n.y.p), para. 44.

[47] Case C-400/10 *PPU-McB* [2010] I-8965, para 53; C-92/09 and C-93/09 *Volker and Schecke*, [2010] ECR I-11063, paras. 51 and 52.

[48] A different opinion, sound founded on case-law: S. Peers, 'Article 52. Scope of Guaranteed Rights', in S. Peers, T. Hervey, J. Kenner and A. Ward (eds.), *The EU Charter of Fundamental Rights* (C. H. Beck/ Hart/Nomos 2014) 1454-1521, 1498. See nevertheless, sustaining an autonomous interpretation of the fundamentals rights of the Charter, the opinions of the General Advocate Cruz Villalón in Case C-69/10 *Diouf* [2011] ECR I-07151, para 39, and in Case C-70/10 *Scarlet Extended*, para 33.

[49] Case C-390/12 *Pflager* (n.y.p), para. 30.

accession of each State applies immediately, as a fundamental right and not as a mere 'general principle of law,' in every EU Member State. In principle, since Article 52(3) CFREU directly chooses to apply the highest fundamental right standard, it must be considered that the national court must require the degree of information and accuracy resulting from the ECHR case law on Article 8 ECHR from the EU inspection authority. However, this demand, whilst it does not conflict with Article 7 CFREU (since Article 52(3) CFREU quells the regulatory quarrel), does conflict with Article III-18(6) which expressly prevents the national court from requesting from the EU authority the assembled file that allows for the on-the-spot check. That being the case, insofar as Article 18-III is fully lawful (since it is in compliance with its primary regulatory standard, i.e. Article 7 CFREU) it has to be fully effective over the national rule. The foregoing is due to the application of the principle of primacy of EU law, even over domestic constitutional law,[50] in the terms of the *Melloni* doctrine.[51] Consequently, although Article 8 ECHR, in its condition of effective rule within each Member State law calls for the national court to have the utmost information, which would provide grounds for the need for entry, search and seizure, the national judicial authority should not be able to require such information from the EU inspection authority, but only the most obtainable information to which Article III-18 refers. This conclusion brings up the issue, either in fact or at least in appearance, that it entails that the national court has to breach a legally binding international treaty (the ECHR). A possible solution to this conflict could stem from the very understanding of the fundamental right to home privacy (Article 8 ECHR) as a right restrictable 'by law.' In other words: Article 8 ECHR expressly acknowledges the possibility of having the law setting restrictions which are proportionate to the content of the relevant right.[52] Since in relation to EU coercive inspections the said 'law' is an EU legislative act, it should be considered that the definitive or final content[53] of the right to home privacy enshrined in Article 8 ECHR, which is binding on the national judicial authority, is in fact that stemming from Article III-18, and with such restricted scope, it has a binding effect on the national court which has to authorize the coercive inspection measure.

Something similar should be stated regarding the application for national judicial assistance, about a hypothetical national privacy standard resulting from national constitutions. In this case, and the *Melloni* doctrine should be brought

[50] B. De Witte, 'Article 53. Level of protection', in Peers, Hervey, Kenner and Ward (n 48) 1523-1538, 1533 § 53.26. See, notwithstanding A. Torres Pérez, 'Constitutional Dialogue on the European Arrest Warrant: The Spanish Constitutional Court knocking at Luxembourg's door' (2012) *European Constitutional Law Review* 8 (2012) 105-127, 118.

[51] Case C-399/11 *Melloni* (n.y.p), paras. 58, 59, 63.

[52] *Niemietz v Germany*, no. 13710/88, 16 December 1992, para.31; *Bernh*, no. 24117/08, 14 March 2013, para. 104.

[53] The concept of 'definitive scope' of a fundamental right after being delimited by the law: R. Alexy, *Teoría de los derechos fundamentales* (Centro de Estudios Constitucionales 1993) 272.

up again, it must be taken into consideration that the national judicial authority authorizing the coercive entry by the inspection authority should not add any further requirements to those provided for in Article III-18. If that were the case, such requirements would account for a denial of the primacy of EU law (Article III-18) over Member State law, having regard to the fact that the abovementioned Article III-18 is in compliance with Article 7 CFREU. In order to avoid an override of a domestic fundamental right, it could be understood that there is a scope for decision-making for the national judicial authority which would not be regulated in Article III-18, and thus not subject to the standards established in Article 7 CFREU, but rather to the protection standard of the national fundamental right.[54] This could be realised in relation to the time extension of the coercive inspection measure, or in relation to the geographical determination of the premises to be inspected, but only to the extent that Article III-18 lacks specific rules, and such rules cannot be found in sector-specific secondary law. In such cases, more stringent national privacy standards (both statutory and those stemming from fundamental rights) than those resulting from Article 7 CFREU, could be deemed acceptable. However, this plausible argument is distorted because it departs from the premise of a false absence of regulation (in Article III-18 or in sector-specific legislation). It can be considered that when Article III-18(6) fails to establish any specific time or geographical limits on the warrant of entry, search and seizure, it is in fact granting the administrative authority some room so it can perform its own weighing on the basis of the needs of the particular case and pursuant to the principle of effectiveness of inspections. Accordingly, the lack of further remarks in Article III-18 would account for a 'false gap,'[55] so there would be no material scope for the application of domestic law.

2. Right to an effective remedy

Concerning the warrant of entry, search and seizure, in the context of an EU on-the-spot inspection, the question of an existing overlap of various rights to effective remedy standards might arise: under Article 6 ECHR, under the applicable national fundamental right, and under Article 47 CFREU. Furthermore, the right to an effective remedy enshrined in Article 47 CFREU applies insofar as Article III-18(6) directly provides that the warrant of coercive entry, search and seizure has to be authorized by a (national) court. Therefore, an EU law provision is the relevant rule which triggers the applicability of the rights of defence and the right to be heard to which the subject being inspected is entitled in the judicial proceedings for the warrant of entry, search and seizure. Given the possible simultaneous effectiveness of the three fundamental rights to an effective remedy, it is necessary to draw up certain criteria aimed at

---

54 This possible interpretation of Article 53 of the Charter in De Witte (n 50) 1534.

55 K. Larenz, *Methodenlehre der Rechtswissenschaft* (6th ed., Springer 1991) 370.

making the three standards compatible. To that end, the abovementioned criteria may be extended in relation to the right to home privacy.

In the first place, it may be considered that Article III-18(6) limits the possible judicial review over the coercive inspection when the former is requested, yet not at the time it is performed. In other words, Article III-18(6) does not expressly provide for the possibility that each specific coercive measure in the course of an inspection already authorized by the competent national court can be challenged before the national court itself. This regulation may raise compatibility concerns regarding the fundamental rights enshrined in Article 47 CFREU and in Article 6 ECHR[56].

a) It is true that the ECHR case law has declared that the judicial review of inspection measures has to be 'certain' as well as not conditioned by the content of the final inspection decision.[57] Notwithstanding, it also has to be taken into account that the fundamental right to an effective remedy is an individual right subject to a statutory formulation, substantially open to legal provisions. To that extent, it could be considered that once an effective legal remedy against the EU inspection decision (before the ECJ), against its coercive enforcement (by means of a national warrant of search and entry), and against the final decision of the procedure during which the coercive inspection has been conducted (before the ECJ), has been guaranteed, an EU rule (such as Article III.18(6)) may exclude the individualized control over each inspection measure (to take samples or to obtain copies of documents) generally covered by the warrant of entry, search and seizure. On the other hand, it also has to be taken into account that EU case law understands the right to an effective legal remedy as a right to a particular outcome: a right to assert one's rights before a court, by means of ex ante or ex post procedural instruments.[58] It seems clear that such a protection can be attained through the ex ante and ex post controls allowed by Article III-18.

b) Concerning domestic law, which could allow for an individualised control over each single coercive measure in the form of statutory or fundamental rights (as happens in France, for instance),[59] the abovementioned *Melloni* doctrine should be applied again, and thus it shall be considered that the competent national judicial authority must not be able to carry out an analytical control of each single inspection measure covered by a warrant of entry, search and seizure, since such judicial review would be far beyond the judicial review provided for in Article III.18(6).

---

56 D. Théofile and I. Simic, 'Legal challenges to dawn raid inspections under the principles of EU, French and ECHR law' (2012) 3 (6) *Journal of European Competition Law & Practice* 511-520, 518.

57 *Primagaz v France*, no. 29613/08, 21 December 2010, para 28.

58 *I ıldak v. Turkey*, no. 12863/02, 30 September 2008, para. 51. Regarding the judicial guarantee of privacy: *Bernh*, no. 24117/08, 14 March 2013, para. 172.

59 Article L-450-4 of French Commercial Code (Code de Commerce). According to this Article, the court can overlook at any time the enforcement of the warrant of entry, search and seizure: 'A tout moment, il peut décider la suspension ou l'arrêt de la visite.'

The restrictive approach on the grounds and information to be attached to the application for a warrant of entry, search and seizure by the EU inspection authority can be assessed on the basis of the right to an effective judicial review. In accordance with Article III-18(6), the administrative application for a warrant of entry, search and seizure must not be accompanied by the assembled file or the evidence held by the EU authority, but only a detailed explanation of the grounds for the need to enter into a private home. Such limitation in the information required does not allow for the national court to have full knowledge of the inspection activities, but only the assessment of to what extent the requested warrant of entry, search and seizure is duly justified. However, such limitation does not infringe the various fundamental right standards stemming from the right to an effective remedy. The truth is that both the ECHR and the ECJ have declared that the right to an effective remedy requires the judicial authority to have 'full jurisdiction' over the subject-matter.[60] Notwithstanding, this assertion entails – in the context of the cited case law – that an appeal before a first instance or single-instance court, should not be limited to questions of law leaving aside the questions of fact. Nevertheless, this is very different from having the law define restrictively the judicial review standards. It must be recalled, and this applies both to Article 47 CFREU and Article 6 ECHR, that the right to an effective remedy has an instrumental nature with respect to a pre-existing individual right.[61] In this case, the right to an effective legal remedy of the subject being inspected (in the context of the warrant of entry, search and seizure procedure initiated by an EU authority) is actually defined by Article III-18(6): it consists in the power to object to judicial searches and seizures which are not based on a previous EU decision, which are arbitrary or excessive. As for this right's protection, the expedited judicial review accounts for an 'effective remedy,' managed in accordance with national procedural legislation, as provided by Article III-18(6). Aside from this, and in reference to current Article 47(1) CFREU, it must be recalled that the ECJ case law on the general principle of an effective legal remedy (currently contained in Article 47 CFREU), explicitly rejects that the assembled inspection file ought to be made available to the judicial authority. Finally, in those cases in which national law (either constitutional or statutory)[62] calls for the court responsible for procedural safeguards to have full access to the inspection-related information, such demand would have been overridden by the express restriction provided for in Article III-18(6).

60 *Incal v. Turkey*, no 41/1997, 9 June 1998, para 72. Case C-506/04, *Wilson* [2006] ECR I-08613, para. 61.

61 Case 222/84 *Johnston* [1986] ECR 1651, para. 17. Case 222/86 *Heylens and Others* [1987] ECR 4097, para.14; Case C-424/99 *Commission v Austria* [2001] ECR I-9285, para. 45; and Case C-459/99 *MRAX* [2002] ECR I-6591, para. 101. For further details see H. C. H. Hofmann, 'Article 47. Right to an effective remedy', in Peers, Hervey, Kenner and Ward (n 48) 1211-1228, 1213.

62 For instance, Article L 450-5 (2) of the French 'Code de Commerce,' according to which: 'Le juge doit vérifier que la demande d'autorisation qui lui est soumise est fondée ; cette demande doit comporter tous les éléments d'information en possession du demandeur de nature à justifier la visite.'

V. Liability arising from assistance activity

A common issue for the European Administrative Union and thus for the 'Administrative Union of Investigation and Inspection,' is the attribution of liability for damages. In other domains of the 'Administrative Union,' the strong functional integration amongst different authorities (domestic and EU authorities) within the same administrative procedure, makes it difficult to identify to which authority the harmful consequences arising from such joint action should be attributed. Within the particular domain of assistance provided to outside inspections (EU inspections or eventually inspections conducted by other national authorities), the starting point could be the separation principle. Accordingly, any harmful consequences arising from the order for an inspection and the subsequent conduction thereof should be attributed to the EU authority (or another Member State authority). In turn, regarding the host domestic authority, only those damages arising from the due assistance (particularly the judicial authorisation or police coercion) provided to an inspection which has not been sufficiently justified should be attributed thereto.[63] However, given the abovementioned twofold legal significance of the judicial or administrative assistance, a joint and several liability for damages between the inspection administration and the authority providing the relevant assistance to the inspection administration is more suitable.[64]

VI. Duties in the shared or joint inspections

Chapter 3 of Book III provides for various forms of participation of several authorities in the same inspection. It departs from the premise that a sole inspection conducted in a given Member State could be of interest to a number of authorities (both to the national authority itself and the EU, as well as to other Member State authorities). The technique for procedural 'participation' of various administrative authorities is already widespread in EU law.[65] Concerning the inspection, there are three forms of participation provided for in Book III: participation of national authorities in EU inspections (Article III-18(1)); participation of EU authorities in Member State inspections (Article III-19); and joint inspections of Member State authorities (Article III-20). Strictly speaking, in every case the subject-matter of regulation is the 'participation' of

63 The restriction of the liability of the 'requested authority' for damages directly caused by its assistance activity follows previous sector specific rules, as for example Article 4 (2) of Council Regulation (EC) No 515/97 of 13 March 1997.

64 As a general possibility, though no immediately proposed for inspections, J. Hofmann, 'Rechtschutz und Haftung im Europäischen Verwaltungsverbund', in Schmidt-Assmann and Schöndorf-Haubold (n 2) 353-382, 377.

65 Schneider (n 20) 38; O. Mir Puigpelat, 'La codificación del procedimiento administrativo en la Unión Administrativa Europea', in F. Velasco Caballero and J.-P. Schneider, *La Unión Administrativa Europea* (Marcial Pons 2008) 51-85, 62; Velasco (n 2) 457.

certain authorities in procedures managed by other authorities. Actually, 'joint inspections' in the strict sense of the term do not account for the subject-matter of regulation. In fact, the 'joint inspections' to which Article III-20 refers, are actually inspections to be conducted by a domestic authority with participation of other outside national authorities.

The general principle which can be deducted from Articles III-18 through to III-20 is the general capacity of every authority within the 'European Administrative Union' to participate in a particular inspection based on EU law. Alongside this general capacity comes the implicit duty to tolerate the participation or involvement of the other authorities. This duty is incumbent on the authority conducting the inspection. The general capacity to participate, and the corresponding general duty to tolerate the inspection-related involvement of another authority, are channelled by means of two instrumental duties. First, the duty to inform the remaining authorities (both domestic and European) of the intention of initiating an inspection procedure; and secondly, the duty incumbent upon the invited authority to submit to the leadership of the main inspection authority. These duties are present, with various wordings, within the three forms of inspection-related participation expressly regulated by Book III.

1. Participation of national authorities in EU inspections

For the case where the inspection is conducted by an EU authority, Article III-18(1) grants the host domestic authority the right to participate in the inspection. In addition, it implicitly lays down the corresponding duty, incumbent on the EU authority, to tolerate the presence of officials from the 'hosting State.' In order to enable the inspection-related involvement of the relevant Member State, Article III-18(2) imposes on the EU authority the instrumental duty to inform in advance and 'in good time' of the inspection activities. Having regard to the fact that the EU authority must tolerate the participation in the inspection of the relevant national authority, the core issue at stake is now to determine the legal significance of such 'participation.'

The participation of the national authority has been previously regulated as a form of 'assistance' provided to the EU authority.[66] As such 'assistance,' the involvement of the national authority takes place in a position of dependence or submission with respect to the EU authority. One could speak about a duty of submission of the national authority to the inspection guidelines issued by the EU authority. This submission duty does not imply that the domestic authority accounts for a mere instrument in the hands of the European authority. In fact, the assistance role played by the national authority gives rise to specific utilities for the Member State:[67] the latter benefits from the information gathered by the EU authority in the inspection conducted thereby. In addition, this allows the relevant Member State to monitor the European inspection activities carried

66 Article 4 of Council Regulation (Euratom, EC) No 2185/96.

67 David (n 2) 244.

out on its soil. Hence, what is actually important in order to talk about a duty of submission does not lie in the existence of domestic or foreign utilities attached to the inspection, but rather in who plays the functional leadership role in the inspection. There is no doubt that this task lies in the inspection EU authority, not in the participating Member State authority.

On the basis of the abovementioned duty of submission, and to the extent that every step of the procedure and inspection measure is agreed and led by the European authority, some consequences can be drawn from the legal framework of the inspection-related 'participation.'

a) In the first place, in its dependent position the national authority can get involved in European inspection activities which, although having been authorized by EU sector-specific legislation, are not provided for in domestic legislation (for instance, the seal of premises).[68]

b) Secondly, the position of submission of the national authority leads to the assertion that judicial review performed over the inspection activities (except for anything concerning coercive entry, search and seizure into private premises) can only be carried out by the ECJ, and that a hypothetical liability of the public authorities' claim for damages has to be filed before the EU.[69] This includes domestic authority action when the latter has acted under the inspection leadership of the EU authority. It obviously does not include the potential national inspection measures which could have been developed de facto independently and in line with European activity.

A particular case of national participation, established in Article III-18(4), consists of the presence of officials from other national authorities, different from that of the hosting State, in the EU inspection. This is quite an exceptional case, and that is why it is strictly subject to the express agreement of the concerned Member State in whose territory the inspection is conducted. Strictly speaking, this does not account for participation of a national authority in an inspection carried out by the EU in another Member State, since the officials of the third Member State only play the role of 'observers' and where appropriate, they provide the EU authority with technical assistance. Accordingly, rather than with an example of participation, herein we are confronted with an organic borrowing,[70] pursuant to which the official from the third Member State acts as

---

68 On the diversity of inspection measures in the Member States see: M. De Benedetto, 'Procedural powers in competition enforcement: a look at inspections', *9th ASCOLA Conference Warsaw 2014 con Procedural Fairness in Competition Proceedings* (http://www.ascola-conference-2014.wz.uw.edu.pl/conference_papers/Maria_De_Benedetto.pdf), 5, and the Report of the European Competition Network (ECN) Working Group Cooperation Issues and Due Process, *Investigative Powers Report*, 31 October 2012. (http://ec.europa.eu/competition/ecn/investigative_powers_report_en.pdf).

69 David (n 2) 259.

70 The theoretical features of the 'borrowed bodies' can be followed in German Law (*Organleihe*): H. Maurer, *Allgemeines Verwaltungsrecht* (14th ed., C. H. Beck 2002) 542; and specifically in the framework of the 'European Administrative Union' see L. Hastings, 'Grenzüberschreitende Zusammenarbeit der Polizei- und Zollverwaltungen', in Schmidt-Assmann and Schöndorf-Haubold (n 2) 127-152, 144.

the official of the EU authority. This explains the blunt terms used by Article III-18(4) when it establishes that 'EU authorities remain responsible for any misconduct or damage caused by these officials and bodies in the course of an inspection.'

2. Participation of EU authorities in Member State inspections

A second possibility is that a national authority has initiated an inspection procedure (obviously in its territory), and an EU authority participates therein. Article III-19 provides for the participation of the EU authority as a potential capacity (since it needs prior agreement with the Member State in question or a special provision in sector-specific EU law). In principle, the participation of the EU authority could be labelled as a form of 'assistance' provided to the national authority. However, such participation does not only account for 'assistance.' It allows the EU to monitor the way in which the national authority carries out its inspection. It also allows for information gathering in order to make a decision of its own. From this perspective, and in line with the central idea of this work, the participation provided by Article III-19 is a form of gathering information (by an EU authority) taking advantage of an already underway national inspection procedure.

Since this participation of the EU authority is the way of gathering information on-the-spot, such participation is subject to certain precautions and limits from the Member State, which translates into duties incumbent on the EU authority.

a) Firstly, Article III-19 expressly declares that the EU authority participation shall take place 'under the responsibility of officials of a Member State.' This implies that it is on the national authority, at any event, to lead the inspection activities.

b) Secondly, the inspection powers of the EU authority are somewhat narrow. According to Article III-19, EU officials 'may not, on their own initiative, use the powers of inspection conferred on national officials or be present at inspections based on national criminal law.' In sum, the capacity of gathering information of an EU authority in the territory of a Member State is carried out in a position of dependence with respect to the national authority,[71] taking advantage of an inspection already ordered and conducted by the national authority.

Given the position of submission of the EU authority to the national inspection authority, the effective remedy safeguards of the subjects being inspected shall be exercised before national courts. The potential liability claims shall be filed against the national authority, except in the extraordinary event (and actually foreign to Article III-19) that on a de facto basis, the EU authority had acted without regard to the national authority.

[71] Referring to the sector-specific law foregoing to the ReNEUAL MR scholars spoke of 'begleitende Kontrolle' (complementary control): David (n 2) 242.

The EU authority participation established by Article III-19 differs from another form of participation, which exists in sector-specific legislation, according to which the inspection of the national authority is carried out 'at the request of the Commission,'[72] and the soliciting Commission can participate therein. Herein we are confronted rather with a case of 'mutual assistance' (regulated in Book V). In this case, the national authority is not managing a procedure which the EU authority joins: the domestic authority is assisting the EU authority (by performing certain inspections required by the EU authority) and when such inspections are being conducted, an agent or person delegated by the Commission can be present or take part therein.

3. Horizontal participation

Finally, the third participation possibility -which accounts for the subject-matter of Article III-20- is that several national authorities can participate in the inspection initiated and conducted by another national authority in its own territory. This provision does not address an existing phenomenon, in which a number of national authorities carry out a joint inspection coordinated by a European agency. These cases could be designated as EU inspections, since they are substantially led by an EU authority. According to this designation, and following the 'separation principle,' the right to an effective remedy and the non-contractual liability safeguard against these inspections coordinated by an EU authority are located in the EU.[73]

Although the reference made to 'joint inspections' in Article III-20 could lead to an impression of an intense horizontality in the inspection procedure, in these inspections there is no actual equality amongst every national authority, since the prominence and the lead lie in the national authority (host authority).[74] In this connection, it must be recalled that the inspection has an instrumental nature with respect to an administrative decision-making procedure (which is the subject-matter of Book III). This obviously gives special functional attention and importance to the national authority managing the procedure.

Strictly speaking, Article III-20(1) does not provide for a specific legal framework applicable to joint inspections. Actually, and according to the reference made by Article III-20(1) itself, the legal framework applicable to the joint inspection shall be established by means of an agreement between Member States or sector-specific legislation.[75] Not even the straightforward reference to the fact that the national authority (the host authority) 'shall invite the inspection authority of each Member State' has actual legal significance apart from the corresponding agreement or sector-specific legislation. In order for this formal

72 In this sense: Article 47(2) of Regulation (EU) No 1306/2013.

73 David (n 2) 259.

74 As precedent in customs law: Article 9(2) of Council Regulation (EC) No 515/97. In food law: Article 36 (3) Regulation (EC) No 882/2004.

75 For example, Article 29(1) of Directive 2000/12/EC.

duty to 'invite' to the participatory procedure to account for a true duty, it can only stem from the formal identification on an ex ante basis (in an agreement or in a legislative act) of the cases in which an inspection can be considered to be of a supranational interest. Otherwise the 'duty to invite' would be at the 'host authority's' discretion, and thus it could not be deemed a true duty.

Although it is included in the regulation of the joint inspection, the potential conferral of executive powers upon a national authority (by another national authority in its territory), foreseen in Article III-20(2) is beyond the notion of participation in a national inspection. Along with the participatory character come distinct features of the 'organic borrowing' (*Organleihe*). In other words, the inspection officials from the 'invited authority' act as host authority bodies.

VII. Duties to inform on an 'ex post' basis

Finally, the last sort of cooperative duties provided for in Book III consist in the administrative authority which has gathered the information informing the host authority (where the information has indeed been gathered) of the results.[76] This duty to inform on an 'ex post' basis is not expressly provided by Book III for the requests of interviews, yet it is in fact foreseen for the on-the-spot checks (Article III-18(3)). Although in principle the duty to inform of the results of the inspection is favourable to the Member State in which the inspection is conducted – as a compensation measure for the general obligation to tolerate an outside inspection in its territory – the truth is that Article III.18(3) gives an additional or complementary sense to the report issued by the outside inspection authority.

Indeed, Article III. 18(3) requires that 'in drawing up their reports account is taken of the procedural requirements laid down in the national law of the Member State concerned.' This complementary duty is actually aimed at providing the final inspection report with probative value in potential administrative and judicial procedures (either subsequent or complementary) in the Member State. Obviously, there is only room for such probative value of the inspection reports, directly set out in Article III-18(3), in a subsequent national procedure (either judicial or administrative) where EU law is applied. For those cases, Article 18-III(3) does not confer a specific value to the inspection report, yet it attributes it the same value attributed to the equivalent report in accordance with domestic law.[77] Hence, where national legislation on administrative procedure grants a specific probative value to inspection reports,[78] that same value should be applied to the inspection report issued by the EU authority. Accordingly, Article III-18(3) does not award EU inspection reports a hypothetical 'presumption of certainty' if such value or quality does not result from domestic law.

---

76 A precedent of this law is Article 9.2 of Council Regulation (EURATOM, EC) No 2185/96.

77 As a precedent, see Article 9.3 of Council Regulation (EURATOM, EC) No 2185/96.

78 For example, in Spanish law, Article 137 of Law 30/1992 of 26 of November.

CHAPTER 7

Investigation and Responsibility – Legal Aspects of Common Interest

Gunilla Edelstam

This paper will deal with some aspects as to questions of fact. Collection of proof and evaluation of proof will be discussed in the light of similar issues in some penal law cases and civil law cases that have been up for debate in Sweden.

The starting-point is that there is one party in the administrative single case that it is handled by a public administrative authority and that the basis of the decision must be reliable and the assessment of it must be correct. Sufficient investigation as to collection of proof as well as correct evaluation of the collected information is needed. This Chapter thus deals with the investigation that takes place after a case has been initiated either ex officio by the public authority or through an application from an individual. The unilateral decision that follows in a case that was initiated ex officio can imply an encroachment in the property of the party. In the application case there is no such encroachment but still the interest of the State or society must be guarded and the party in the application cases shall not have a positive decision unless his right has been proven.

In all legal cases there are questions of law as well as questions of fact. The focus in legal cases is often on the meaning of a certain regulation or of some terms in a provision. The focus is then on a question of law where interpretation of legal sources is made in order to find, amongst others the preconditions, for a certain decision. As regards questions of fact the focus is instead on the circumstances in the actual case. This is not about interpretation of law but about fact-finding. In a penal law case the meaning of the term murder is a question of law where interpretation of law might be needed. The question of fact however concerns who committed that crime and fact-finding is needed.

Demarcation between law and fact might be difficult to draw. Nevertheless there is a difference and different legal methods[1] are used as regards questions of law and questions of fact. In addition there are also questions of discretion where the law contains broadly-framed conditions that have to be established before the power or duty can be exercised at all. Such questions of discretion must be regarded as a kind of question of law.[2] For questions of law one needs to go to the legal sources, the texts and the principles. As regards the questions of fact, that is, how to find the facts, legal sources do not give much assistance.

In Sweden fact-finding and evaluation of proof in some penal law cases has been up for debate as to whether there are system failures related to questions of fact and a special commission, *Bergwallkommissionen*, was appointed to analyze whether the legal system had structural faults. The context for this was that a man (T Quick who later changed his name to S Bergwall) was convicted in seven different court cases for having committed eight murders. The convicted person had drug problems and had taken drugs when speaking about – what were considered to be – repressed memories. He wanted to be convicted. The

1 Legal methods are often referred to only as questions of law with regard to legal sources. Compare A. Peczfenik, *Juridikens teori och metod (Theory and methodology of law)* (Norstedts juridik 1995). Legal methods can however concern handling of facts and the evaluation of proof. Compare C. Sandgren, *Rättsvetenskap för uppsatsförfattare (Legal science for authors of essays)* (Norstedts juridik 2007) 37 f.

2 Compare P. Craig *EU Administrative Law* (Oxford University Press 2006) 429 ff.

person, who some years later changed his mind about his guilt, has now been freed in all the cases. The *Bergwallkommission* has recently[3] given its report. It found that though there was some lack in the legal procedures there were no systematic faults regarding the legal system as such. The cases were considered to be too special. The commission found[4] that "The district courts did not assess the completeness of the investigations sufficiently carefully, nor did they analyse the impact of any flaws in the investigations on the evaluation of evidence. Moreover, the district courts do not seem to have set sufficiently high standards for the evidence required to be able to convict a person for murder. The absence of opposition may also have been contributing factor in this." The commission stressed[5] that courts should always maintain an independent attitude to the parties, and direct proceedings with particular attention to the legal security of the individual, seeking the best possible basis for assessments and that weaknesses in the evidence should lead to the prosecution being dismissed. The Commission also stressed that despite the fact that expert statements usually have a major impact on the courts' assessment of the evidence, expert statements cited in court are not quality-assured and it therefore found that the possibility of establishing a system of quality assurance of expert statements should be investigated. Furthermore it stated[6] that the duty of objectivity should be more strongly emphasized.

It has been up for debate whether uncritical "group-thinking" and negative "bureaucratic intellectual fellowship" that is like a "warm shelter" for some of those that work with investigations, takes place during investigations. One of the members of the Bergwall commission stressed[7] that there had been "group-thinking" in the relations between the psychiatric care and the legal system. There had been a lack of critical thinking between them.[8] The investigators were driven by uncritical group-thinking and demand for loyalty. "Group-thinking consists of a strive for uniformity. The members of the group strives to reach a similar way of looking at the case by repressing divergent opinions and by isolating themselves from other facts and opinions".[9] The demand for loyalty within the group makes the member avoid controversial issues or look for other solutions. Through the inner dynamics of the group each member is assured that the decisions are correct and a feeling of invulnerability develops.[10]

The *Quick/Bergwall* cases have been called legal scandals. It is not the legislation and the questions of law but the investigation and the questions of fact that are in focus when calling it such. During the investigation as to fact and

---

3 *Bergwallkommissionens* report: SOU 2015:52.

4 *Ibid.* SOU 2015:52 p. 25.

5 *Ibid.* p. 27 f.

6 *Ibid.* p. 27.

7 *Ibid.* p. 684 ff.

8 Statement by Prof. K. Asplund in the report from the Bergwallcommission, *Ibid.*

9 M. Zaremba, *Kaijsa Ekis Ekman skriver in sig i narrkvoten* DN 2015-06-16.

10 *Ibid.*

evidence something goes wrong. The circumstances in the actual case are not clarified and the judgment is made on insufficient information regarding the facts of the case.

Could similar things happen in administrative law cases? Could group-thinking and negative intellectual fellowship replace a sufficient and objective investigation of the actual case? The question of facts and how they are handled by the legal system is closely connected to legitimacy and trust in the legal system.

The investigation of facts can be divided into collecting proofs and evaluating proof. In order to then assess whether there is enough proof there is a need for standard of proof that is of a certain level that the collected proof must reach in order to satisfy it, and after this evaluation if there is still doubt it might be necessary to use the burden of proof.

Collection of proof is of course dependent on how the law is interpreted but once the provisions have been interpreted, the collection of evidence can begin. A complication is that there are framework laws where the norms give space for choices between several possible interpretations.[11] Appropriateness and different interests might have to be taken into consideration. Discretion as to the interpretation or choice between possibilities within the frame of a provision and thus the establishing of the preconditions that are to be applied can in addition be possible to a greater or lesser extent.

Collection of proof depends upon the type of case. Administrative cases can either be application cases where the party has applied for some kind of decision, an allowance for example, or they can be ex officio cases where the public authority starts a case that is unfavorable for the party, regarding for example a prohibition. It is either the public authority itself or the individual that can bring forward the proof. If the individual party is adduce evidence to the public authority he might need some guidance as there generally is no proxy to help a party in administrative cases. The party in an application case will lose the case if the requisite standard of proof cannot be reached.

Who shall collect the information needed? As regards collection of proof there are some special administrative provisions according to which the public authority has a duty to investigate. In the Swedish general administrative act there is however no such duty expressed but there is a duty to guide the party. As a general principle it is considered that in application cases the party shall provide the public authority with proof and in ex officio cases the public authority shall collect the required proof. However in legislation that gives the public authority a duty to ex officio start a case (for example on a prohibition) there are an increasing amount of provisions on duties to give information to the public authority. This way the duty to investigate is less heavy for the public authority and it can put pressure on the party to give information. This can be done

11 A complication as regards collection of proof can in addition be that while some cases administrative law deals with facts that happened in the past (tax cases for example) others deal with predictions for the future (compulsory care of children for example).

unless such pressure would be in contradiction to Article 6 of the ECHR where the party shall be presumed to be innocent until found guilty of a crime following proof adduced by the prosecutor and the penal law court.

Without proven facts an administrative unilateral single case decision will have a lack of legitimacy. Administrative law is rather close to politics, political goals shall be fulfilled through unilateral single case decisions but the decisions must be judicial. A precondition for legitimacy is that the collection of facts is handled in the correct way. Guidance from the public authority should be a precondition for the proper collection of evidence, and should be required in application cases as well in such ex officio cases where there are duties for the party to give information to the public authority.

A regulation of the guidance as regards relevant facts and proof could help to create a more judicial administrative law, at least if the fulfilment of such provision is kept up to date with the case law by the court.

For ex officio cases, where there are no duties for the party to give information to the public authority, guidance is not needed. The public authority must collect all needed information itself.

There is a freedom as regards adducing proof. Any available evidence must be permitted to be brought before the public authority or the court. A party may thus bring forward whatever he finds to promote his case. This means that the public authority must assess the importance of all information given by the party.

A fundamental principle is that evaluation of the proofs is free. That is, the officials that make the investigation and the public authority has freedom to evaluate the proof. Some administrative law states what evidence can be, but the principle of freedom as regards evaluation is primary and the party or the public authority can rely on other proof. Otherwise there would be no freedom as regards submission of evidence.

The official must evaluate the evidence in order to see if further investigation is needed. The evaluation is a legal activity where the investigating official (or other decision-maker or judge at the court) uses his knowledge and experience. He will not find the answer as to how to evaluate certain information in legal texts. There might be provisions stating that for example a certain certificate is needed. Furthermore a standard assessment or a presumption might be used instead of further investigation. As regards for example handling of refuse from households it can be presumed that there will be some waste even if the party claims that all waste is taken care of.

If presumptions or similar ways of replacing investigation with standards that are easy to handle, are used instead of other relevant information or further investigation, this can be a way to minimize work and manage work-loads. However it can undermine the legitimacy of administrative law.

As regards evaluation of proof a basic principle stated in the constitution of Sweden.(RF 1:9) states that courts of law, administrative authorities and others performing public administration functions shall observe objectivity and impartiality. It is furthermore stated in the Administrative Procedure Act that the person charged with handling a matter is disqualified if he is challengeable. The principle of objectivity and impartiality in the Constitution is more comprehensive as regards the evaluation of proof than the provision in the Administrative Procedure Act. As it is stipulated as a Constitutional provision its importance is emphasized.

It is however rather obvious that investigations that are made before taking an administrative unilateral single case decision can imply insufficient investigation and imply errors as regards evaluation of the proof. It might be easy to hide such matters behind some statement of the case being too special but nevertheless there is a demand for legitimacy that can be promoted by objectivity and impartiality. The issue of evaluation of proof is complicated by the fact that it is unclear what the standard of proof should be in administrative unilateral single cases. Evaluation of proof is furthermore complicated as regards burden of proof, which is not the same thing as the duty to investigate. The burden of proof in administrative unilateral single case decisions concerns how to handle doubts when no further investigation can be made. If the level of the standard of proof is clear in a case and there are still doubts as to whether the facts are beyond or below this standard the burden of proof can be used. The issue then is whether the burden of proof can be placed on the party in the case or not. In general the authority can place the burden of proof on the party in application cases but not in ex officio cases. The level needed, as regards the standard of proof in administrative cases, is unclear, thus leaving uncertainty as regards the burden of proof.

Simplifying the collection and evaluation of proof could be a way of minimizing the work-load and maximizing the efficiency of decision making. Especially when discretion exists as regards the question of law and the investigation is complicated, "discretion" might "fly over" to the question of fact when for example irrelevant values are taken into the evaluation, but discretion cannot be used on fact-finding. Another way might to give too much importance to some information, for example statements from so called experts.

In Swedish civil law cases the court shall decide whether the mother or the father shall have the custody of a child after a divorce when it does not serve "the best interest of the child" that the parents have joint custody. If one of the parents fails to care for the child in such a way that there is lasting danger to the health and development of the child the other parent will have sole custody of the child. The social board and its officials make the investigation in such cases. A Swedish journalist, Maciej Zaremba has studied such investigations from the social authorities. He has found that "When a couple breaks up and start arguing on custody of the child the legal procedure invites to mutual murder of character". The parent that "wins" is the one that manages to convince the social authority that the other parent is a bad person, even a "monster". In several newspaper articles he showed how this was done and shows how there was a lack of objectivity during investigations.[12] He stressed that where power can be misused it will be misused. Feministic values played a role. The parents were not treated equally. Opposing information was not presented to the court. Zaremba found[13] that psychologists and therapists of a similar kind had played important roles in the cases. They discovered the asserted crime (such as sexual crime by the father), they helped the victim and they convinced the court that the memories are real. These "experts" were similar to a sect. Their belief was strong and if they had enough time to question a child they would almost always find terrible things. Science was neglected by the investigators and the courts.

"Warm shelters" with group-thinking, where negative bureaucratic intellectual fellowship prevails that excludes objectivity and impartiality rules, might exist within public authorities when investigating administrative single cases. Corruption is a strong word to use as it can imply severe crimes such as taking bribes and it is therefore more convenient to speak of irregularities when the acting of the public authority should have been different in a certain case. The content of corruption is not clearly defined from a legal point of view. Corruption within public authorities is not necessarily criminal activity. Criminal corruption is in general easier to find because there is often money involved. It involves pecuniary benefits for the official. Taking of bribes in order to give a certain permit, for example a residence permit to a third country national or an environmental permit to a certain company, are examples of such corruption. Three kinds of corrupt action can be distinguished:[14] pecuniary corruption, institutional corruption and intellectual corruption. Institutional corruption occurs "when members of institutions take advantage of their institutional role for personal aggrandizement, in ways not prohibited by law but incompatible with their mission".[15] Intellectual corruption is more difficult to define but can be situations where authority would replace justification.[16] This implies that investigating activities such as collection of evidence or evaluation of proof could involve corruption if it is not done correctly. In the penal law murder-cases the "bureaucratic intellectual fellowship" has been pointed out as something that can have far reaching consequences for all of us when this fellowship is used as a "warm shelter" for incompetent bureaucrats.[17] Even if the great majority of

[12] M Zaremba, *Demons of Justice, five articles on the Swedish legal sytem and the hidden driving force of the social authorities.* Dagens Nyheter (DN): 'Varför dog Matilda? (Why did Matilda die)' (19/4), 'Därför försvann Ellens pappa' (That is why the father of Ellen disappeared) (23/4), 'Så blev Olle berövad sin mamma (This is how Olle lost his mother)' (29/4), Därför levde lögnerna om Julias pappa (That is why the lies about Julia´s father continued)' (7/5) och 'Så förvandlas männen till rättvisans demoner (How men are turned into demons)' (13/5).

[13] Why did Mathilda die?, *Ibid.*

[14] HP Glenn, *Legal Traditions of The World* (4th ed., Oxford University Press 2000) p. 28 ff.

[15] *Ibid.* p. 30.

[16] *Ibid.* p. 30.

[17] LGW Persson, 'Inkompetensen gynnas av värmen (Incompetence profits from warmth)'. Expressen, 2015-05-10,

officials do very good work the bureaucratic intellectual fellowship can be of a negative kind where incompetence plays a role and that could involve institutional and intellectual corruption.

Whether group-thinking in "warm shelters" replaces correct investigations with objectivity and impartiality is seldom controlled by the administrative courts. Instead the public authority is often considered by administrative courts to be better suited to the investigation of the proof. The Swedish Ombudsman (JO) is not allowed to look into such issues as the Constitution states that "No public authority, including the Riksdag (Parliament), or decision-making body of any local authority, may determine how an administrative authority shall decide in a particular case relating to the exercise of public authority vis-à-vis an individual or a local authority, or relating to the application of law".[18]

Objectivity, impartiality, as well as guidance and some investigation ex officio are fundamentals of good administration as regards questions of fact. In administrative law these issues have different importance when compared to similar issues in penal and civil law and even if they cannot be more closely regulated they could be given more attention by the administrative courts.

[18] Instrument of government, chapter 12 sector 2.

CHAPTER 8

Third Parties Protection in Administrative Procedure Law

Jacques Ziller

A. By Way of Introduction: Third Parties as the Parent Pauvre of Administrative Procedural Law?

A quick review of literature indicates that overall there is rather little interest in the topic of third parties to administrative procedures.[1] The issue that is most often explored seems to be that of standing of third parties to challenge administrative decisions,[2] as well as the notion of 'public' – which in my view is different of that of third party (see sections B and D) – and to a certain extent that of participation of persons other than the addressee in specific procedures,[3] but further exploration of the impact of procedural rules remains seemingly unattractive to scholars. Clearly I do not exclude that there are useful considerations on the point in more general studies dedicated to administrative procedure law, but the absence of monographic studies (not only volumes, but also articles) is in my view a clear symptom of lack of interest.

More important than the foibles of scholarship is the fact that amendments to existing administrative procedure acts in recent decades – such as in Germany or in Italy[4] – have tended to focus on the relationship between the

* This chapter is part of in the framework of PRIN project 2012 (2012SAM3KM) on Codification of EU Administrative Procedures, financed by the the Ministero dell'Istruzione, dell'Università e della Ricerca, Italy, as a written and further developed version of the remarks I presented in the Rome Seminar.

1 To my knowledge, there is only one book entirely dedicated to the issues regarding third parties in administrative procedure law: T. Tanquerel and F. Bellanger (eds.) *Les tiers dans la procédure administrative* (Schultess 2004).

2 This point is also stressed by Tanquerel and Bellanger (n 1) in their presentation of their edited book: "L'étendue de la faculté pour des personnes qui ne sont pas directement destinataires d'une décision administrative de contester celle-ci par un recours est un sujet de débat certes classique, mais en perpétuelle évolution. Quant à la participation de ces tiers à la procédure administrative non contentieuse, elle est restée relativement peu étudiée, hormis le cas de l'aménagement du territoire. Or, l'exigence de participation s'est considérablement accrue, d'une part, avec le développement de procédures administratives dont la portée concrète, notamment économique, dépasse largement le cercle de leurs destinataires directs et, d'autre part, en raison de l'approche souvent plus énergique adoptée par les tiers intéressés. Le moment était donc opportun de clarifier les enjeux de la participation des tiers, en les confrontant à la réglementation juridique de la qualité de partie à la procédure administrative et aux problèmes pratiques qui se posent dans quelques domaines particulièrement intéressants à cet égard". Ten years later, however, it does not seem that the interest in third parties has grown. For literature on the USA see e.g. K. A. Coyle, 'Standing of Third Parties to Challenge Administrative Agency Actions', 76 *California Law Review* (1988) 1061-1107.

3 See in Tanquerel and Bellanger (n 1): T. Tanquerel, 'Les tiers dans les procédures disciplinaires'; J.-L. Duc, 'Les tiers dans la procédure administrative non contentieuse dans les assurances sociales'; C. Bovet, 'Les tiers devant les Commission fédérales des banques, de la concurrence et de la communication'.

4 See H. Hill, K.-P. Sommermann, U. Stelkens and J. Ziekow, *35 Jahre Verwaltungsgesetze – Bilanz und Perspektiven* (Duncker & Humblot 2011).

applicant/addressee and public administration with the legitimate goal of reducing the burdens imposed on both parties, but with scarce concern to what used to be called 'general interest', a seemingly outdated concept in the light of trends in political and social science. The main motto of those reforms are 'de-bureaucratisation', 'suppressing red-tape' etc. The target of such reforms is not only the wording of procedural rules per-se but also important issues of principle such as the choice in handling authorizations to proceed with regulated activities, as expressed in the recitals of the 2006 services directive, amongst others:

> (42) The rules relating to administrative procedures should not aim at harmonising administrative procedures but at *removing overly burdensome authorisation schemes, procedures and formalities* that hinder the freedom of establishment and the creation of new service undertakings therefrom.
>
> (43) One of the fundamental difficulties faced, in particular by SMEs, in accessing service activities and exercising them is the complexity, length and legal uncertainty of administrative procedures. For this reason, *following the example of certain modernising and good administrative practice initiatives undertaken at Community and national level,* it is necessary to establish principles of administrative simplification, inter alia through the *limitation of the obligation of prior authorisation to cases in which it is essential and the introduction of the principle of tacit authorisation* by the competent authorities after a certain period of time elapsed. Such modernising action, *while maintaining the requirements on transparency and the updating of information relating to operators,* is intended to eliminate the delays, costs and dissuasive effects which arise, for example, from unnecessary or excessively complex and burdensome procedures, the duplication of procedures, the 'red tape' involved in submitting documents, the arbitrary use of powers by the competent authorities, indeterminate or excessively long periods before a response is given, the limited duration of validity of authorisations granted and disproportionate fees and penalties. Such practices have particularly significant dissuasive effects on providers wishing to develop their activities in other Member States and require coordinated modernisation within an enlarged internal market of twenty-five Member States.[5]

Who would oppose such a reasonable proposal, especially when indicated that what should be removed are overly burdensome schemes, procedures and formalities? What should be understood by maintaining the requirements on transparency and the updating of information relating to operators? Indeed the same directive, in recital (63) indicates that:

> In the absence of different arrangements, failing a response within a time period, an authorisation should be deemed to have been granted. However, different arrangements may be put in place in respect of certain activities, where objectively

[5] Directive 2006/123/EC of the European Parliament And Of The Council of 12 December 2006 on services in the internal market, OJ, 27.12.2006, L 376/36, emphasis added.

justified by overriding reasons relating to the public interest, including a legitimate interest of third parties. Such different arrangements could include national rules according to which, in the absence of a response of the competent authority, the application is deemed to have been rejected, this rejection being open to challenge before the courts.[6]

Article 13 of the Directive contains indeed a concretization of the idea stated in recital (63).

The Directive is not a problem as such but it may be used as a pretext by national legislators or rule makers who want to be 'more royalist than the King'. I submit that the application of the principle in judicial review or even in the legislative or regulatory choices is not enough, and that it is necessary to reflect upon in-built safeguards for third parties' interests, both in the wording of procedures and in institutional design.

My personal interest in the issues of third parties has been fostered by my participation in the drafting work of Book IV on Contracts[7] of the ReNEUAL Model Rules on EU Administrative Procedure (Model Rules). This interest has developed further in the framework of a research project on European Administrative Procedure Law financed by the Italian Ministry of Education and Research.[8] This Chapter is thus very much work in progress. The considerations presented here are based largely upon the issues relating to third parties in Book III of the Model Rules (section 3). The chapter however goes beyond Book III and touches also upon the issues relating to third parties in rule making (section 4 – Model Rules Book II) and in contracts (section 5 – Model Rules Book IV), as well as to the research agenda of the group I am coordinating in the above mentioned research project which will focus on autonomous organizational structures (bodies, offices and agencies in the jargon of EU primary law) and their working procedures and routines as specific tools for inclusion of third parties or 'non parties' to procedures (section 6). A first question to be addressed – to which there is not necessarily an answer – is that of a definition of 'third party', a question which we will look at from the point of view of the Model Rules as a whole.

B. Third Parties in the ReNEUAL Model Rules

Not being an English native speaker, I have to signal my discomfort with the use of the word 'party' as it seems that the noun 'third' is only used for a fraction of a number, differently from German (der Dritte) or Roman languages (el tercero, il terzo, le tiers, o terceiro) where on the contrary elegant

---

6 *Ibid.*, rec. 63.

7 I owe special thanks to the other two-team leaders of ReNEUAL WG 3 on Contracts as well as the members of the drafting team of Book IV: J.-B. Auby, M. Mirschberger, H. Schröder, and U. Stelkens.

8 See above n *.

legal writing implies the use of the sole noun. I might be wrong, but my impression is that speaking of 'third parties' tends to exclude persons who are not a party to the procedure in even a broad sense (see section A) whereas speaking of a Dritte, tercero, terzo, tiers, or terceiro leads to a broader perspective.

Book I of the Model Rules on General provisions applies all rules including those of Book III on single case decision making. In side number 27 of the general part we wrote that:

> "[t]oday, the design of composite procedures is geared predominantly towards achieving efficiency and optimal use of pre-existing resources, but their multi-jurisdictional nature may diminish protection of individual rights and possibilities of effective judicial review. Rules of administrative procedure are, therefore, necessary to prevent that the rights and interests of addressees and third parties in the implementation of EU law fall in a 'black hole' between situations covered by the EU-level review and accountability mechanisms and those of Member States".

This statement is complemented by the commentary of side number 27 about the definition of composite procedure:

> "Paragraph 4 defines 'composite procedures', which are a distinctive and important element of EU administrative law. The wording is based on a definition formulated in 1999 by the Committee of Independent Experts who reported on needs to reform the Commission. The second sentence of this paragraph reflects the situation in which procedures at EU level are preparing decisions by EU authorities which *are directly addressed to a Member State whilst having also direct effects on third parties*; the latter happens because the EU decision obliges the Member State to take a precisely determined action against that third party in a national procedure, such as, for instance, a beneficiary of a national state aid" (emphasis added).

In the EU context, there are a series of situations where the EU institutions, bodies, offices and agencies acting in their administrative functions deal with the Members States as addressees, whereas their decisions directly impact upon other persons; those situations are only to a limited extent comparable to the situation where a central State administration is dealing with local authorities. The typical case of such a situation is that of State aids, where the Commission addresses a decision on a new aid to the relevant Member State whereas the decision will primarily affect the recipient of the proposed aid. Indeed, there are rules in secondary EU law as well as jurisprudential principles, which have been developed to enable the recipient – as well as possible competitors – to participate in the administrative procedure leading to the Commission's decision. More broadly, whenever the Commission is exercising its function of oversight and with the exception of the application of competition rules based upon Articles 101 to 106 TFEU – which are designated in the title of the relevant

Section of the treaty as 'Rules applying to undertakings', the oversight function has Member States as direct addressees. For the purpose of administrative procedural rules, there are no specific reasons to distinguish between the executive function – which is usually the locus of administrative activities – and the oversight function.[9]

The cited comment from number 27 general Part Model Rules Book I addresses a more complex issue, that of composite procedures which are a fundamental issue in EU administrative procedural law. Composite procedures[10] can be broadly characterized as procedures which are not only located in either the EU administration or in one Member State's administration, but in both, or even in the EU administration and/or that of several Member States. In composite procedures it can happen that the same person is the addressee of all intermediary decisions as well as the ultimate decision – as is the case in the famous *Oleificio Borelli* situation[11] -, and therefore is without any doubt a party to the procedure; but it happens also very often that intermediary decisions have different addressees, which are also different from the final formal decision, and thus are not easily identifiable as parties to the same procedure. The latter type of situations are mainly addressed in Book V of the Model Rules.

That being said, what is a 'third party'? The only definition to be found in the Model Rules[12] is in Book IV on contracts in Article IV-2 (10): "Third party' means any person who is not a party to the EU contract". If transposed to administrative procedures in general without qualifications, 'third party' would

9 For more details on the differences between oversight and executive function in the strict sense see J. Ziller, 'Separation of Powers in the European Union's Intertwined System of Government. A Treaty Based Analysis for the Use of Political Scientists and Constitutional Lawyers', in 3 *Il Politico* (2008) 133-179 also available at http://papers.ssrn.com/sol3/papers.cfm?abstract_id=1398902, as well as J Ziller, 'Multilevel Governance and Executive Federalism: Comparing Germany and the European Union', in P. Birkinshaw and M. Varney (eds), *The European Union Legal Order after Lisbon* (Kluwer Law International 2010) 257-275.

10 The definition of composite procedures in Art. I-4 (4) is: "`Composite procedure´ means an administrative procedure where EU authorities and the authorities of a Member State or of different Member States have distinct functions which are inter-dependent. A composite procedure may also mean the combination of two administrative procedures that are directly linked."

11 The reference is to the Judgment of the CJEU of 3 December 1992, *Oleificio Borelli SpA v Commission of the European Communities*, Case C-97/91, ECLI:EU:C:1992:491; for the very interesting situation created in the framework of, see L. Wissink, T. Duijkersloot and R. Widdershoven, 'Shifts in Competences between Member States and the EU in the New Supervisory System for Credit Institutions and their Consequences for Judicial Protection', 10 *Utrecht Law Review* (2014) 97 s., accessible at http://www.utrechtlawreview.org.

12 A reference to third parties is also to be found in the comments to Art. I – 4 (6) on the definition of 'persons', which indicates that "A [...] definition is to be found in Regulation 1049/2001 on access to documents, where according to Article 3 'third party' is defined as meaning "any natural or legal person, or any entity outside the institution concerned, including the Member States, other Community or non-Community institutions and bodies and third countries".

thus mean 'a person who is not a party to the procedure'. The problem is that there are a series of different positions of the persons that are not a party to the procedure, which are taken into account indirectly in the different Books of the Model Rules. An overall definition of different categories of third parties has not been attempted in the Model Rules as there was no practical purpose in establishing it. Trying to establish typologies is on the research agenda for scholarship. My experience is that an ex-ante typology might take much time and resources without being satisfactory when it comes to the application of it. I see it therefore as a future hoped outcome of the research, which will only emerge gradually and will be consolidated at best at the end of the period of the PRIN project mentioned above.

C. Third Parties in Book III of the ReNEUAL Model Rules

A (too) quick reading of the Model Rules Book III on single case decision-making might give the impression that there is little concern for third parties in those rules; but the definition of a party to the procedure shows on the contrary great concern for inclusiveness. In Book III, the commentaries (let alone rules) refer very little to third parties.

Indeed there are only two provisions referring explicitly to third parties: Articles III-35(4) and III-36(4) on Rectification and withdrawal of decisions provide in an identical wording that: "[t]he public authority when exercising the power in this article shall take into account the effect of the rectification or withdrawal *on other parties and on third parties*" (emphasis added). The differentiation between 'other' and 'third' parties is due to the fact that the decision has one or more addressees; we will see that the definition of a party to the procedure in Book III is not limited indeed to the addressee of a decision.

In Book III there is only one explanation referring to third parties: side number 73 about Article III-20 on Joint inspections of Member State authorities: "Moreover, the host authority remains responsible for actions of the visiting authority vis-à-vis third parties in its territory." Third party means here persons other than the person whose premises or documents are being inspected.

That being said, Book III contains a series of provisions of critical importance for third parties, beginning with Article III-2 Definitions, which provides that:

> (3)'Party' means the addressee of the intended decision and other persons who are adversely affected by it and who request to be involved in the procedure. Sector-specific EU law may assign the status of party to persons not adversely affected.

The main point is that, as already mentioned, it is not only addressees of a decision that are considered as parties to the procedure, but also other persons who

i) are adversely affected and ii) request to be involved in the procedure. In order to understand fully the provision, two other definitions in Article III-2 need to be taken into account:

> (1) 'Decision' means administrative action addressed to one or more individualized public or private persons which is adopted unilaterally by an EU authority, or by a Member State authority when Article III-1(2) is applicable, to determine one or more concrete cases with legally binding effect.
>
> (4)'Interested public' for the purposes of Article III-25 means every natural or legal person and other associations, organizations or groups expressing an interest in the administrative procedure.

It derives from the three definitions that there are four categories of 'parties' with respect to administrative procedures: i) the addressee of a decision, ii) the person who, being adversely affected, has requested to become a party to the procedure, iii) the person who expresses an interest in the procedure and iv) persons who have not even expressed an interest in the procedure; there are thus at least three types of 'third parties', depending upon the way EU secondary law and jurisprudence defines a party to the procedure.

The relevant explanations of Book IV indicate (side number 7) that: "[...] The definition of 'party' does not cover persons who are merely interested. A person who is merely interested does not qualify as being adversely affected merely because he or she subjectively thinks that this is so. It is an objective test, determined by the body providing the procedure, albeit subject to judicial review." Furthermore, in side number (8) it is explained that "it is only those 'adversely' affected by the intended decision who enjoy procedural rights. [...] This formulation does not require that the contested measure should be initiated against the claimant [...]".

The explanations say nothing about the 'applicant' which derives from Article III-5 Initiation;[13] indeed a number of provisions of Book III provide for duties and rights of the applicant. It derives from these provisions that applicants are by definition fully fledged parties to the procedure – with an important provision relating to the definition of a 'decision' – with the exception of pointless or manifestly unfounded applications, which may be rejected as inadmissible by means of a briefly reasoned acknowledgement of receipt according to Article III-6 (3) Model Rules.

The question which remains to a certain extent open in the framework of the rules of Book III is the status of a party who makes an application to a procedure that does not necessarily lead to a decision in the sense of Article III-2 (1). Indeed the definition of 'decision' in Book III is rather restrictive as it is intended to determine one or more concrete cases with legally binding effect. The mention that decisions 'adopted unilaterally' has hardly any restrictive effect due to the fact that Book IV on contracts explicitly provides for the

[13] Administrative procedures can be initiated ex-officio or by an application.

application of most provisions of Book III to procedures related to contracts. The important point is that only decisions "which determine a case with legally binding effects" are considered as decisions in the sense of Book III, thus excluding a series of intermediary decisions or others. The explanations of Book III stress in side number (5):

> [...] it is important to note that decisions for the purpose of this Book 'determine' one or more concrete cases with legally binding effects. This Book regulates certain aspects that are preparatory to the final decision, such as a decision that a responsible official should be excluded from the administrative procedure, but these do not constitute themselves decisions for the purposes of this Book, because they do not determine the concrete case with legally binding effect. The definition of decision also means that decisions made by the Commission pursuant to an infringement procedure against a Member State are not covered by Book III.

The latter indication about infringement procedures is of particular importance taking into account the very high number of requests made to the Commission by natural or legal persons asking to start an infringement procedure. The European Ombudsman has developed an 'ombudsprudence' which fully recognises the discretionary power of the Commission to decide if, when and how to start an infringement procedure against a Member State or to stop it. According to that 'ombudsprudence'[14] the Commission is bound by Article 41 CFREU in handling this type of request, and in particular it is obliged to inform the applicant about the follow-up to the request and to give reasons. The latter obligation has often been criticised as limiting discretion;[15] however I submit that it suffices that the Commission indicate for instance that it decided not to initiate or continue an infringement in view of political considerations, without qualifying those considerations more in detail or explaining them. To my view the central consideration here is that explained by the Court in *Heylens*:[16]

> *effective judicial review, which must be able to cover the legality of the reasons for the contested decision, presupposes in general that the court to which the matter is referred may require the competent authority to notify its reasons. But where, as in this case, it is more particularly a question of securing the effective protection of a fundamental right conferred by the treaty on community workers, the latter must also*

14 See European Parliament, Working Group on EU Administrative Law, State of play and future prospects for EU administrative law, Brussels, European Parliament, 14 October 2011, p. 17-19, available at http://www.europarl.europa.eu/meetdocs/2009_2014/documents/juri/dv/juri_wdadministrativelaw_/juri_wdadministrativelaw_en.pdf

15 See for instance a hint in this direction by J.-P. Jacqué, *Droit institutionnel de l'Union européenne* (7th ed., Dalloz 2012) 702.

16 Judgment of 15 October 1987, *Union nationale des entraîneurs et cadres techniques professionnels du football (Unectef) v Georges Heylens and others*, Case 222/86, ECLI:EU:C:1987:442, para. 5.

> *be able to defend that right under the best possible conditions and have the possibility of deciding, with a full knowledge of the relevant facts, whether there is any point in their applying to the courts. Consequently, in such circumstances the competent national authority is under a duty to inform them of the reasons on which its refusal is based, either in the decision itself or in a subsequent communication made at their request* (emphasis added).

That being said, the national rules on judicial review usually contain very strict time-limits which hinder very strongly the effectiveness of the right to be given reasons in that perspective. What matters here to me is to take stock of the existence of a quantitatively and qualitatively quite important category of third parties, i.e. the persons that have an interest in a Member State's procedure – where they would often also be a party to the procedure or a potential party to the procedure if the definition of a party in Article III-2 (3) Model Rules applied to the relevant Member State, but are only a third party at EU level due to the definition of a decision.

On the whole the definition of a party in Article III-2 (3) is quite broad in that it permits any person who might be negatively affected to become a party to the procedure, without any discretionary power of the administration. However, the consideration of the need to be negatively affected means that there are a number of persons who might have an interest of some kind in a procedure and cannot become a fully-fledged party, unless they have been indicated as such by relevant secondary EU law.

Any further research on third parties based upon the rules defined in ReNEUAL Book III will thus have to take into consideration the three categories of parties as indicated above.

Having in mind the definition of a party, there are other provisions of Book III which are of direct relevance to third parties, beyond Articles III-35(4) and III-36(4) on Rectification and withdrawal of decisions which I have already mentioned.

Even though Article III-3 on the General Duty of Fair Decision-making and Impartiality is supposed to apply to parties,[17] its wording is taken from Article 41 CFREU, which in my view remains applicable to any party, even third parties, and cannot be limited by secondary law. True, the Court has not yet taken a clear position on the applicability of the notion of *Gesetzesvorbehalt* or *riserva di legge* to the fundamental rights guaranteed by the CFREU. We do not yet know if, similar to those notions, only legislative acts may define the conditions of application of fundamental rights[18] and if there is a nucleus of the fundamental rights that even the legislator may not reduce.

---

[17] "(1) Every person has the right to have his or her affairs handled impartially, fairly and within a reasonable time by public authorities *as specified in these model rules*". (Emphasis added).

[18] See however point 56 of the Judgment of the Court of 8 April 2014, *Digital Rights Ireland Ltd* (C-293/12) *v Minister for Communications, Marine and Natural Resources and Others and Kärntner Landesregierung* (C-594/12) and *Other*, ECLI:EU:C:2014:238.

Article III-4 on online information on existing procedures is particularly interesting. According to Article III-4 (1) "Public authorities shall promote the provision of general updated online information on the existing administrative procedures, wherever possible and reasonable. Priority shall be given to application procedures". The explanations to the rules of Book III (side numbers 21 to 24) clarify the notion of online information. Importantly, what is meant is not information on ongoing procedures, and thus Article III-4 should not be misunderstood as a procedural guarantee for the potential party to be informed of the existence of a procedure to which it would like to become a party. The mention that "priority shall be given to application procedures" makes it clear to the attentive reader of the sole rules, who has not yet read the explanations. It has also to be stressed that this provision does not create a subjective right for parties and third parties. However the commented provision is particularly interesting in that it shows how the legislator can use nudging[19] in order to try to get better administrative routines and practices that, if applied, will indeed result in a better protection of parties and third parties.

D. Third Parties in Books II as Well as IV, V and VI of the ReNEUAL Model Rules

In order to understand the choices made in the definition of decisions by the drafting team of Book III Model Riles, the other Books have clearly to be taken into account as is clear from the definition of 'administrative action' in Article I-4 (a)[20] and from the absence of a definition of 'party' let alone 'third party' in the same article.[21] The idea of the ReNEUAL Steering committee is that it is perfectly manageable to have different definitions of 'party' – and hence of 'third party' for each of the books, as the issues are quite different.

As already mentioned, Book IV is the only one which gives a definition of 'third party', namely in Article IV-2: (10) "'Third party' means any person who is not a party to the EU contract". The definition is self-explanatory and unavoidable, as – differently from a procedure – the identification of parties to a contract

19 On the notion of nudging in the context of EU law see A. Alemanno and A. L. Sibony (eds.) *Nudging and the Law. What Can EU Law Learn from Behavioural Sciences?* (Hart Publishing 2015).

20 "(1)'Administrative action' means activity of a public authority as defined in paragraph (7) that results in: (a) a legally binding non-legislative act of general application as defined in Book II, (b) a decision as defined in Book III, (c) a contract as defined in Book IV, (d) mutual assistance as defined in Book V, (e) information management activities as defined in Book VI."

21 Art. I-4 only gives a definition of person: "(6)'Person' means any natural or legal person. Other associations, organizations or groups may be considered as a person on the basis of EU law or the case law of the Court of Justice of the European Union."

is a quite banal operation. The definition of 'third party' is functional to Articles IV-31[22] and IV-37(40).[23]

One issue about third parties is particularly interesting in the framework of contracts, that of subcontractors. Indeed, subcontractors are by definition not parties to the contract between the EU authority and their own contractor, but in the framework of the contract's execution they are usually affected – and more than often negatively affected – by decisions of the EU authority that are formally addressed to the contractor. As indicated in the Explanations to Chapter IV in side number (77): "Subcontractors are third parties that are in a particularly weak position due to the combination between principles of sound management and rules of standing in court procedures."

Article IV-2 (9) defines a subcontractor as "any person who has entered into a contractual relationship with the contractor for the purpose of implementing an existing EU contract". In practice, especially in the framework of contracts for the implementation of EU policies such as research and technological development; economic, social and social cohesion; development aid, the habit is for the Commission or relevant EU agency to have to deal only with one legal or natural person who will act as leader of a consortium, network or team. It is then part of the contractor's duties – who is usually remunerated as such – to manage the entirety of the relationship with subcontractors. As we explain in side number 77 of the explanations of Book IV:

> As far as sound management is concerned, when a number of activities for the performance of a contract have to be performed by different persons, it is advisable for the sake of overview – especially for sound financial management – that an EU authority delegate the burden of managing those persons to a sole contractor, who in turn will establish the necessary subcontracts. Having delegated that burden, EU authorities usually consider that nothing in the relationship between a contractor and its subcontractors is of their concern.

However often the contract contains clauses that enable the EU authority to have a say not only on the selection of subcontractors, but also on the evaluation of their performance and on the continuation of their contractual relationship with the contractor. A contractor who is not satisfied with the performance of a subcontractor often needs a formal request or decision of the EU authority in order to put an end to the contractual relationship with that subcontractor.

In this framework there have been a certain number of attempts of subcontractors to apply for judicial review of those decisions. But as we explain in side number 78:

[22] On Termination due to an infringement of the provisions of Chapter 2: "(1) For the purpose of complying with Article IV-8(4), or if the EU authority becomes aware that the rules on the procedure regarding the conclusion of an EU contract have not been respected to the detriment of a third party, the EU authority may terminate the contract in order to re-open this procedure".

[23] The EU authority is not liable to third parties for the negligence of a subcontractor.

> On the side of standing rules, decisions taken by an EU authority in the implementation of a contract are not considered by the EU courts as decisions in the sense of Article 263 TFEU. While contractors have the possibility to have such decisions reviewed by the judge of the contract, which may be an EU court or a Member State's or other court, subcontractors have therefore no standing to bring an action for annulment, or an action for failure to act under Article 265 against the EU authority. In turn, the judge of the subcontract (which furthermore is normally not an EU Court) cannot review the decisions made by the EU authority in the implementation of the EU contract, as these are not formally addressed to the subcontractor: this solution also is clear in the (rather limited) case law of the GC on actions introduced by subcontractors.

The only solution for subcontractors has thus been to turn to the European Ombudsman, as explained in side number 79, "who has developed an ombudsprudence on the applicability of the principles of good administration to the actions, or to the inaction, of EU authorities that have implications for the situation of subcontractors". The three articles on subcontracts of Book IV have therefore been drafted in view of trying to give a more precise view of the procedural rules and principles of good administration that have to be complied with by the EU authority in situations that impact on the subcontractor (Article IV-39).[24] Our experience in drafting those provisions – with the same technique that has been used in order to allow a number of provisions from Book III to benefit also parties to contracts – has convinced me that there is room for further research on differentiating procedural rules according to the different kinds of parties and third parties according to what has been mentioned above in section 2.

Book II on the other hand does not give a definition of party, a word which is used in the explanations, but not in the provisions of Book II itself. Of particular relevance is the explanation to Article II-1 (1) on the scope of application:

> which applies to all procedures leading to acts that affect or are intended to affect in a legally binding manner an a priori undetermined group of third parties. Applying the rules only to the adoption of such acts would be too limited because amendment and even repeal of such acts might have significant impact on rights of individuals or other protected values of EU law. Acts of general application, in any case, should be understood as acts that affect or are intended to affect in a legally binding manner *an a priori undetermined group of third parties* (emphasis added).

---

[24] Which refer to the following articles of Book III: III-3 – General Duty of Fair Decision-making and impartiality ; III-5 – Initiation; III-7 – Responsible Official; III-8 – Management of procedures and procedural rights; III-9 – Time limits for concluding procedures; III-10 – Principle of investigation; III-11 – Investigation by request; III-13 – Duties to cooperate of parties; III-14 – Privilege against self-incrimination and legal professional privilege; III-15 – Witnesses and experts; III-22 – Access to the File; III-23 – Right to be heard by persons adversely affected ; III-29 – Duty to give reasons; III-30 – Duty to indicate available remedies; III-31 – Formal and language requirements; III-32 – Decisions in electronic form.

Indeed, Book II on rule-making, as it deals with consultation and participation, works with different concepts that go from the very broad notion of the 'public' to 'targeted third parties' (see side number 44).

In Book V on mutual assistance deals with parties that are usually the EU and Member States' authorities, but interestingly the notion of 'third party' appears in the explanation in relation to 'documents to be served to a third party',[25] 'disclosure of data to a third party'.[26] Book VI on information indicates in side number 12 of its introduction that "a framework should ensure that the various stages of the composite information management activities comply with the procedural rights afforded to concerned persons and third parties in EU administrative procedures" and there is a specific provision for that purpose in Article VI-24.

Confronting the use made of the notions of 'third party', 'concerned person', addressee', 'interested party', 'third party' and 'the public' in the various Books of the Model Rules gives thus ample food for thought in order to develop a broader research agenda on the protection of third parties in administrative procedures.

E. Protection of Third Parties Through Rules of Administrative Procedure and Organisational Design

By way of conclusion, I will give a few indications on the directions followed by the Pavia research unit of the Codification of EU Administrative Procedures; this is work in progress.

A first direction of research is that of the possible development of a typology of parties to procedures ranging from the most restrictive notion, that of a party to a judicial procedure, to the broadest one, i.e. 'the public', with intermediate concepts such as the addressee of an administrative decision to the 'third party' to an administrative procedure who has been admitted to become a party upon request, such as in the Book III Model Rules definition. Such a typology, if any, will only be the outcome of the research programme of the unit and its assessment of other work done in the framework of the general PRIN project, of ReNEUAL, to which the PRIN is linked, and to the work of the Dornburg Group and other similar research groups, associations etc.; it is mentioned only pro memoria.

A second direction of research is the further exploration by way of a series of case studies of the guarantees offered to third parties in the different types of administrative procedures as identified by ReNEUAL, i.e. procedures leading to rule-making, to single-case decision, to contracts, as well as in administrative mutual assistance and information management. Here also work will be

25 Side number 12.

26 Side number 36(3) "The dissemination of data and information shared between public authorities to third parties requires a specific legislative authorisation".

compared with other work as mentioned in the previous paragraph. Clearly, and contrary to the attempt to establish a typology, this second direction of research can only lead to a patchwork of results that will at best enable to formulate some general ideas about the protection of third parties – ex-post, as in the case of the general typology. In order to come to some useful conclusions, this second direction of research should include comparisons with judicial procedures and also, as far as rule-making is concerned, with legislative or quasi-legislative procedures.

A third direction of research, conceptually more innovative, will try to work with a far broader concept of administrative procedure that will include not only administrative procedural rules, but also operational rules and organisational rules that either are consciously designed as a tool of protection for third parties or appear to be protective albeit not being conceived as such. To give just one example I am presently working on the progressive evolution of the European Ombudsman from a 'médiateur' adjudicating in cases where there are clearly opposing parties – the EU administration and the applicant – to a guarantor of rights of third parties and 'the public'.[27] This evolution is based upon the rules of the Maastricht treaty (Article 228 (1) TFEU).[28] The fact that the European Ombudsman has been granted from the beginning the power and duty to enquire upon his own initiative – a power which has been granted by the 'masters of the Treaty' in full knowledge of its consequences – deserves further reflection from a legal point of view. More generally for all kinds of EU autonomous bodies, offices and agencies, there may be similar kind of guarantees that are of a formal/procedural nature: organisational structure (boards, advisory councils etc.), the supervisory mechanisms, the possible existence of internal mechanisms and, last but not least, the decision making procedures as laid

---

27 The European Ombudsman's 20th Anniversary Colloquium, the programme of which has been established by Herwig Hofmann and myself, has taken place on 22 June 2015 (see http://www.ombudsman.europa.eu/activities/calendarevent.faces/en/983/html.bookmark) and will lead to a publication.

28 "A European Ombudsman, elected by the European Parliament, shall be empowered to receive complaints from any citizen of the Union or any natural or legal person residing or having its registered office in a Member State concerning instances of maladministration in the activities of the Union institutions, bodies, offices or agencies, with the exception of the Court of Justice of the European Union acting in its judicial role. He or she shall examine such complaints and report on them.
In accordance with his duties, the Ombudsman shall conduct inquiries for which he finds grounds, either on his own initiative or on the basis of complaints submitted to him direct or through a Member of the European Parliament, except where the alleged facts are or have been the subject of legal proceedings. Where the Ombudsman establishes an instance of maladministration, he shall refer the matter to the institution, body, office or agency concerned, which shall have a period of three months in which to inform him of its views. The Ombudsman shall then forward a report to the European Parliament and the institution, body, office or agency concerned. The person lodging the complaint shall be informed of the outcome of such inquiries.
The Ombudsman shall submit an annual report to the European Parliament on the outcome of his inquiries". (Emphasis added.)

down in the agency's basic act and in its legally binding procedural rules as well as in soft law documents. I acknowledge that this is a very ambitious research agenda, for which only partial results can be expected in the short and medium term.

Comment by Andrew Le Sueur

A. Craigs's Argument

The ReNEUAL project team's collective decision was that the Model Rules, including those in Book III (on single case decision-making), should apply to EU authorities whenever they make administrative decisions but should not generally be applicable to Member States taking administrative action in a field of EU law. Only in situations where EU sector-specific legislation requires application of the code, or if a Member State choses to adopt the code, do they envisage the rules applying to national institutions.[29] Paul Craig's chapter ends with a note of dissent from the view of his colleagues on the ReNEUAL drafting team. His call for action is that Model Rules should normally be applicable to EU Member States when they act in the sphere of EU law. The subtext is that lawyers working in the common law tradition have nothing to fear from codes in general and the ReNEUAL Model Rules in particular. Everybody concerned with administrative decision-making would benefit from the clarity and simplicity of a code, Craig argues.

As a gloss on Craig's essay, this comment adds a note on issues related to current constitutional politics and legal culture, neither of which feature strongly in Craig's chapter.

B. Constitutional Politics

Craig's elegantly written essay is a politics-free zone. From a British perspective, the brooding presence of the European Referendum Act 2015, which completed its legislative passage through the UK Parliament and received Royal Assent in December 2015, goes unnoted. On a date to be determined by the government before the end of 2017, British, Commonwealth (including Maltese and Cypriot) and Irish nationals living in the United Kingdom or Gibraltar will vote on the question 'Should the United Kingdom remain a member of the European Union?'. In a departure from the normally strict constitutional convention of collective Cabinet responsibility, Prime Minister David Cameron conceded in early 2016 that government ministers would be free to campaign either to 'remain' or 'leave'. Opinion polls in January 2016 (admittedly before the campaigns have started) show voting intentions at 41 per cent 'leave', 42 per cent 'remain'. The political parties and the people are divided down the middle.

---

29 *ReNEUAL Model Rules on EU Administrative Procedure: Book III – Single Case Decision-making* (2014) 70-71.

The world of high politics may seem a world away from the technocratic debates about the reach of a detailed legal code on administrative decision-making; and so it is. But I would like to suggest that the constitutional and political context is an important matter in debating whether, as a default position, a code of EU law should apply to national public bodies as they exercise functions relating to EU matters.

Most obviously, it needs to be be borne in mind that the technical arguments over the merits or otherwise of an EU administrative procedure applied to national decision-making may become hypothetical should the outcome of the UK referendum be to leave the EU. Integration will be put into reverse gear, though the technical legal work involved in extracting a long-serving Member State from the *acquis*, where possible, will surely take a decade or more. The shadow influence of the EU on UK law and procedure will last long after the 2-year withdrawal period under TEU Article 50.

Less obviously, we in the United Kingdom live in politically sensitive times. What ever the merits of Craig's proposal, Eurosceptics will detect EU 'mission creep'. As the drafting team recognised, 'there are doubts as to whether the EU has legal competence to enact a general law on administrative procedure that is applicable to Member States as well as the EU'.[30] When in doubt, at least in the current climate, it is unwise to push at boundaries.

C. Legal Culture

The earlier parts of Craig's chapter provide a brilliant grand tour of the development since the 16th Century, though the common law cases, of standards of administrative procedural propriety in England and Wales. He goes on to show, through the discussion of relatively recent procedural rules of the new tribunal system established under the Tribunals, Courts and Enforcement Act 2007, that the British are proficient at drafting modern procedural codes.

Craig's assessment is that the coverage of ReNEUAL Book III 'is not different in significant respects' from that of the UK procedural codes (such as the Tribunal Rules) and where there are differences, they 'do not signal issues that are particularly difficult in terms of principle'.

Injecting some legal culture into the debate helps highlight a potential challenge to Craig's preference for an EU procedure code being extended to national institutions when they act in the sphere of EU law. One reason for the ReNEUAL team's decision to restrict the reach of the code to decision-making by EU institutions is that 'it might at this stage of European integration be perceived as an undue intrusion into national legal traditions'.[31] This observation is especially pertinent to the British situation.

30 *ReNEUAL Model Rules* (n 1) 71.

31 *Ibid.*

The common law tradition and UK approaches to making legislation have been notably permeable and welcoming of 'European law', both in the relation to EU law and the European Convention on Human Rights (incorporated into national law as recently as 1998 by the Human Rights Act). We are now, however, in times of a push-back. At political level there are strong currents of opinion against continued EU integration (see above) and also against Convention rights. The Conservative government, elected for a 5-year term in May 2015, has a manifesto commitment to 'scrap the Human Rights Act' and replace it with a more indigenous British Bill of Rights.[32] Push-back is also taking place in the legal sphere. In several cases decided over the past three years, the UK Supreme Court has emphasised the continuing vitality and importance of common law principles and approaches in contexts where European law (EU and the Convention) also applies.[33] Detailed examination of these cases falls outside the scope of this brief comment but they reveal, in different ways, judicial impatience with the idea that European law always provides better solutions than the common law.

Craig writes that 'while national diversity is an important value, it should surely be kept in perspective'. His argument is that 'there have to be compromises in relation to substantive issues related to trade, good, services, and the like. There is no a priori reason to place national rules of administrative procedure on a higher plane in this regard'. From an entirely rational perspective, the logic of this approach is undeniable. But arguments for law reform need also to have regard to questions of legal culture. In 2016 in the United Kingdom, the senior judiciary are choosing to emphasise the continuing importance of common law values and techniques.

For this reason, and the background of constitutional politics discussed above, in relation to the United Kingdom the ReNEUAL proposal to limit the application of the administrative procedure code to EU institutions seems a wise judgement.

---

32 Overlooking the role of British lawyers in drafting the ECHR. The new government has been slow to publish its thinking on how British human rights differ from European human rights (or indeed universal human rights).

33 See for example *R (on the application of HS2 Action Alliance Ltd) v Secretary of State for Transport* [2014] UKSC 3 at [207] (EU law) and *Osborn v Parole Board* [2013] UKSC 61 (on ECHR and rights to oral hearings).

CHAPTER 9

Expert Influence in Unilateral Single Decision Making

Jean-François Lafaix

In their Article III-15 the ReNEUAL Model Rules on EU Administrative Procedure[1] sketch the status of expertise in the unilateral single decision-making process. The first paragraph states that "Witnesses and experts shall be obliged to make a statement or prepare opinions, when the law specifically requires this". The second paragraph adds that "The parties may propose witnesses and experts".[2] The relevant explanations specify that the public authority finally makes the choice: "According to Article III-10 (1) sentence 3 it is the authority that takes the final decision as to which experts and witness shall be asked for a statement. Therefore, the parties may propose such experts and witnesses without thereby legally binding the investigating authority. However, the authority is obliged under Article III-10 to consider whether a proposed expert or witness should be interviewed in order to investigate the case carefully".[3]

The Model Rules deals with three issues: *(a)* the situations in which an expert may or ought to be asked for an opinion; *(b)* who decides upon the choice of expert; *(c)* what the expert's functions are. But these three points are dealt with in a relatively vague way. The reason for this lack of detail is to be found in the variety of expertise in the field of public administration. Therefore there is work to be done on the Model Rules in relation to experts.

In order to suggest some general principles about expertise, it is necessary to consider more closely the role of experts in the decision-making processes. Indeed, any legal status of expertise presupposes some (even implied) conceptions of an expert's influence on administrative decisions. An inquiry into the expert's influence is therefore a preliminary stage in order to conceive legal rules about expertise.

Experts' influence on public affairs and political, administrative or judicial decisions is a *leitmotiv* in contemporary society, often pushed forward as a sign and result of its "technicalization". Modern society is supposed to be a society of knowledge and information, but also a society of uncertainty and risk. In such a context experts' influence seems to be obvious and doubtless. It illustrates the relationship between knowledge and power.[4] But the reality of this influence is more complex. One has to establish differences between the types of decision and the types de expert's participation. To put it in few words: "It depends"[5]!

In order to assess the influence of experts it is necessary to clarify the role of an expert. According to the Model Rules, experts (like witnesses), "shall be obliged to make a statement or prepare opinions, when the law specifically

1 http://www.reneual.eu/publications/ReNEUAL%20Model%20Rules%202014/ReNEUAL-%20Model%20Rules-Compilation%20Books%20I_VI_2014-09-03.pdf

2 *Ibid.*, p. 82

3 *Ibid.*, p. 116.

4 N. Stehr and R. Grundmann, *Die Macht der Erkenntnis* (Suhrkamp 2011) 22-23.

5 M. Ambrus, K. Arts, E. Hey and H. Raulus, 'The role of experts in international and european decision-making processes: setting the scene', in M. Ambrus, K. Arts, E. Hey and H. Raulus (eds.) *The Role of "Experts" in International and European Decision-Making Processes* (Cambridge University Press 2014) 15.

requires this". But this text does not clearly specify what the object of this statement or opinion is, nor the stage at which the expert should contribute to the decision-making process. One should therefore view the different conceptions of expertise (A), as well as its political and juridical importance (B). It will then be necessary to set out the various levels of expert involvement in the decision-making processes (C, D, E, F). Finally, some general principles about a potential legal status of expertise in European administrative procedure will be proposed (G) in order to complete the Model Rules.

A. The Diversity of Expertise

I. Expertise and science

An expert is to be defined by his/her competence (in a technical and scientific sense), meaning his/her specialised knowledge and proficiency. An expert is someone who possesses a "cognitive resource"[6] socially recognised as knowledge with a technical and scientific value,[7] but also as "topical knowledge"[8] useful to solve social problems and take decisions. Experts are responsible for "giving a scientifically or technically justified advice about issues in which they are considered specialists".[9] So expertise consists of a "scientific contribution to decision-making"[10] or of a "knowledge production for action".[11] According to their competence, experts possess the legitimacy to play a specific "social role" in the decision-making process.[12]

From this perspective experts are not defined merely as scientists, but also as scientists who participate in the decision-making process. One must emphasize that experts, as experts, do not play the same social role as scientists, even if scientists are chosen to assume the role of experts. Experts then play a different social role, as far as the temporality of their activity or the formulation of their knowledge are concerned.[13]

---

6 C. Delmas, *Sociologie politique de l'expertise* (La Découverte 2011) 18.

7 S. P. Turner, *The Politics of Expertise* (Routledge 2014) 3: "the scientific expert, possessing models and theories, and cognizant of the data and its significance, delivers truths that are policy relevant, speaking in a way that non-experts can understand the conclusions, if not the reasoning behind them".

8 Delmas (n 6) 17.

9 Delmas (n 6) 9; Ambrus, Arts, Hey and Raulus (n 5) 2.

10 R. Encinas de Munagorri and O. Leclerc, 'Théorie du droit et expertise: conclusion prospective sur les apports de l'analyse juridique', in R. Encinas de Munagorri (ed.) *Expertise et gouvernance du changement climatique* (LGDJ 2009) 203.

11 P. Lascoumes, 'L'expertise, de la recherche d'une action rationnelle à la démocratisation des connaissances et des choix', 103 *Revue française d'administration publique* (2002) 369.

12 Delmas (n 6) 10.

13 S. Jasanoff, 'Judgment Under Siege: The Three-Body Problem of Expert Legitimacy', in S. Maasen and P. Weingart (eds.) *Democratization of expertise? Exploring novel forms of scientific advice in political decision-making* (Springer 2005) 209-225.

II. Expert participation

The way experts participate in decision-making varies depending on the type of decision or the type of legal system. For this reason there is no uniform model of expertise.

A first distinction is to be drawn depending on whether the expert takes part in a judicial or an administrative procedure.[14] The Model Rules deal with the latter, but the former cannot be dismissed for several reasons. The stakes are common from a substantive point of view. Judicial expertise is also a major model for administrative procedure because it concentrates reflections and its legal status is more accomplished. Finally judicial expertise is dominant because administrative decisions can be reviewed in a court and so the judicial standards of expertise will be imposed in an administrative procedure.

1. Judicial expertise: common versus civil law tradition

As far as judicial procedure is concerned, the expert's task is to help the judge to answer factual questions that require specialist knowledge. But the model of expertise traditionally depends on the legal system.[15] In the common law tradition expertise is a type of proof and experts are "hired" by the parties. The expert is a witness, even though a special type.[16] Continental legal systems have traditionally used only court-appointed experts. So experts are considered to be neutral and impartial auxiliaries of the court appointed in order to give "judgement" on factual issues.[17] Expertise belongs to judicial inquiry.[18] Of course, these different conceptions are based on the distinction between the adversary system and the inquisitorial system. But the differences should be kept in proportion, and in fact the differences are fading away. The common law tradition obviously inspires the Model Rules as far as it deals with experts and witnesses together, without any legal distinction. But it also can be seen as a mixed procedural model.

---

14 On this distinction between "judicial expertise" and "governance expertise", see Encinas de Munagorri and Leclerc (n 10) 204-205.

15 Institut de droit comparé de Paris, *L'expertise dans les principaux systèmes juridiques d'Europe* (éd. de l'épargne 1969); R. Verkerk, 'Comparative aspects of expert evidence in civil litigation', 13 *International Journal of Evidence & Proof* 3 (2009) 167-197; R. Encinas de Munagorri, 'Le rôle de l'expert dans la formation de la décision de justice' (2014) *Actualité juridique Droit administratif* 1377.

16 N. Monaghan, *Law of Evidence* (Cambridge University Press 2015) 412.

17 Encinas de Munagorri (n 15) 1377.

18 O. Leclerc, *Le juge et l'expert. Contribution à l'étude des rapports entre le droit et la science* (LGDJ 2005) § 83, p. 69.

2. Administrative expertise: embedded versus independent third-party experts

From the point of view of public administration, the expert's influence on decision-making takes place in a historical rationalization process.[19] Expertise takes part in the secularization of political power in the modern State and bureaucracy.[20] Expertise is still a way of legitimating political or administrative decisions.[21] This phenomenon is even more important for the European Union institutions because of their lack of democratic legitimacy.[22] The conception of expertise is nevertheless variable. The expert can be embedded in the public authority or be consulted as an independent person or institution.

The model of the embedded expert consists of conferring a decision-making power to a body due to the specific knowledge of its members. This model has been used in US regulatory agencies that accumulate the functions of assessment, supervision and regulation.[23] This is not the case in the sphere of EU agencies, even if some are empowered to make regulatory decisions.[24] The EU agencies exemplify rather the model of expert as independent third-party. They are of course organs of the EU and they cannot be completely independent from European policy-making. But they participate, on demand, in the decision-making processes and do not decide themselves. Moreover, they have to be independent in carrying out their advisory functions. For example, this is the case with the European Food Safety Authority, whose "scientific Panels shall be composed of independent scientific experts" and whose "scientific Committee shall be composed of the Chairs of the Scientific Panels and six independent scientific experts who do not belong to any of the Scientific Panels".[25]

The Model Rules obviously conceive the expert as an independent third-party who does not belong to the public authority empowered to decide. So we should focus on this model.

---

19 Lascoumes (n 11) 369-377; J. Chevallier, *Science administrative* (3rd ed., PUF 2002) 485-486.

20 Delmas (n 6) 19.

21 Jasanoff (n 13) 221; Chevallier (n 19) 485; Delmas (n 6) 22.

22 Turner (n 7) 197-208.

23 É. Zoller, 'Les agences fédérales américaines, régulation et démocratie' (2004) *Revue française de droit administratif* 757-771.

24 D. Dero-Bugny, 'Agences européennes', *JurisClasseur Europe*, fasc. 245, (2010); R. D. Kelemen, 'European Union Agencies', in E. Jones, A. Menon and S. Weatherill (eds.), *The Oxford Handbook of the European Union* (Oxford University Press 2012) 392-403.

25 See article 28 § 4 and 3 of the Regulation (EC) n° 178/2002 of the European Parliament and of the Council of 28 January 2002 laying down the general principles and requirements of food law, establishing the European Food Safety Authority and laying down procedures in matters of food safety.

3. Timing of expertise

As far as the decision-making process is concerned, experts may participate in two different perspectives. Retrospective expertise consists of analysing a set of facts that already exist but the significance and the meaning of which cannot be understood without specific knowledge and may also be debated in a judicial procedure. On the contrary, prospective expertise consists of giving advice about the likely evolution of a relevant situation. So experts try to "anticipate the future".[26] Retrospective expertise may be more usual in judicial procedures than in administrative ones, especially when the court has to deliver a judgment determining responsibility, for example. But prospective expertise may also be relevant in judicial procedure when the court has to review an administrative decision, the legality of which depends on the likely evolution of a situation of facts. So this distinction should not be overestimated and the two types may both also be relevant in administrative procedure, even if prospective expertise probably increases the role of experts, as we will see.

B. Expertise Issues

The expert's influence on the decision-making processes is a result of scientific advance. The progress of scientific and technical knowledge leads to the capacity of explaining and assessing many phenomena, actions and consequences that were not previously understandable to the decision makers. Taking decisions on the basis of new scientific knowledge and debating conditions and consequences of decisions that are related to the results of scientific research thus become options.

From a general point of view, there are some questions concerning the expert's role in the decision-making processes.

I. Political science

Considering political science, the issue with expertise concerns the place of experts in democracy and the relationship between knowledge and power. Expertise may have a normative significance that compels political deliberation. Even if the political deliberation preserves its substance and autonomy, the expert's involvement in conflicts of interests turns expertise into a political resource. This social role is not neutral because those who cannot get access to this resource are put at a disadvantage.

[26] Delmas (n 6) 5.

II. Legal science

Regarding legal science, the issue is the difficulty of containing experts in a cognitive function concerning facts and of preserving autonomy in decision-making. Indeed, we need a clear distinction between different operations concerning legal implementation: in particular fact recording, fact assessment, subsumption and norm interpretation. If the borders between these operations are clear-cut and actually followed, then the expert's role is kept distinct from the public authorities. Thus the decision-making power does not slip to the expert, even if his/her influence is very important when the decision strictly depends on factual considerations. But if these borders are porous the power of decision is shared with the expert, even if the public authority formally takes the decision. This is the reason why expertise questions the relevance and the solidity of the categories of legal science.

In order to understand the reasons for and the scope of the expert's influence from a legal point of view, we have to consider an abstract model of the decision-making process. First of all, according to the rule of law, decision-making is framed by legal rules that determine legal conditions. These conditions relate to the relevant factual situation, the object and content of the decision and its purpose. The expert's influence then exists at several levels.

C. The Expert's Influence on the Rule-Making Process

The expert's influence is first of all to be identified in the conception of legal statutes or regulations that bind the action of public authorities. The Model Rules do not deal with this question because legislative procedure does not enter its scope. But single individual decision-making is the implementation of legal rules that experts may have contributed to conceive and draw up. So individual decisions bear the stamp of an expert's influence in a rule-making process that occurred upstream.

I. Expertise in the legislative process

Legal rules specify conditions under which the public authority is empowered to decide and so direct the content of these decisions. These actions and the relevant legal conditions are conceived on the basis of scientific knowledge expressed by experts and often at the instigation of experts.

Environmental law or law protecting human health illustrates the influence of experts well. Indeed, "environmental law particularly depends on scientific knowledge upstream and downstream from rules".[27] Upstream, "scientific

[27] M. Hautereau-Boutonnet, 'Quelle place pour le "risque de la preuve" en droit de l'environnement?', in L. Cadiet, M. Mekki and C. Grimaldi (eds.), *La preuve: regards croisés* (Dalloz 2015) 89.

knowledge drives the creation and the consistence of legal rules because scientists detect the most important environmental issues".[28]

At an international level, the Intergovernmental Panel on Climate Change is an instructive example,[29] even if this panel is a hybrid institution.[30] Indeed, the Principles Governing IPCC Work (§ 2) state that "The role of the IPCC is to assess on a comprehensive, objective, open and transparent basis the scientific, technical and socio-economic information relevant to understanding the scientific basis of risk of human-induced climate change, its potential impacts and options for adaptation and mitigation. The IPCC reports should be neutral with respect to policy, although they may need to deal objectively with scientific, technical and socio-economic factors relevant to the application of particular policies". So the IPCC is expected to propose solutions in order to reduce the human impact on climate change. And these propositions consist of norms that are to be followed to achieve such environmental goals. This is the reason why the IPCC is also expected to discuss the relevant means that should be used in particular policies.

At the regional level, EU law explicitly integrates expertise into the rule-making processes. For instance, Article 114 of the Treaty on the Functioning of the European Union, concerning the approximation of laws for the establishment and functioning of the internal market, states that the "Commission, in its proposals [...] concerning health, safety, environmental protection and consumer protection, will take as a base a high level of protection, taking account in particular of any new development based on scientific facts". So legislative rule-making at the EU level has to be based on scientific assessment. The European Commission recognizes that "scientific advice is of the utmost importance at all stages of the drawing up of new legislation and for the execution and management of existing legislation".[31] This is also the reason why Council Directive 67/548/EEC of 27 June 1967 (on the approximation of laws, regulations and administrative provisions relating to the classification, packaging and labelling of dangerous substances) has been amended several times for the adoption of "adaptations to technical progress".

Additionally Article 31 of the EURATOM Treaty states that the basic standards for the protection of the health of workers and the general public against the dangers arising from ionizing radiations "shall be worked out by the Commission after it has obtained the opinion of a group of persons appointed by

---

[28] *Idem*, p. 89. See also Stehr and Grundmann (n 4) 166.

[29] R. Colson, 'L'observance des traités sur le changement climatique. Une gouvernance des experts par le droit, in R. Encinas de Munagorri (ed.), *Expertise et gouvernance du changement climatique* (LGDJ 2009) 159-174; Stehr and Grundmann (n 4) 166-241; S. Andresen, 'The role of scientific expertise in multilateral environmental agreements: influence and effectiveness', in Ambrus, Arts, Hey and Raulus (n 5) 105-125.

[30] It includes scientists and representatives from governments, see Stehr and Grundmann (n 4) 192-193.

[31] European Commission, *Consumer Health and Food Safety*, COM (97) 183 final, 30 April 1997, p. 9.

the Scientific and Technical Committee from among scientific experts, and in particular public health experts, in the Member States".

Beyond these particular occurrences, one should try to explain the expert's normative function.

II. Normative dimension of expertise

The role of experts in the public debate and the legislative process is not only based on "objective" reasons concerning the complexity of the matter. It can also be explained by the fact that a relevant position is conditioned by scientific and technical knowledge about the debated questions or decisions, in a way that this knowledge has become a social and political resource in order to defend a position about what the relevant norms should be. And so knowledge turns into normativity, not because of any theoretical necessity, but due to the structure of the public debate.[32]

Why may this normative dimension of expertise be considered legitimate? It may be justified if the objective of the political or administrative action obtains a consensus. Then the experts are expected to find the means in order to achieve this aim. And so experts will conceive proposals for legal requirements the implementation of which is supposed to lead to the desired result. But this kind of reasoning presupposes a consensus about the aim of action that is often put into question. And even if a consensus actually exists about the aim, the means may be various and the social costs are often unequal for the social groups and interest groups.[33] This is the reason why the power of expertise is often put into question from a democratic point of view.

The expert's influence in rule-making processes is of course limited because lobbies and ideologies often counterbalance experts' positions.[34] That is the reason why experts' influence is probably more effective, because it is more concrete, at the individual decision-making level.

D. The Expert's Influence on Statutory Interpretation

Public authorities executing legal statutes interpret these rules in order to gather the relevant facts and legally characterize them. They choose the adequate action as far as they have a discretionary power. Experts nevertheless participate in the legal implementation of statutes in the decision-making process.

---

32 For a study concerning vaccinations, see J. Kivits and F. Jabot, 'Du débat à la décision: discours croisés d'experts, de praticiens, de citoyens', 20 *Santé Publique* 4 (2008) 371-385.

33 Turner (n 7) 4.

34 Stehr and Grundmann (n 4) 213-216.

I. Interpretation of technical or scientific information

Experts are expected to put their scientific and technical knowledge on issues of facts at the court's disposal. But they also take part in the legal interpretation, especially when legal rules use scientific concepts.

Environmental law once more provides us with an example, because legal statutes borrow "scientific concepts such as biodiversity, ecosystems, biotopes, natural habitat".[35] So the interpretation of the legal concept closely depends on the state of development of the relevant scientific knowledge.

This is also the case with medical or bioethics issues. Let us consider the example of the medical treatment concerning a person suffering from a persistent vegetative state. In France, Article L. 1110-5 of the Public Health Code refuses unreasonable obstinacy, that is to say the performance of medical procedures that appear to be "useless, disproportionate and with the only effect of artificially keeping a person alive". In 2014, the Council of State had to decide whether the refusal of unreasonable obstinacy could justify stopping the treatment even if it would lead to the patient's death. The Council of State actually answered in the affirmative.[36] The interesting point in this case is that it raised questions about the interpretation of the relevant statute concerning the concept of "unreasonable obstinacy". Here the Council of State did not decide without consulting three medical experts about the patient's clinical status and three *amici curiae* about the interpretation of the concept of "unreasonable obstinacy". In fact, the Council of State consulted the National Academy of Medicine, the National Comity of Ethics and the National College of Physicians. Then the Council of State interpreted the statute and the concept of "unreasonable obstinacy" having been "informed and enlightened" by these three scientific, moral or professional authorities.

II. Expert opinion as legitimation resource

It appears that the court itself asks for an expert's opinion about a statutory interpretation. Of course, the court is not bound to this opinion. But the court may use it in order to legitimate its own interpretation, especially when the issues trigger debate in society. This is the reason why it may be difficult to distinguish between an expert's influence and the instrumentalization of expertise.

The expert's influence also exists at a later stage of the decision-making process, concerning the assessment of the relevant facts and the content of the adequate action.

---

35 Hautereau-Boutonnet (n 27) 89.

36 CE 14 February 2014 and 24 June 2014, *Lambert*, n° 375081. The ECtHR later judged that the patient's rights protected by arts 2, 3 and 8 of the ECHR had not been violated, see ECHR 5 June 2015, *Lambert v. France*, n° 46043/14.

E. The Expert's Influence on the Determination of Facts

Decisions are legally conditioned by a set of facts that permit or oblige an authority to begin action. When this set of facts cannot be assessed without a specific knowledge, an expert has to participate in the decision-making process.

I. Establishing the facts

Once again, environmental law or the law protecting human health provide various examples. For instance in France, when someone's mental state may constitute a risk or danger for law and order, the competent authority (the *Préfet*) is empowered to decide to place the person under psychiatric care without his/her consent. But the *Préfet* has to decide "on the basis of a detailed medical certificate".[37] Moreover the *Préfet* has to choose the type of psychiatric care according to the psychiatrist's proposals.

The *Lambert* case described above about stopping the medical treatment of a person suffering from a persistent vegetative state also illustrates the expert's influence on issues of fact. Indeed, in order to know whether a medical treatment has no other effect than artificially keeping a person alive, one needs medical information about the change in the patient's health status and a clinical prognosis. In this case the French Council of State held its judgment on the basis of a statement delivered by three physicians specialized in neuroscience agreeing on the persistent vegetative state and on the effect of the treatment.

It is up to the court or up to the administrative authority to specify what factual conditions are legally required to take a decision. However, experts are expected to state whether these factual conditions actually exist and the court or the public authority has no reason to set aside the opinion of experts. The expert's influence is therefore very important, especially when the relevant set of facts is so complex or sophisticated that its observation and assessment depends on a whole field of scientific knowledge[38] and that "facts" are intellectually built – a holistic approach in the philosophy of science explains that no empirical observation is free from theoretical presupposition.[39]

The expert's influence finally depends on the diversity and the complexity of factual conditions. Their influence is reduced when statutes lay down conditions that are easy to observe or assess beside conditions about which the authority needs a scientific advice. This plurality preserves the autonomy of the public authority.

In the field of environmental law the relevant factual condition may even be relative to the scientific uncertainty. The expert's influence is therefore more significant in such a situation. Indeed, expertise then does not only consist of

[37] See art L. 3213-1 of the French Public Health Code.

[38] Leclerc (n 18) 171 and et seq.

[39] P. Duhem, *La théorie physique* (Vrin 1981) 273-332.

an opinion about the state of things but more precisely in a statement concerning the state of scientific knowledge itself. So this state of specialized knowledge becomes a legal condition.[40] This phenomenon can be illustrated by the precautionary principle enshrined in Article 191 of the TFEU. It follows from this principle that there must be uncertainty as to the existence or extent of risks, even if these risks must be plausible enough, according to EU regulations[41] or to the case-law of the Court.[42] This is the reason why the Court of First Instance requires that "in such circumstances a scientific risk assessment must be carried out before any preventive measures are taken".[43] Of course the degree of scientific uncertainty is assessed by the scientists themselves, namely by the experts. The scientific knowledge reflexively becomes its subject-matter.

II. Characterization of the facts

After having determined what the facts are, the expert's role may spread to the process of characterizing the facts in legal terms. Once again, this is particularly the case when the law uses legal categories that are closely related to a special field of scientific knowledge.

In environmental law, the concepts of "natural habitat" or "biotope" are good examples, in respect with the Council Directive 92/43/EEC of 21 May 1992 on the conservation of natural habitats and of wild fauna and flora (which in Article 1 defines the "habitat of a species" as "an environment defined by specific abiotic and biotic factors, in which the species lives at any stage of its biological cycle"). When an area is to be delimited or a decision is taken that may affect this habitat, an expert is to be asked to characterize the relevant geographic area as natural habitat.

This issue has already been raised several times for the application of the Council Directive 79/409/EEC of 2 April 1979 on the conservation of wild birds.[44] In accordance with this Directive, the Member States shall classify in particular the most suitable territories in number and size as special protection areas (SPAs) for the conservation of these species in the geographical sea and land area (Article 4). The European Commission repeatedly brought actions

[40] Hautereau-Boutonnet (n 27) 90.

[41] For instance, see art 7 § 1 of the Regulation (EC) n° 178/2002 of the European Parliament and of the Council of 28 January 2002 laying down the general principles and requirements of food law, establishing the European Food Safety Authority and laying down procedures in matters of food safety: "In specific circumstances where, following an assessment of available information, the possibility of harmful effects on health is identified but scientific uncertainty persists, provisional risk management measures necessary to ensure the high level of health protection chosen in the Community may be adopted, pending further scientific information for a more comprehensive risk assessment".

[42] CJEC 9 September 2003, *Monsanto Agricoltura Italia*, C-236/01, § 111.

[43] CFIEC 11 September 2002, *Alpharma*, T-70/99, § 168.

[44] See the codified version as amended, Directive 2009/147/EC of the European Parliament and of the Council of 30 November 2009 on the conservation of wild birds.

before the Court for a declaration that, by failing sufficiently to designate special protection areas the Member States had failed to fulfil their obligations. In these cases, the Court referred to an inventory of areas, which are of great importance for the conservation of wild birds in the Community. That inventory was prepared for the competent Directorate-General of the Commission by the Eurogroup for the Conservation of Birds and Habitats in conjunction with the International Council of Bird Preservation and in cooperation with Commission experts.[45] As Advocate General Julianne Kokott observed in her opinion about case C-418/04, an "inventory of areas such as IBA 2000 can provide substantial evidence that a Member State has failed adequately to meet its obligation to classify areas as SPAs. The Court held that in view of the scientific value of IBA 89, and of the absence of any scientific evidence to show that the obligations flowing from Article 4 (1) and (2) of the Directive could be satisfied by classifying as SPAs sites other than those appearing in that inventory and covering a smaller total area, that inventory, although not legally binding on the Member State concerned, can be used by the Court as a basis of reference for assessing whether that Member State has classified a sufficient number and area of territories as SPAs for the purposes of the abovementioned provisions of the Directive".[46]

These examples account for the expert's influence on decision-making as far as the process of characterizing the facts in legal terms is concerned. Indeed, this process consists of connecting a concrete object (e.g. a piece of territory) to a legal category (giving this territory a legal status). When the law uses a scientific concept as a legal category, the decision-maker has no reason to set the expert's opinion aside.

F. The Expert's Influence on the Content of the Decision

The expert's influence is at its maximum when the expert is asked for an opinion about the content of the decision, i.e. for their opinion is about the "good decision" that is to be taken. In such a situation, the expert's role involves all intellectual tasks of the decision-making process that have been already analysed: the statutory interpretation, the determination of facts, and the characterization of facts in legal terms. But it also incorporates an assessment of the appropriateness of the decision to its context and its purpose.

I. Legally binding influence

The expert greatly influences the result of the decision-making process when their opinion is legally binding for the public authority, even if this situation is unusual. The expert draws up a recommendation that binds,

[45] CJEC 19 May 1998, *Commission v. Netherlands*, C-3/96, § 68 à 70.

[46] J. Kokott, opinion about the case C-418/04, *Commission v. Ireland*, § 17.

even partially, the public authority. This authority is not entitled to decide against the expert's opinion or has to satisfy an additional requirement in order to take a different decision. Let's take, once again, the example of a person that is placed under psychiatric care without his/her consent. In France, the opinion of the physician partly determines the type of medical care. In particular, when the physician does not recommend complete hospitalization, the administrative authority cannot choose such medical care without asking opinions from other physicians.[47]

II. Other forms of influence

Even if their opinion is not legally binding, the expert may influence the content of the decision for several reasons.

1. Binary choice

First, when the content of the decision relies on a binary choice, for instance when the authority has to decide whether an authorization is to be delivered or not (without any option concerning the content of the authorization), the role of the expert in the determination and the legal analysis of facts mechanically influences the result of the process, that is to say the content of the decision.

2. Choice of options

Secondly, when several options are offered to the public authority, the most appropriate is to be chosen. It often depends on the effect of the decision on the relevant situation of facts. The legality of administrative decisions depends more and more on their consequences and not only on the preceding events. The decision is legal or illegal according to its foreseeable effects. Such a normative situation relies on a causal analysis. When the relevant factual situation is complex, this analysis requires scientific competence. To put it in other words, as the decision is to be taken with respect to the effects that are assessed by experts, the experts' influence on the decision-making process is most important at this stage.

For example, the Directive 2001/18/EC of the European Parliament and of the Council of 12 March 2001 on the deliberate release of genetically modified organisms (GMOs) into the environment has contributed to the establishment of a common methodology for risk assessment and has introduced compulsory monitoring after GMOs have been placed on the market. Article 4 states that the "Member States and where appropriate the Commission shall ensure that potential adverse effects on human health and the environment, which may occur directly or indirectly through gene transfer from GMOs to other organisms,

[47] See art L. 3213-1 of the French Code of Public Health.

are accurately assessed on a case-by-case basis". So the legality of the authorization depends on its effects, that is to say the effects of the authorized GMOs on human health and the environment. But this assessment is very complex. Indeed, the effects at stake are both "direct effects" (that is to say "primary effects on human health or the environment which are a result of the GMO itself and which do not occur through a causal chain of events") and "indirect effects" (that is to say "effects on human health or the environment occurring through a causal chain of events, through mechanisms such as interactions with other organisms, transfer of genetic material, or changes in use or management"). It even takes into account the "cumulative long-term effects" (that is to say "the accumulated effects of consents on human health and the environment, including inter alia flora and fauna, soil fertility, soil degradation of organic material, the feed/food chain, biological diversity, animal health and resistance problems in relation to antibiotics").[48]

In this case, the expertise comes from the European Food Safety Authority, according to Regulation (EC) n° 178/2002 of the European Parliament and of the Council of 28 January 2002 laying down the general principles and requirements of food law, establishing the European Food Safety Authority and laying down procedures in matters of food safety. When the authorization procedure is about GMOs in food and feed, the Regulation (EC) n° 1829/2003 of the European Parliament and of the Council of 22 September 2003 on genetically modified food and feed shall be applied. According to Article 7, the European Commission draws up a draft of the authorization to be taken, taking into account the opinion of the European Food Safety Authority. And "where the draft decision is not in accordance with the opinion of the Authority, the Commission shall provide an explanation for the differences".

So the opinion of the European Food Safety Authority is not legally binding, but when the decision is not in accordance with this opinion, it has to be specially justified. That means that the "normal" solution consists in following the opinion of the experts. At any rate, the opinion is about the content of the decision to be taken and it is quite difficult to illustrate these "explanations" that justify setting the expert's opinion aside.

III. A cautious approach

The expert's influence on the content of the decision should nevertheless be put into perspective. This is especially the case in the context of scientific uncertainty and with respect to the precautionary principle. In such a case, the public authority must decide beyond the scientific discussions. The authority may then even use the context in order to promote its political intention.

Indeed, the precautionary principle can "apply only in situations in which there is a risk, notably to human health, which, although it is not founded on

[48] See Annex II of the Directive, setting up principles for environmental risk assessment.

mere hypotheses that have not been scientifically confirmed, has not yet been fully demonstrated".[49] As a result, the risk, "although the reality and extent thereof have not been fully demonstrated by conclusive scientific evidence", has to appear "nevertheless to be adequately backed up by the scientific data available at the time when the measure was taken".[50] But, at the same time, "in a situation in which the precautionary principle is applied, which by definition coincides with a situation in which there is scientific uncertainty, a risk assessment cannot be required to provide the Community institutions with conclusive scientific evidence of the reality of the risk and the seriousness of the potential adverse effects were that risk to become a reality".[51]

Thus, in a situation of scientific controversy, "it is for the Community institutions to determine the level of protection which they deem appropriate for society".[52] It is for the public authority to determine whether the risk is acceptable or not and it may use expert opinions that support the intended decision. So the judge of the EU accepts, for instance, that the European institutions can revoke an authorization in the context of their broad discretion and their responsibility for defining the public health policy which they deem most appropriate, without awaiting completion of more thorough research. It is sufficient that they adopt preventive measures on a provisional basis and in reliance on available scientific knowledge.[53]

In such a case, a risk of political instrumentalization of expertise does exist. The prevention of potential adverse effects of mobile phone antennas is a good example. Ideologies have an influence on the opinion whether a risk is "founded on mere hypotheses" or is "in reliance on available scientific knowledge". The French Council of State recently judged that a risk of harmful effects was not serious enough while the authority had taken its decision on the basis of a report calling for a reduction of the exposure to radiofrequency fields for sensitive persons (elderly, children, etc.).[54]

These examples show that expertise may become an argumentative resource used to legitimate the content of a decision.

G. Conclusion

The expert's influence is double. It is "objective" because the expert, as they are officially supposed to do, helps an administrative authority or a court to take a decision about a subject-matter which requires specific knowledge to analyse. But this influence is also strategic, because expertise is

49 CFI 11 September 2002, *Alpharma Inc.*, T-70/99, § 159.

50 *Idem*, § 157.

51 *Idem*, § 155.

52 *Idem*, § 164.

53 *Idem*, § 318.

54 CE 21 October 2013, *Sté Orange France v. Commune d'Issy-les-Moulineaux*, n° 360481.

also used as an argumentative resource in order to justify decisions. Of course, these dimensions are not mutually exclusive. So the expert's influence first of all means that the expert is a major actor in the decision-making process. Expertise has become a "necessary illusion".[55]

The legal status of expertise has to take these different elements into account. In this perspective, the Model Rules have to be completed. They provide that experts shall be obliged to make a statement or prepare opinions, when the law specifically requires this and that parties may propose experts even if this proposal is not legally binding for the public authority. But the Model Rules do not specify the principles that determine the choice of experts, nor their precise status in the process, nor the definition of their task. We need to examine these questions in light of the above discussion.

I. The role of an expert

The nature of the expert's role is not as simple. This role may concern several aspects of the decision-making process. So the Model Rules should focus on the content and limits of the public authority's power in order to determine the expert's role, at least when there is no regulation defining it. The decision about the expert's role is important, because the public authority could give the expert too broad a function, even if the expert's opinion is not legally binding.

The question is consequently whether the expert's function should be defined by default, when the law does not predefine it. Should the expert's role be limited to a statement about facts? Or should the expert also state an opinion about the interpretation of a statute or even about the relevant content of the decision to be taken? There is no right answer, but we have to keep in mind that the frontier between the "pure description" of the facts, the legal characterisation of these facts and the statutory interpretation is porous. These legal operations are closely interdependent in legal practice. So the most important point is that the public authority should be obliged to justify the use of third party expertise and the consistence of the expert's mission, when the law does not predefine it.

II. Decision to involve an expert

The public authority takes the final decision as to who shall be asked for a statement, even if the parties may propose such experts. But three issues nevertheless arise.

55 As François Ewald wrote, see Lascoumes (n 11) 370.

1. Power to request an expert opinion

The first is about the power to ask an expert for an opinion. The Mode Rules stipulate experts shall be obliged to make a statement or prepare opinions when the law specifically requires this. But should the public authority be empowered to ask for expertise even if the law does not specifically require it? This power may be implicitly admitted because the parties may propose experts. When the law requires expertise, it often specifies who is to be chosen, specifically at the EU level. If we admit the power, even when the law does not specifically require it, we have to determine who is to be chosen as an expert and what status should be established.

2. Selection of an expert

The second issue is about who is to be chosen as an expert. The parties may propose experts and the public authority takes the final decision as to which experts shall be asked for a statement. But does it mean that the parties may propose experts even when the law has predetermined who is to be chosen? And does it mean that the public authority may ask several experts for an opinion in any case?

The law would lose its useful effect if the public authority could choose another expert in order to have a different opinion where the law predetermines who is to be chosen as an expert, especially when this expert is a European agency. Certainly, the public authority may sometimes take a decision that is not in accordance with the opinion of the agency and then shall provide an explanation for the differences.[56] Then different expertise could be the basis of this kind of decision. But such an interpretation is questionable because European norms may also be interpreted in a way that gives an exclusivity of expertise to the agency. For instance, Regulation n° 178/2002 of 28 January 2002 (Article 22) states that the European Food Safety Authority "provides scientific opinions which will serve *as the scientific basis for the drafting and adoption of Community measures* in the fields falling within its mission". This exclusivity of expertise is also based on the attempt to avoid diverging scientific opinions.[57]

This issue concerning the exclusivity or plurality of expertise is sensitive, because it is related to the objectivity of expertise and the risk of instrumentalization. Several experts may appear as defenders of antagonistic interests. Such a situation may produce harmful effects on the expert's utility or their authority. But where a substantive divergence on scientific issues exists, the plurality and the diversity are more objective and more transparent than any artificial agreement.

The Court of Justice admits the plurality of expertise where the law does not impose a predetermined expert. For instance, in a case about the conservation

[56] For example, see art 7 of the Regulation (EC) n° 1829/2003 of 22 September 2003.

[57] See article 30 of the Regulation n° 178/2002 of 28 January 2002.

of wild birds,[58] the Court judged that the report of the Commission's experts "has proved to be the only document containing scientific evidence making it possible to assess whether the defendant State has fulfilled its obligation". But the Court also admitted that "the situation [would have been] different if the Kingdom of the Netherlands had produced scientific evidence in particular to show that the obligation in question could be fulfilled" by classifying a less wide area. The plurality of expertise is obviously implied in this judgment.

A reasonable solution could be a single expert whose legal status prevents any risk of instrumentalization by the public authority or the parties.

3. Legal status of experts

The third issue is precisely the question of the expert's legal status. What conditions does the expert have to satisfy in order to fulfil their function adequately? The Model Rules remain silent on this point. But the European Commission has already dealt with this issue in its Communication on consumer health and food safety"[59] and in its Communication on the precautionary principle.[60] According to the Commission, the "three principles which must be at the basis of the good performance of the scientific committees are the excellence of their members, their independence and the transparency of their advice". These principles imply that the expert's scientific authority must be unquestionable. Every kind of conflict of interest must be avoided because it would be contrary to the principle of equality.[61] The expert's opinion should be published in a way that non-specialists can understand. But it may also be useful to integrate pluralism into expertise by using peer review or by establishing interdisciplinary bodies of expertise.[62]

The expert's legal status also raises the issue of the scientific quality of expertise. When the expert is not pre-identified, the public authority must choose the competent experts or the recognized studies. But this may be quite complicated. Once again, a case concerning the conservation of wild birds is interesting.[63] In this case, the Court approved of the use of a study published by an "association of national organisations for the protection of birds", "drawn up with the help of high-level Irish ornithological experts", and "based mostly on available data on numbers and distribution of birds and on studies carried out with the financial support of the competent authorities". According to the

58 CJEC 19 may 1998, *Commission v. Netherlands*, C-3/96, § 68-71.

59 See: http://ec.europa.eu/food/fs/sc/comec1en.pdf

60 See: http://ec.europa.eu/dgs/health_consumer/library/pub/pub07_en.pdf

61 CJEU 12 March 2015, *eVigilo Ltd*, C-538/13, § 32-35.

62 P Boistard, 'Expertise scientifique et débat démocratique', in Université de tous les savoirs, *La philosophie et l'étique*, (Odile Jacob 2002) vol. 11, 35-51.

63 CJEC 7 December 2007, *Commission v. Ireland*, C-418/04, § 45: "it is appropriate to consider whether IBA 2000 carries scientific value comparable to that of IBA 89 and whether it may thus be used as a reference to appraise the alleged failure to fulfil obligations".

Court, "a list of scientific references shows, moreover, that the experts relied largely on studies published and carried out with the participation of scientists from the competent conservation authorities".[64] As a result, where the expert is not pre-identified, the public authority has to justify its choice on the basis of the expert's scientific authority or the number and the up-to-date validity of empirical data and scientific references.

Finally, one way to deal with these issues consists in imposing on the administrative authority the duty to give the reasons for using expertise, for choosing a particular expert, for defining the content of their mission, and possibly for taking a decision that is not in accordance with the opinion of the expert. So transparency is the most important principle that should guide the development of the Model Rules in relation to experts.

64 *Idem*, § 57.

Expert Influence in Unilateral Single Decision Making

Comment by Wolfgang Hoffmann-Riem

The topic of expert influence in unilateral decision-making is part of the large field involving the generation and use of knowledge in sovereign decision-making. With regard to the ReNEUAL Model Rules provisions relate only to "public authorities". In other words, they consist of "administrative action addressed to one or more individualized public or private persons" (see III-2(1)). Such decisions require information about facts and their judgmental allocation to the task at hand, including as a basis for forecasting potential effects. Such information may have to do with individual facts involving the specific problem, such as a legal dispute. But it should also include legislative facts, i.e. general factual assumptions that formed the basis for the creation of the laws to be applied. They can assist in better identifying the law's meaning and purpose, including where the assumptions have since changed, and in focusing on both the desired and the undesired consequences, in order to be able to ward off the latter with the aid of the decision.

In general, experts are presumed to have special knowledge in their field. They are tasked with conveying to the public authority the particular experiences and findings in their respective field and/or the conclusions to be drawn from the established facts based on the particular experiences and findings known to them. However, this must be broadened to account for the fact that public authorities often require knowledge about the larger factual (i.e. empirically discernible) contexts in which a rule is found or in which it can trigger consequences.

To generate knowledge is often difficult in our so-called knowledge society, due to the complexities and dynamics in many areas. We know today that knowledge – which means more than a mere description of a superficial appearance but also includes cause-and-effect relationships – can usually be acquired only through a process replete with conditions. Assuming that causation chains are linear is often insufficient. It is also necessary to take into account dynamics, recursive interweavings, and discontinuities. To this extent, public authorities can and should also rely on their own experiences and heuristic assumptions, but they always need to test whether they are consistent with the expertise of other actors and the scientific community.

Since those charged with applying the law cannot themselves know everything, customary administrative procedure laws set forth rules about how facts are ascertained. The ReNEUAL Model Rules on Single Case Decision-Making contain general rules (Chapter 3, III-10 to III-15). It is striking that the use of experts as a source of knowledge is dealt with so sparingly: public authorities are permitted "to hear the evidence of ... experts or gather statements in writing or electronically from ... experts" (III-10(2)(b)). Such experts are selected by the public authority itself. Although the parties may propose experts, the public authority is not bound by this. Experts are obligated to furnish an expert opinion only if a special law envisions this. Public authorities moreover have broad discretion in engaging and selecting experts.

Since the Model Rules made use of the specialised knowledge of a large circle of experts from nearly all EU Member States and strive to conform to best practices, the experiences of other legal systems may also be indirectly significant when it comes to interpreting and applying the Model Rules.

Scientific policy advice, public disputes, and special expert hearings have taught us that today there is no longer any such thing as unique expert knowledge. Rather, we find repeated disagreements, including among experts. In many cases, this has shaken the confidence in the impartiality of experts, particularly where it is apparent that the results ostensibly stemming from expertise are framed in a selective manner so as to comport with the way that the party that commissioned the study wants to use them. In controversial fields, such as risk law, one often finds that for every expert, there is a counter-expert.

Public authorities are to be obligated to "take into consideration the relevant factors ... and give each of them its proper weight in the decision [and to] use such evidence as, after due consideration, [they deem] necessary in order to ascertain the facts of the case" (III-10(1)). Such rules leave unresolved how to handle the uncertainty associated with many expert assumptions. Also unresolved is how to treat value judgements that experts necessarily draw on in most cases in order to evaluate facts. From a legal standpoint, the decision-making authority is the relevant one for making value judgements. It must ensure that decisions are based only on those value judgements that are compatible with value judgements legitimated by law. Accordingly, this is consistent with the principle – recognised in Germany and elsewhere – that public authorities are not bound by the value judgements of experts but must instead independently review them.

Where antithetical expert opinions are furnished, public authorities are at liberty to engage additional experts. But in many cases, there are no available studies pertaining to the given case that can aid in making important findings of fact, such as with regard to the causes and attendant circumstances associated with the emergence of risks, as well as for the forward-looking evaluation of measures designed to ward them off. The Model Rules leave open here whether public authorities can require experts to undertake an independent study relating to the specific problem. Since public authorities are responsible for ascertaining the facts, they certainly will be empowered to do so.

However, it becomes important here, as elsewhere, whether temporal and, above all, financial resources are available for this.

The Model Rules are silent on the issue of remuneration of experts. In many legal systems – in Germany, for instance – the compensation of experts is subject to hourly rates. However, those rules do not address how the costs are to be borne for more involved empirical studies whose results are to form part of the decision-making process.

The Model Rules clarify that experts are generally not obligated to act. As mentioned above, corresponding duties presuppose rules in a special law. It is generally appropriate to leave such rules to special laws where the characteristics of those rules also suggest legal characteristics. But there are also issues that can be resolved with a generally applicable rule. This includes the issue of how a public authority can respond when an expert obligated to comment fails to meet this duty. Under German law, public authorities are not empowered to take compulsory measures against the expert. But they can ask the competent court to enforce the furnishing of an opinion with procedurally legitimate compulsory measures (section 65 of the German Administrative Procedure Act (*Verwaltungsverfahrensgesetz*, VwVfG), with reference to sections 376, 383-385, and 408 of the German Code of Civil Procedure (*Zivilprozessordnung*, ZPO)).

One final observation: In the topic area that I addressed, the ambitious project of the Model Rules is limited to relatively meagre statements. It therefore trusts that the courts will flesh out the Model Rules through the way they apply and perhaps control them and in so doing take into account the substantial, though not always identical, body of experience available in Europe. This is very comprehensible strategy for the Model Rules. On the other hand, this results in a certain shifting of responsibility for the details about how the Model Rules are applied from the legislative branch to the executive branch. There are good reasons for this, given the flexibility and responsiveness needed for each specific set of circumstances. But it should also be considered that this could have an impact on the allocation of legislative and executive decision-making power. However, this sentence applies to the Model Rules as a whole.

CHAPTER 10

Decision-Making and Information Management

Diana-Urania Galetta

A. The Reasons for the Inclusion of Rules on Information Management in the Reneual Model Rules

Information management is a core feature of each administrative procedure. The sharing of information is a key element of decentralised yet effective implementation of EU law within the internal market.[1]

Information-related activities are therefore often the very essence of composite decision-making procedures already partially addressed in Books II-IV of the ReNEUAL Model Rules. This is especially true for Book III which contains extensive rules on information gathering, inspections and hearings, participation of third parties and consultation of other authorities.

In addition, mutual assistance, as regulated in Book V, is a core element of EU administrative law and consists to a large extent of informational mutual assistance.[2]

Book V of the ReNEUAL model rules establishes mutual assistance between public authorities as a generally applicable default obligation. It is directly applicable to all fields of EU law as long as no more advanced forms of inter-administrative cooperation such as those for information exchange established in Book VI are applicable. It creates a set of minimum rules for mutual assistance which is applicable between authorities – both horizontally, between authorities belonging to different Member States, as well as vertically, between a Member State and an EU authority – and aims at equipping, in all such cases, administrative authorities with a set of default rules. These basic rules structure EU mutual assistance proceedings and provide authorities with a greater amount of clarity in their inter-administrative dealings.

This implies that, on the contrary, Book VI only regulates a specific set of information activities[3] and, that it supplements the other books by regulating

---

* The paper presents some results of the collective efforts who lead to the drafting of Book VI of the ReNEUAL Model Rules on EU Administrative Procedure. Therefore I owe special thanks to the other two team leaders of ReNEUAL WG 4 on Information Management, Prof. Herwig C. H. Hofmann and Prof. Jens-Peter Schneider, for having consented to the publication of this paper, the content of which is largely the product of our collective efforts within WG 4. This paper is part of the publications related to project PRIN 2012 (2012SAM3KM) on Codification of EU Administrative Procedures.

1 See D.-U. Galetta, H. C. H. Hofmann and J.-P. Schneider (eds.) 'Special edition: Information Exchange in the European Administrative Union' *European Public Law* 20 (2014), Issue I, *passim.*

2 See on this point the general remarks of E. Schmidt-Aßmann, ‚Strukturen Europäischer Verwaltung und die Rolle des Europäischen Verwaltungsrechts', in A. Blankenagel, M. Kotzur and P. Häberle (eds.) *Verfassung im Diskurs der Welt. Liber Amicorum für Peter Häberle zum siebzigsten Geburtstag* (Mohr Siebeck 2004) 395 et seq. See also F. Lafarge, 'Administrative Cooperation between Member States and the Implementation of EU Law', *European Public Law* 4 (2010) 597 et seq.

3 See Art. VI-1, para 1, at http://www.reneual.eu/.

certain horizontal aspects which give rise to distinct problems of information law.[4]

Rules on information management are included in the Model Rules because such provisions on information management are essential pre-conditions for the realisation of the right to good administration provided for in Article 41 of the EU Charter of Fundamental Rights.[5] Indeed, in requiring fair and impartial decision making, good administration depends on procedures which allow administrations to take into account and to reason about the relevant facts of a case, including those which arise from other jurisdictions within the EU.

A legal framework for composite information management activities is therefore necessary in order to:

a) steer the informational course of composite administrative procedures and provide the various actors involved in such procedures with legal certainty as to their tasks and their obligations;

b) ensure that the various stages of the composite information management activities comply with the procedural rights afforded to concerned persons and third parties in EU administrative procedures;

c) provide solutions to overcome the challenges stemming from the inherent fragmentation of composite procedures.

B. The Scope of Application of Book VI and its Meaning

The Model Rules on Administrative Procedures do not follow the same definition of their scope of applicability in all books. Unlike Books I-IV, Book VI follows (as with Book V) a comprehensive approach concerning its scope of application. It includes not only information management activities of EU authorities but also those of national authorities. In other words, Book VI is applicable to all forms of composite information management activities.

The reason for the extended scope of applicability is that procedures covered by Books V and VI address issues which cannot be solved without taking into account the relationship between EU institutions, bodies, offices and agencies, on the one hand, and Member States' authorities, on the other hand. Given the reality of Member States being more often than not involved in the implementation of EU law and policies, the Model Rules of Books V and VI are designed to be applicable also to implementation activity by Member States.

However, book VI does not apply to information management activities legally confined to a single Member State, with no information exchange with either another Member State or an EU authority. Nevertheless the Model Rules were also drafted in order to be useful to Member States' authorities, who might

4 As stated in Art. VI-1, para 2, "Rules in books I to V of these model rules on other information management activities remain unaffected".

5 See on this topic: D.-U. Galetta, 'Inhalt und Bedeutung des europäischen Rechts auf gute Verwaltung' (2007) *Europarecht* 57 et seq.

choose to always apply them for their activities when implementing EU law and policies and even beyond that, when implementing their national laws.

As to its inherent meaning, Book VI is an important gap-filler enabling judicial review of decision-making procedures with inputs from various jurisdictions and aims to contribute to ensuring effective judicial review within the EU under the principle restated by Article 47 of the CFREU.[6]

C. The Structure of Book VI: Rules on Structural Issues Combined with Data Protection Aspects of Information Law

The peculiarity of Book VI is that it combines rules on structural issues (procedures, organisation, inter-administrative obligations) as well as on data protection aspects of information law.

The rationale behind this choice is that, in the opinion of the drafters of the Model Rules, data protection needs to be integrated into general information law provisions in order to be effective. At the same time, data protection must be applied in the context of the general objectives of information law so as to avoid being excessively burdensome.[7] Therefore, Book VI attempts to find a fair balance between these objectives of information law, by not simply duplicating general data protection rules but rather by adequately adapting them to the problems and needs of inter-administrative information exchange and databases.

One example of this attempt to find a fair balance is the obligation of data controllers – provided for in Article VI-15 para 1 – to inform the person concerned about his or her data processing. There is a complementary right for the person concerned – provided for in Article VI-15 para 2 – to request access to the data relating to him or her processed by a data controller. Such provisions are central instruments of good information management as well as of data protection law required by Article 8 para 2 of the CFREU.[8]

Book VI Model Rules does not cover, at this stage, rules on access to documents or the proactive display of data held by public authorities.

---

6 The right to judicial review of Art. 47 of the CFREU is not subsidiary to other Charter rights in the way of Art. 13 of the ECHR. It empowers individuals to challenge a measure affecting any right conferred to them by the law of the Union taken as a whole and not only in respect of the fundamental rights guaranteed in the Charter. In that respect the scope of Art. 47 is wider than that of Art. 6 (1) of the ECHR which is restricted to the determination of the civil rights and obligations of an applicant.

7 See in this vein: P. Hustinx, 'Opinion of the European Data Protection Supervisor on Promoting Trust in the Information Society by Fostering Data Protection and Privacy', Brussels, 18 March 2010, at https://secure.edps.europa.eu/EDPSWEB/webdav/shared/Documents/Consultation/Opinions/2010/10-03-19_Trust_Information_Society_EN.pdf.

8 See J.-P. Schneider, ‚Informationssysteme als Bausteine des Europäischen Verwaltungsverbunds' (2012) *Neue Zeitschrift für Verwaltungsrecht* 65.

The reasons for such a limitation is, as a matter of fact, twofold: in some cases comprehensive legal provisions already exist for such activities. This is especially the case for rules on access for private parties to documents held by public authorities (Regulation 1049/2001;[9] Directives 2003/4;[10] INSPIRE Directive 2007/2[11]). In the specific case of the (public) use of public sector information to inform or warn the general public, this remains at present outside the scope of the Model Rules, due essentially to limited resources.

This obviously leaves open the problems of transparency issues and open data policies in the Member States, which are very sensitive issues at present,[12] but too far reaching to be dealt with at this stage of the ReNEUAL project.

D. Book VI: No Information Management Activity Without a Basic Act, Yet with "A Touch of Flexibility"

According to Article 3 of Book VI "A basic act shall be adopted before an information management activity within the scope of this book may be performed. No duty to perform such an activity shall exist without a basic act".

This fundamental obligation is justified for mainly two reasons: first, such an approach guarantees legal certainty, as in many cases it might still be possible that an information management activity also comprises the processing of personal data. Second, information management activities regulated in Book VI concern the information exchange between at least two and in most cases among a large number of distinct public authorities from various jurisdictions. Under such circumstances a clear and stable legal basis for the interaction among those authorities provides not only for a clear allocation of responsibilities but also for administrative effectiveness and efficiency.[13]

The derogation clause provided for in Article VI-3, para 4, assures that flexibility which is needed in the case of pilot projects. This choice is based on the finding that, as a matter of fact, informality of cooperation is very often the best

---

9 Regulation (EC) No 1049/2001 of the European Parliament and of the Council of 30 May 2001 regarding public access to European Parliament, Council and Commission documents [2001] OJ L 145/43.

10 Directive 2003/4/EC of the European Parliament and of the Council of 28 January 2003 on public access to environmental information and repealing Council Directive 90/313/EEC [2003] OJ L41/26.

11 Directive 2007/2/EC of the European Parliament and the Council of 14 March 2007 establishing an Infrastructure for Spatial Information in the European Community (INSPIRE) [2007] OJ L108/1.

12 See on this topic: D.-U. Galetta, 'Transparency and access to public sector information in Italy: a proper revolution?' 2 *Italian Journal of Public Law* (2014) at http://www.ijpl.eu.

13 See the critical remarks concerning the actual situation in H. C. H. Hofmann and M. Tidghi, 'Rights and Remedies in Implementation of EU Policies by Multi-Jurisdictional Networks', in Galetta, Hofmann and Schneider (n 1) p. 147 et seq. (153).

working solution in the first stages of development of cooperation networks.[14] This is also the solution proposed in the new IMI Regulation, which suggests the idea, that procedural (and technical) rules such as those contained in the new IMI Regulation should perhaps not apply from the very beginning of an informal cooperation, but only after a certain period time, after having tested that they can be well adapted to that specific form of cooperation.[15]

Always in order to ensure the necessary flexibility, according to Article VI-3, para 2, the basic act must not necessarily be a legislative act. Thereby, the administration is empowered to choose between different levels of formalization. If feasible and lawful the information management activity may also be based on a cascade of basic acts with different legal nature. Nevertheless, it is expressly specified that such basic act must take the form "of a regulation, directive, decision, or any other instrument which has binding legal effect". Pursuant to Article VI-3, para 2, Recommendations and opinions shall therefore not constitute basic acts.

E. Different Regulatory Standards Applying to Different Types of Information Management Activities

In order to establish a legal infrastructure for information management activities which is not excessively burdensome on the one hand, and to provide the legal standards necessary in an EU based on the rule of law on the other hand, Book VI takes a differentiated approach. Book VI also provides for a very flexible legal infrastructure. We preferred such a comprehensive, while at the same time differentiated and flexible, legal arrangement to a very selective approach with only a few minimum standards.

As a consequence, in the Model Rules we provide different standards for five different types of information management activities:[16]

a) the first type of information management activity we refer to in Book VI is databases, which are necessarily supported by an information system. According to Article VI-2, para 3, a database means a structured collection of data supported by an IT system and managed by a public authority, which provides at

[14] See D.-U. Galetta, 'Informal Information Processing in Dispute Resolution Networks: Informality versus the Protection of Individual's Rights?' in Galetta, Hofmann and Schneider (n 1) p. 71 et seq. (87).

[15] According to Recital n. 12 of Regulation of the European Parliament and of the Council, of 25 Oct. 2012, On administrative cooperation through the Internal Market Information System and repealing Commission Decision 2008/49/EC (the IMI Regulation – Regulation (EU) n. 1024/2012), "Pilot projects are a useful tool for testing whether the expansion of IMI is justified and for adapting technical functionality and procedural arrangements to the requirements of IMI users before a decision on the expansion of IMI is taken".

[16] For a general reconstruction of the starting points of the model rules in this regard see: J.-P. Schneider, 'Basic Structures of Information Management in the European Administrative Union', in Galetta, Hofmann and Schneider (n 1) 89 et seq.

least one other competent authority at EU or Member State level with access to stored data without prior request.

b) The second type of information management activity we refer to is the duty to inform other authorities, if they are supported by an information system as defined in Article VI-2 para 4. A duty to inform – according to Article 2, para 2 – is an obligation for an authority, which exists under EU law, to provide data or information to another authority without prior request. An information system – according to Article VI-2 para 4 – is either a specific software or IT infrastructure (IT system) or an organizational infrastructure supporting inter-administrative information exchange or establishing a database.

c) The third type of information management activity we refer to is the structured information mechanisms, if they are supported by an information system as defined in Article VI-2 para 4. According to Article 2, para 1, a structured information mechanism means a pre-defined workflow allowing authorities to communicate and interact with each other in a structured manner beyond the general obligations of mutual assistance according to Book V.

d) The fourth type of information management activity is the (simple) duty to inform other authorities. Information provided under a duty to inform should in general be exchanged in electronic form and only in exceptional and duly justified cases in writing or orally.[17]

e) The fifth type of information management activity is the (simple) structured information mechanisms.

E. The Principles Ruling Information Management According to Book VI

Article VI-5 specifies, first of all, a general duty of sincere cooperation. Such sincere cooperation is imperative for composite information management and may inter alia oblige the participating authorities to establish or to comply with a set of interoperability standards.

Articles VI-9 and VI-10 highlight two other very important principles for composite information management and joint data processing: the principle of transparency and the principle of data quality. Both principles serve two distinct but interrelated objectives: the provision of reliable inter-administrative information exchange and the protection of subjective rights of persons concerned.

The principle of transparent information management includes, for instance, duties to record data processing activities. This duty supports data protection but it also fosters inter-administrative accountability and interaction with regard to collaborative information gathering.

Information exchange is reliable only if the data provided meets high standards of data quality. In as far as the principle of data quality is concerned,

---

17 See Art. VI-12, para 4.

Article VI-19 establishes therefore different obligations, to update, correct or delete data.

While Article VI-19 para 3 explicitly provides an individual 'subjective' right for persons concerned (including data subjects) in line with general data protection principles, other paragraphs are predominantly concerned with establishing obligations and rights applicable in the inter-administrative relationships which are not confined to data protection.

Article VI-19 para 5 on data flagging combines the latter two approaches.

Finally, Article VI-34 provides an obligation to establish internal supervision by data protection officers. This rule is declaratory with regard to EU authorities,[18] but innovative for national authorities (at least at present)[19].

As a matter of fact, obligations to regularly prepare general evaluative reports exist for most information management activities to which Book VI is applicable. They allow for the relevant administrative bodies as well as for legislative bodies to reconsider the existing organizational and legal arrangements and to propose modifications to optimize them, adapt them to new circumstances or to abolish duties to implement information management activities no longer needed or proved dysfunctional.

The supervisory and judicial procedures should ensure the efficiency of administrative action while at the same time guaranteeing that concerned persons are in a position to obtain enforcement of their rights.

F. Conclusions

As Book VI regulates inter-administrative information exchange and databases used by different authorities, many of its rules contain obligations of authorities or establish organizational structures. The creation of such innovative organizational structures contributes to the objective of clear allocation of responsibilities and transparent information management. This would benefit legal certainty and real possibilities of supervision and accountability, either through control by a supervisory authority or through the Commission when starting an action for infringement (under Articles 258, 259 TFEU) before the EU Court of Justice. From this perspective Book VI contributes to the legal infrastructure for implementing EU law in a decentralised structure. Decentralized implementation is, in fact, a way of enforcing EU law for which

[18] See the general obligation in Art. 24 of Regulation (EC) No 45/2001 of the European Parliament and of the Council of 18 December 2000, on the protection of individuals with regard to the processing of personal data by the Community institutions and bodies and on the free movement of such data.

[19] See Art. 49 of the Commission's Proposal for a Regulation of the European Parliament and of the Council on the protection of individuals with regard to the processing of personal data and on the free movement of such data (General Data Protection Regulation – COM(2012) 11), which provides that "Each Member State shall provide by law within the limits of this Regulation: (a) the establishment and status of the supervisory authority".

well-structured information management activities and general supervisory powers are essential.

Nevertheless, an equally important element of the legal infrastructure provided for by Book VI consists in rules which provide, explicitly or implicitly, subjective rights for individuals in order to effectively protect their legal interests.

Some rights and the corresponding obligation are explicitly provided. These include, for example: access to data for the persons concerned; obligations to correct, block or delete data; rights to be heard by the Supervisory Authorities; obligations of National Supervisory Authorities to assist and advise a person concerned; obligations of an incompetent authority to transfer a request of a person concerned to the competent authority and the right to compensation in relation to composite information management activities.

Other provisions contain obligations which might also be interpreted as to contain rights, such as in: Article VI-13 (General standards for databases); Article VI-14 (Verification); Article VI-16 (Access for competent authorities); Article VI-19 (Obligations to update, correct or delete data); Article VI-21 (Duty to independently assess information provided through information systems); Article VI-24 (Restrictions on the use of data and information); Article VI-28 (Confidentiality); Article VI-29 (Security standards for IT systems).

Therefore – and to conclude – the overall philosophy of ReNEUAL underlying the Model Rules and those of Book VI too is that, if the complexity of composite procedures enhances the quality of administration in the common interest, at the same time such complexity should not come at the cost of complying with procedural rights.

CHAPTER II

Conclusions

Eberhard Schmidt-Aßmann

I would like to focus my conclusions on asking three questions:

- Do the Model Rules follow a convincing concept of law?
- Are the Model Rules based on a realistic conception of the European Administration and its special features?
- What is innovative in the Model Rules?

A. Do the Model Rules Follow a Convincing Concept of Law?

The concept is discussed in the introduction of the whole project No. 11: "Constitutional principles constitute decisive normative standards for the design of administration in the EU".

This is true, but it is not new. Other proposals (like the European Parliament Resolution of January 2013 or the Council of Europe's Recommendation on good administration) share the same starting point.

What is convincing in the Model Rules is what follows: "Rules on administrative procedure need to be designed to equally maximize the twin objectives of public law: to ensure that the instruments in question foster the effective discharge of public duties and, at the same time, that the rights of individuals are protected". This double function of administrative law is to be underlined emphatically, because in many text books you can find a perspective which is too narrow mentioning the protection of individual rights only.

Procedural rights are necessary; but the realization of public duties is necessary too. Procedural law has to be construed in a manner so that administrative decisions can still be taken. It is not a collection of impediments and brakes.

To "equally maximize the twin objectives of public law", means balancing procedural justice and effectiveness, fairness and efficiency.

How does Book III manage this duty of balancing? We shall examine this focusing two topics: first the single case decision itself (A) and second the gathering of information (B).

I. The single case decision

The single case decision is to be found in many national legal orders. The historical background is different, although not as different as it is suggested between the UK and the continental systems. What is more important is that its instrumental function nowadays is broadly accepted. An administrative action, adopted unilaterally and with legally binding effect (Article III 2) is not a relic of an authoritarian state, but a well known instrument in the administrative law of the Member States and in EU Law.

Its central position is based on its distinct contents, clearing the responsibilities and the duties. This is not only an advantage for the administration; it is an advantage for the addressee and sometimes even more importantly, for other persons who are adversely affected by the decision.

The Model Rules balance the interests adequately:

(1) The administration has an instrument to regulate affairs effectively by acting unilaterally and imposing sanctions (although sanctions are not part of the Model Rules).

The persons affected by the decision not only possesses some rights but also a procedural status, which takes their interests seriously and enables them to express their point of view. They are not acting in a subordinate position.

(2) This is underlined especially by the following provisions:

- The procedural rights of Article 8 are given to all parties.
- Access to the file (Article 22) and the right to be heard (Article 23) are guaranteed extensively; exceptions are restricted and the authority has the burden of proof.
- The decision "shall be clearly specified in order to enable the parties to understand their rights or duties" (Article 28).
- The public authority has to give reasons (Article 29) and to indicate available remedies (Article 30), which is especially important in fields of composite administration.
- The decision is binding not only on the parties but for the administration too. Rectification and withdrawal are possible, but under strict conditions only (Articles 35 and 36). These provisions keep the administration flexible. But the withdrawal is an extra decision, demanding an extra procedure:
  - The authority "shall take in account the legitimate expectation" of the parties, even when the decision is unlawful.
  - Lawful decisions may be withdrawn, when the party has not complied with an obligation, or "to prevent a serious harm"; this alternative leads to compensation.

II. Gathering of information

What does Chapter 5 ("Gathering of information") say about the balancing of private and public interests? This is a crucial point in every administrative law concept: is it up to the parties to care for information (in a more adversarial process) or is it the duty of the administration even in application procedures?

(1) The Model Rules take a clear position: "When taking decisions, the public authority shall investigate the case carefully and impartially" (Article 10).

The principle of investigation fits best with the principle of legality, and it is a huge advantage for the parties, who are no longer subject to the formal burden of proof. It is the administration which has to take into consideration all relevant factors, "including those favourable to the parties". Article 10 underlines the serving function of the administration.

(2) However, the Model Rules are not biased. I quote from the Explanations No. 47: "Nevertheless the authority does not bear the responsibility for accurate

fact finding alone. According to Article 13 the parties are obliged to assist the authority in this regard". They have a duty to cooperate.

Article 13 tries to balance the interests in a specific way: § 1 stipulates the generally applicable standards: the parties shall state such facts which can reasonably be expected to be presented by them. § 2 intensifies this duty in the application procedure. Nevertheless the duty to cooperate must not compromise the principle of investigation (Explanation No. 52). The main responsibility remains with the administration, but the parties are not allowed to twiddle their thumbs.

In this respect, Article 13 is an important expression of the procedural culture. Nobody can expect to be taken seriously when he is not ready to communicate in a procedure. Thus Article 13 not only supports the administration in gathering information but also prevents a paternalistic approach in the relations between the state and the individual person.

B. Are the Model Rules Based on a Realistic Conception of the European Administration and its Special Features?

Two special features are mentioned in the Explanations; and I would like to add a third one:

- European Administration is mainly done by gaining and exchanging information, far less by decisions.
- European Administration in large sectors is a shared or composite administration, cooperating with national administrators.
- European Administration is a high level administration, while national administration which the administrative law of the Member States addresses, are mostly acting at the local and regional level.

Conceptualizing a procedural codification for an administration characterized by these features needs a high level of sensitivity to the differences, especially to national codifications.

(1) The striking proof for this sensitivity is the structure of the Model Rules itself, adding to the more traditional objects (rule making, adjudication, contracts) Book V and especially Book VI on information management, corresponding to the most challenging phenomena, the administrative networks.

Once more the Model Rules keep in consideration the double function of the administrative law: "Today, the design of composite procedures is geared predominantly towards achieving efficiency and optimal use of pre-existing resources, but their multi-jurisdictional nature may diminish protection of individual rights and possibilities of effective judicial review" (Introduction No. 27). Book VI is the answer to information, cooperation and high level action.

(2) But Book III also pays attention to the special features of EU Administration:

- In a specific way in the provisions concerning inspections, which are more or less a rather complex form of mutual assistance (Article 18-21).
- More generally Article 24 concerning the right to be heard in composite procedures. The provision is very detailed, but convincing in substance. There might be a need for further provisions of this structure, differentiating concrete types of composite procedures and their relevance for other central problems, e.g. for rectification and withdrawal of decisions. But for the moment, we can wait to see what future case law brings.
- Compared with these very detailed provisions Article 15 on experts and witnesses might not be as useful as this delicate subject warrants: it is true that the balancing between provisions of a more general nature and provisions of a more detailed character is the responsibility of the Working Group. We should not review their results in this respect too narrowly. But the neutrality of experts and the conflict of interests is such an important topic (cf. Article 3 (5)), that it would be reasonable to formulate a few guidelines for the administration to take into account when it has to choose experts. A clause like Article 23 (5) seems to be helpful to support the educational function that codification has for the administration. Public authorities often are not aware of the importance of guaranteeing the objectivity of experts.

(3) Another question is the complexity of most of the provisions.

The EU Administration is a high level administration. The sector-specific law deals with regulating competition, states' subsidies and licensing drugs. The addressees of most of the decisions taken by the EU Administration are enterprises (often multi-national companies), research institutions and public persons. Most of the case law is of this character too.

Thus the existing procedures share this high-level structure; they are of good quality: written documents, step by step information exchange, and duties to give reasons for extensions and exceptions.

- In the face of this complexity I am not sure if it is realistic to stipulate a time-limit for concluding a procedure of three months (Article 8 § 1). Exceptions are of course possible, but three months are fixed as the norm for the standard situation.
- A broader question is: should some of the standards of the Model Rules be reduced? Are they too complicated, for instance, in freedom of information procedures? A reduction could be an option, especially if decisions of the EU Administration in future operate at a lower level and deal more with the affairs of the man in the street. This might occur for instance in some areas of police law or it might be a consequence of building up more and more EU agencies, but it is by no means certain that this will occur. Thus it seems reasonable to stick to the high procedural standards of the Model Rules. Notwithstanding, sector-specific law is always entitled to provide its own solutions for a special field.

C. What is Innovative in the Model Rules?

Let me quote the Introduction to the whole project one last time. No. 4 read as follows: "The Model Rules follow an approach of "innovative codification'". What that means is explained in No. 17: not only collecting the existing principles and rules in one document, but also modifying them and adding new rules, if needed.

(1) Innovative in this respect especially in Book III are (inter alia) the following rules:

- Online information on existing procedures (Article 4).
- Appointment of a responsible official (Article 7).
- Transfer of applications, addressed to a non-competent service, to the competent one ex officio (Article 6 § 2) – in my opinion however too narrow.
- Time-limits for concluding procedures (Article 9).
- Consultation of the interested public, using online consultation (Article 25).
- Duty to indicate available remedies including the ombudsman (Article 30).

The overall innovation is the better integration of persons that are adversely affected by the decisions; the cooperative procedures, and the detailed provisions for certain problems, which in Article 41 of the CFREU are mentioned in a very broad manner only, such as impartiality.

(2) How far can the Model Rules guarantee their own openness to future innovation?

Inflexibility and "petrification" sometimes are an argument against codification projects. However, in my opinion there is no real danger of inflexibility (cf. Introduction N. 18):

- The Model Rules are a codification of binding law, but they are not an isolated rock.
- They often refer to sector-specific law. In legal terms, the sector specific law is the first reference for the administration and the courts. The Model Rules come in when there is no special rule or existing special rules are incomplete.

There is a permanent exchange between Model Rules and sector-specific law, which has to be seen in the light of the Model Rules, while the Model Rules use sector-specific law as a source of inspiration.

The codification process itself serves as a driving force for creativity and openness. The idea is a permanent learning process between codification and special needs, between legislation and case law and between practicing lawyers and legal scholarship. This learning process is the best guarantee for further innovation.